A Fragile Balance

A Fragile Balance

Emergency Savings and Liquid Resources for Low-Income Consumers

Edited by

J. Michael Collins

palgrave
macmillan

A FRAGILE BALANCE

First published in 2015 by
PALGRAVE MACMILLAN®
in the United States—a division of St. Martin's Press LLC,
175 Fifth Avenue, New York, NY 10010.

Where this book is distributed in the UK, Europe and the rest of the world, this is by Palgrave Macmillan, a division of Macmillan Publishers Limited, registered in England, company number 785998, of Houndmills, Basingstoke, Hampshire RG21 6XS.

Palgrave Macmillan is the global academic imprint of the above companies and has companies and representatives throughout the world.

ISBN: 978–1–137–48781–0

Library of Congress Cataloging-in-Publication Data

A fragile balance : emergency savings and liquid resources for low-income consumers / J. Michael Collins, editor.
pages cm
Includes bibliographical references and index.
ISBN 978–1–137–48781–0 (hardback : alk. paper)
1. Saving and investment. 2. Low-income consumers.
3. Poor—Finance, Personal. I. Collins, J. Michael.

HB822.F735 2015
332.0240086'942—dc23 2014036604

A catalogue record of the book is available from the British Library.

Design by Newgen Knowledge Works (P) Ltd., Chennai, India.

First edition: March 2015

10 9 8 7 6 5 4 3 2 1

Contents

Illustrations

Figures

Tables

Acknowledgments

This edited volume is the culmination of an effort organized by the Center for Financial Security at the University of Wisconsin-Madison to promote an innovation dialogue around emergency savings for low-income households (see also the Emergency Savings Project's website at emergencysavings.org). The success of the project was made possible by the contributions of a multitude of individuals who played valuable roles.

The initial impetus for studying emergency savings at the Center for Financial Security grew out of an event at the US Capital Building in 2011 organized by the New America Foundation. Caroline Schultz, Pamela Chan, Alejandra Lopez-Fernandini, and many others generously shared their time and insights, which influenced an early working paper I coauthored with Stephanie Chase and Leah Gjertson funded by MDRC. At a subsequent UW-Madison webinar, Mae Watson Grote of the Financial Clinic expanded the conversation to the potential role for community-based programs in developing savings strategies.

In the fall of 2012, the Center for Financial Security issued a call for proposals for papers describing new products, policies, and programs to support emergency savings. An advisory committee selected the strongest concepts, which were developed more fully for a Salon in May 2013 that brought together the authors and other experts from across the country. JPMorgan Chase hosted the Salon at its offices in Chicago, greatly enhancing the quality of event. The Salon was organized by the Center for Financial Security and supported by the Charles Stewart Mott Foundation, which provided generous support throughout the project and is chiefly responsible for making this book possible. The concept for the Salon, and ultimately this volume, would not have been possible without the creative force and vision of Benita Melton at the Mott Foundation and the insights and ongoing advice of Tom Shapiro at the Institute on Assets and Social Policy at Brandies University.

The chapters in this volume would not have been developed without the advice and counsel of the Emergency Savings Project Advisory committee: Ray Boshara, Sarah Gordon, Johnette Hartnett, Gary Koenig,

Benita Melton, Jonathan Mintz, Robin Newberger, Ida Rademacher, Nancy Register, Ben Rogers, Tom Shapiro, and Josh Wright. I am grateful for their time and critical reviews. Other participants who enhanced discussions at the Salon included Desmond Brown, Haidee Cabusora, Sol Carbonell, Kant Desai, Keith Ernst, Nathalie Gons, Chris Herbert, Jeanne Hogarth, Sarah Bainton Kahn, Frank Kaplan, Melissa Koide, Ben Mangan, David Marzahl, Signe-Mary McKernan, Robin McKinney, Kent Mitchell, Sherrie Rhine, Irene Skricki, Margery Spinney, and Jennifer Tescher. The input of practitioners, researchers, public policy professionals, and others have shaped and formed this project over its two-year development.

I would like to thank all of the authors in this volume for persevering through multiple cycles of critical commentary and rigorous editing. I am hopeful the final product has achieved the goal of advancing the dialogue and I am grateful to the authors for sharing their creativity, insights, and expertise.

Finally, my colleagues at the Center for Financial Security were critical in making this project a success. Coordinating all of the moving parts was no small feat. Nicole Truog organized the call for papers and the Salon. Leah Gjertson guided the authors through the process of assimilating the feedback of the advisory committee. More recently, Collin O'Rourke coordinated the final steps with the authors and publisher to complete this volume. MaryAnne Gobble ably offered reviews and careful editing. This book would have never come to fruition without their tireless efforts.

I am grateful to all those who have been engaged in this work; the level of commitment to the issue of emergency savings illustrated by all involved is a testament to the need for ongoing research into the motivators of and barriers to emergency saving. I look forward to continued development of new ideas that will help vulnerable families accumulate the resources needed to make ends meet in a pinch.

J. MICHAEL COLLINS
August 24, 2014

Chapter 1

Paying for the Unexpected: Making the Case for a New Generation of Strategies to Boost Emergency Savings, Affording Contingencies, and Liquid Resources for Low-Income Families

J. Michael Collins

Introduction

Low-income households' accumulation of liquid savings is an important and growing issue, and one that has not yet attracted significant attention in the United States. Financial advisors commonly recommend that people have three to six months of income as liquid savings, stored as cash, demand deposits, or other funds that can be accessed within a few days. This rule of thumb is based at least in part on the fact that it could take three to six months to find a new job in case of unemployment, and liquid funds can provide an emergency safety net for this period (Chang, Hanna, and Fan 1997). However, for lower-income families, a three-month savings cushion is difficult to accumulate. As these households face lower incomes and higher relative costs for housing, transportation, food, and other essentials, just making ends meet is a challenge.

In surveys, low-income households report being worried about their ability to respond to financial emergencies (Lusardi, Schneider, and

Tufano 2011). It is important to note that "emergencies" encompass a wide range of situations, not just job loss. For low-income households, even relatively small unexpected expenses can have significant impacts on financial stability (Abbi 2012). A lack of resources can result in material hardships such as housing instability or food insecurity (McKernan, Ratcliffe, and Vinopal 2009). And a lack of financial flexibility can leave households unable to take advantage of opportunities for upward economic mobility, such as job training or enrichment activities for children. In fact, "emergency savings" might better be labeled "contingency savings" since it is a pool of resources used to manage unexpected, extraordinary expenses that current income cannot accommodate.

Without savings, low-income households may have no choice but to turn to credit to make ends meet. For example, Babiarz, Widdows, and Yilmazer (2013) show that households, especially low-wealth households, take on debt following an illness or health difficulty. Demand for short-term, high-cost credit suggests an underlying need for liquidity. In theory, this sort of borrowing is a reasonable substitute for savings. However, emerging research suggests that using high-cost credit could make families worse off overall, relative to using other forms of financial support or savings (Carrell and Zinman 2014; Melzer 2011). Emergency savings may not just be a recommended practice among financial experts; it may actually have a material impact on the quality of life of low-income families. In fact, Xiao (2013), in a broad review of literature, concludes that having an emergency fund is a key factor in overall financial satisfaction and well-being (see also Gjertson, this volume). Yet, low-income families lack much in the way of savings of any kind, including savings to cover unexpected expenses or income shortfalls (Scholz, Seshadri, and Khitatrakun 2006).

The Failure of Precautionary Savings for Low-Income Families

In a review of the literature, Chase, Gjertson, and Collins (2011) identify studies on emergency savings and alternative sources of liquidity for households in times of unexpected income shortages or expenditure shocks. About 30 of these articles focus on forms of precautionary savings, and 5 focus specifically on emergency savings. This set of papers highlights the emerging interest in this area among researchers and policymakers, as well as its potential for growth as an area of study.

The economics literature generally defines savings as the accumulation of financial assets to store resources for future consumption—that is, the intertemporal substitution of income now for income later. These might be in the form of long-term savings, such as a retirement account, or more liquid funds to provide short-run consumption smoothing. This form of savings is unrestricted in its use but intended to accommodate variability in income and expenses. The life-cycle hypothesis commonly used in economics (Ando and Modigliani 1963) suggests people will save less (and borrow more) when their earnings are lower relative to their future earning potential. This implies that younger people with expectations of income growth will save less and borrow more, using their future income to pay down debt. In old age, as incomes decline, people tend to consume savings. Likewise, people will recognize that if they have short-run fluctuations in income, they should save in peak earnings periods to prepare for less prosperous periods.

Saving for a potential income loss is the focus of studies of precautionary savings. Researchers often focus on savings that households accumulate based on expectations of future income losses. For example, Lusardi (1998) finds that people who have a higher risk of an income decline save more than those with more stable incomes; for example, individuals who work on commission may save more when their income is relatively higher to prepare for future periods when income could be lower. In the aggregate, households also respond to income uncertainty by increasing savings as the risk of an income shock rises, consistent with research findings regarding precautionary savings motives (Wilson 1998).

Acs, Loprest, and Nichols (2009) examine within-year income changes among individuals age 25–61 in families with children. They find highest incidence of substantial income declines (50 percent or more) among those initially in the lowest income quintile. Yet, savings levels are substantially lower for these households. Like all forms of savings, precautionary saving levels rise with income (Guiso, Jappelli, and Terlizzese 1992), and lower-income households save relatively less in precautionary funds. Thus, while overall savings is related to households anticipating income drops, low-income households often have little or no liquid reserves. The group that might most benefit from precautionary savings lacks access to that resource.

Precautionary savings can also be defined as funds stored in anticipation of increases in expenditures, in addition to anticipation of declines in income (Nocetti and Smith 2010; Feigenbaum 2008; Browning and Lusardi 1996; Hubbard, Skinner, and Zeldes 1994a, 1994b). However, income shocks appear to be more widely studied than expenditure shocks (Gorbachev 2011). In part this is because there are a wide range of expenditure shocks—including medical costs, the costs of repairing or replacing durable goods, and other expenses that are outside of typical spending patterns. Most households will incur variable expenditures for which the exact timing is difficult to predict, such as car repairs, heating bills, or home maintenance expenses. Other expenditure shocks, such as medical expenses not covered by insurance, changes in family size or status, support for relatives, and costs of relocating or moving, are less predictable but can be large in magnitude. Even households who do not anticipate income drops may therefore prefer to have emergency savings to protect against some form of an expense shock.

Using data from the Survey of Consumer Finances, in which respondents were asked to estimate their own "optimal" savings amounts, Kennickell and Lusardi (2004) find that the vast majority of households report they in fact want to have precautionary savings funds. However, when subjective estimates for desired savings are compared to how much households report *actually* saving, it becomes evident that many households, particularly low-income households, are far below their stated savings goals. Furthermore, the amounts households say they need often fall below their actual emergency spending; Brobeck (2008) finds that among the lowest income quintile, households perceive annual emergency savings needs at about $1,500, yet these households typically spend around $2,000 on emergencies each year. Very few households approach even the perceived amount required; less than half the households studied by Kennickel and Lusardi (2004) had savings accounts, and less than half of those with a savings account had emergency savings of at least $500. It appears low-income families would prefer to save more but often fail to do so.

It is important to note that smaller irregular spending or income shocks might have amplified effects on lower-income families. A low-income family may be forced to cut back on essential expenses, while a higher-income family can reduce nonessential expenditures. Thus, poorer families may be more profoundly affected by a lack of emergency savings. Lack of liquidity can result in substantial and tangible hardships that threaten family well-being.

The Increasing Need for Emergency Savings

Increased volatility in both income and expenditures have heightened the need for precautionary savings among low-income households in recent decades. Gottschalk and Moffitt (2009) show increasing variance in income over the last few decades, especially for low-skilled, lower-wage workers. Dynan, Elmendorf, and Sichel (2012) also find that low-income people today face a greater likelihood of a drop in income than did prior generations. This change is due to several factors, including welfare reform that has reduced income supports, an increase in part-time employment, the decline of labor unions, and the greater use of contracting by employers. These factors, combined with shifts in demand for both skilled and unskilled labor in international labor markets, mean that low-income households need to be prepared for greater income shocks than in prior generations.

Gorbachev (2011) shows expenditures have also become more volatile. Household-level volatility in the consumption of nondurable goods has increased by at least a quarter since the 1970s, with much of the effect among households with lower incomes, such as minorities and those with lower education levels.

These two trends combine to make cash-flow management more challenging for low-income families. Households today are more likely to experience drops in income and increases in expenses. Emergency savings can provide liquidity to bridge these fluctuations, but low-income households have limited emergency savings available.

Measuring Emergency Savings

Lusardi (1998) notes that estimating precautionary savings is complex, requiring detailed information about current net wealth, lifetime income, spending, and the relative risk of an income shortfall. As a result of this complexity, studies of emergency savings use a wide variety of definitions of emergency funds. Some are based on a benchmark relative to income. For example, a benchmark of three months of income would suggest that someone who earns $36,000 per year should have an emergency fund of at least $9,000. Other approaches might be based on a portion of current consumption, such as three months' rent or housing payments.

Often, studies define emergency funds based on how they are stored; cash and savings accounts that are accessible in short order are considered "emergency liquid funds" (Bhargava and Lown 2006). Of course, even equities and personal property can often be liquidated in a few days, potentially resulting in a larger range of assets that could be included. Other studies rely on subjective assessments of emergency funds, rather than labeling financial accounts. For example, Babiarz and Robb (2014) use a survey question: "Have you set aside emergency or rainy day funds that would cover your expenses for 3 months, in case of sickness, job loss, economic downturn, or other emergencies?" This approach has the advantage of incorporating the context of the family given their stage in the life course, as well as geographic cost of living differences, but becomes more challenging to quantify in terms of savings levels.

Finally, some studies ask people if they can access a fixed dollar amount, such as $500 or $2,000, within a set time period (Mills and Amick 2010). In this vein, Lusardi, Schneider, and Tufano (2011) define liquidity as "coping capacity" and link it to the family's ability to come up with funds from any source in short order. Both, assets owned by the household and the household's perceived ability to access credit or tap into resources provided by family or other networks may be included. The amount of funds and the number of days required to acquire funds both seem likely to be important. Smaller amounts could more likely be accessed via the most informal and liquid means, often in a few days. Larger amounts might require working with financial institutions or liquidating assets, taking a few weeks. Both may be of interest for practice, research, and policy, but these measures are likely to be distinct constructs depending on the amounts and time frames involved.

Barriers to Emergency Savings

While economic theory would suggest that households should save based on expectations regarding future income and expenses, numerous studies show many people lack liquid savings, especially low- and moderate-income households (Gjertson, this volume). Without easy access to liquid savings, people turn to other alternatives, including short-term credit, friends and family, and potentially even public subsidy programs. Why do people fail to save even small amounts for contingencies? The literature suggests a range of reasons, from program rules to a lack of knowledge. Ultimately, a lack of resources is a major factor, along with behavioral biases such as procrastination.

Some researchers suggest that the existence of public assistance might reduce savings motivations (Carter and Barrett 2006). This discussion focuses on whether welfare and unemployment policies might inhibit savings, since people facing an income loss could claim unemployment benefits rather than having to rely on precautionary savings (Lise 2013). Unemployment insurance does not cover unexpected expenses in the absence of a loss of employment, however, and access to unemployment insurance is not universal (Ben-Shalom, Moffitt, and Scholz 2011). Thus, the existence of unemployment coverage is not sufficient to explain the lack of emergency savings.

Another potential barrier to saving is that public assistance programs may include asset tests, which could preclude people who have emergency savings from accessing benefits. For example, Supplemental Social Security (SSI) benefits restrict a single person to a savings balance below $2,000 and a married couple to a balance below $3,000. In some states, Supplemental Nutrition Assistance Program (SNAP) and Temporary Assistance for Needy Families (TANF) have asset tests, typically around $3,000. However, the connection between asset tests and savings is unclear. Hurst and Ziliak (2006) find no connection between asset limits and low savings rates among low-income households, but O'Brien (2008) suggests that even the perception that savings may make a household potentially ineligible for welfare supports may discourage some savings. It seems asset tests are worthy of scrutiny, but they are not the only barrier to emergency savings.

Emergency savings can be stored in a variety of forms, including cash, but the prototypical form of savings is a demand deposit savings account at a financial institution. Since about one in ten households lacks a bank account, and an even higher share of low-income people lack savings or checking accounts, not being banked could be one barrier to saving for an emergency (Rhine and Greene 2013). An explicit link between the use of mainstream banking and the accumulation of emergency savings is unlikely, however, since even the unbanked can use alternative mechanisms to store funds. Nevertheless, the formality and safety of these savings accounts may be associated with accumulating emergency savings. However, there are not many savings products that are well designed for low-balance emergency savings. Even among banked households, fees for maintaining small-balance accounts might discourage using a savings account as a store of liquidity. Although inflation has not been a concern in recent years, low-yield accounts also run the risk that inflation could outpace the rate of return on the savings account. Moreover, many low-income households tend to use alternative financial services such as check cashers or payday lenders, and these providers may not offer any savings account option.

A barrier that is well supported in the literature, and obvious from our own experiences, is that people often fail to behave in ways that they know are beneficial. Karlan, Ratan, and Zinman (2014) discuss barriers to savings generally and conclude that behavioral biases and failures are central reasons people fail to save. We all tend to push off difficult tasks with delayed rewards, even though we know that in the future we will regret not taking action today (Laibson 1997). Some people realize their self-control problem and correct for it using commitment devices (O'Donoghue and Rabin 1999). For example, using automatic deposit to transfer funds directly into a savings account allows individuals to commit today to saving in the future. Pre-commitments can be powerful, but the application depends on context. If a worker is self-aware and has a reliable paycheck and an employer that offers direct deposit, signing up for automatic savings is feasible. It may be much more difficult for those with irregular paychecks or no access to direct deposit. Another technique to reduce the temptation to divert savings to nonemergency uses is to use peer pressure to encourage people to set up and maintain accounts. If people know that their friends, family, or peers are monitoring their progress toward savings goals, they may be more likely to cooperate with a savings plan (Karlan, Ratan, and Zinman 2014 for a discussion).

Mullainathan and Shafir (2009) describe the lack of financial liquidity as lacking financial "slack." Credit can provide financial slack today, at the expense of committing resources in the future to repay the debt. The authors observe that people often mistakenly expect slack to be greater in the future than in the present. This results in people systematically discounting how hard the debt they incur today will be to manage in the future—that anticipated slack fails to materialize. This bias results in people underestimating needed savings today and a tendency to use overuse credit.

A related behavioral bias is that people act as if they have only a limited supply of attention that can be applied to financial issues (Stango and Zinman 2014). They neglect to pay attention to cash-flow management and consequently fail to save for an emergency. Savings does not become "top of mind" in the same way that bill payments, which have concrete due dates, dominate attention. Innovations like saving deadlines, penalties for undersaving, and simple reminders (e.g., through mobile phone messaging) can all help to focus attention on savings that otherwise might be neglected.

Finally, a lack of financial knowledge may lead people to underestimate the need to set aside resources for unexpected emergencies or to overlook beneficial financial products or services. Many people—at all income levels—lack basic knowledge related to financial management and planning (Lusardi and Mitchell 2007). Despite these associations between knowledge and behavior, research on the effectiveness of financial literacy education interventions has been far from conclusive (Fernandes, Lynch, and Netemeyer 2014). In a literature review, Karlan, Ratan, and Zinman (2014) conclude there is little evidence that financial literacy education would substantially improve savings decisions, especially given the relative costs of delivering such education.

Overall, there are a number of potential barriers to emergency savings, including policies and regulations, poorly designed financial products, and behavioral biases. Well-designed innovations need to consider all of these factors; simply introducing an exciting new financial product is not sufficient. Behavioral issues may prove to be both the most challenging barrier to address and the one most likely to yield substantial gains.

Credit Market Alternatives for Liquidity

Cash-flow management is a major task of any corporate financial officer. Firms use lines of credit, commercial paper, and other instruments to meet short-term expenses. Households manage cash flow in similar ways. Even low-income people can access a wide array of credit instruments; the major factors being interest rates, fees, and other costs (see Chase, Gjertson, and Collins 2011 for a review of alternatives). One form of short-term liquidity is to delay or skip a payment on a bill that is due, redirecting the money to another use. This will incur fees, may result in service shut-offs or repossession, and could undermine an individual's credit history. An alternative is to borrow, for example, in the form of a payday loan. These short-term loans can cost less than missed payments, but they can also become very expensive if the borrower extends the loan by rolling it over at the end of the initial period, resulting in additional fees and interest.

Pawn loans offer a similar way to borrow for a short term, but these are loans against property. Pawn loans allow people to borrow a portion of the value of an item for a short period, with the risk of losing the pledged possession in case of default. When the pawn loan involves an automobile title, failing to repay the loan may mean losing the vehicle, which may be the borrower's transportation to work and other important functions. Another example of short-term liquidity is a bank overdraft. Consumers can run a negative balance on a checking account to access short-term credit from the bank, for a fee. All of these instruments have features that are attractive to low-income households, such as convenience and accessibility. But they also come with significant costs, some of which may undermine long-run financial stability (Carrell and Zinman 2014).

Traditional wisdom in personal finance is that households should pay off debt (which charges a higher interest rate) rather than holding savings (which pays a lower interest rate). In practice, however, saving and borrowing both provide liquidity, and both may be appropriate, depending on the consumption the household needs to cover (Chetty 2012). Savings amounts tend to be smaller and slower to accumulate, but they can be used more flexibly. Telyukova (2013) shows that consumers may carry credit card debt at high interest rates even when they have money in a bank account earning low yields because they anticipate needing that money to cover situations where credit cannot be used. Because the need for cash-only expenses can be uncertain, households may maintain high-cost revolving debt while holding low-yield liquid savings. Programs and products need to recognize the dual and complementary role that savings and credit play.

Developing New Models

The low levels of emergency savings among low-income households and the increased need for the liquidity offered by emergency savings represent opportunities for new financial products, innovative programs, and improved public policies. Currently there are no specific policies or programs to support the development of emergency savings (Lusardi, Schneider, and Tufano 2011). Innovative new approaches like those outlined in this volume have the potential to help low-income people better manage their cash flow in the modern economy. Entrepreneurs in the private sector, as well as social innovators, should find emergency savings a fertile ground for new ideas.

However, it is worth reflecting on the goals of any new approaches before investing public and private resources in a new idea. Several factors must be considered in evaluating new strategies. First, any new product or program needs to be effective at scale. Good ideas that cannot be widely replicated become more like a lottery, where a lucky few people benefit but a large portion of families gain little. Second, new products or programs must have an effective delivery mechanism to reach the target population. Too often, financial innovations aimed at low-income consumers are not sustainable because there is not enough institutional capacity to expand them beyond an initial pilot. Innovations that leverage existing markets, systems, and infrastructure may be most successful. Third, any new approach must be developed with a keen eye toward regulatory feasibility. In the post–Dodd-Frank Act era, consumer credit products are under increased scrutiny, as are costs associated with transactions and payments. Regulators need to be included in the development process to aid in the design or propose new flexibility in existing rules to accommodate new approaches. Fourth, any new approach needs to take into account ideas emerging from behavioral economics and psychology. The use of commitment devices, reminders, and mechanisms to leverage peer and family relationships to encourage cooperation are all examples of tools that may facilitate savings. These features have the potential to help people adhere to their financial goals, reduce procrastination, and overcome limits to attention. Finally, before a new emergency savings strategy can be expanded or brought to market, there needs to be evidence of its effectiveness. Researchers need to develop evaluations that can show the impact of new approaches to emergency savings using randomized field experiments as appropriate and including cost-effectiveness measures.

Failure of Policy: Opportunities for Private Innovations

Encouraging saving and investment is a frequent topic of policy discussions, but typically the emphasis is on savings for a specific, restricted purpose, for example, retirement or education savings. Most savings incentives provided by the government come in the form of tax subsidies for particular savings goals. Tax subsidies can be defined as either tax deductions or tax credits.

Most savings incentives are deductions—for example, contributions for qualified retirement saving are deducted from taxable income in federal (and most state) tax calculations. Deductions are claimed by taxpayers on their tax returns to reduce the taxable income and hence the total tax due. The value of the deduction depends on the taxpayer's marginal tax bracket. Reducing taxable income by $1 is worth $0.33 to a taxpayer in a 33 percent marginal tax bracket, but only $0.15 to a taxpayer in a 15 percent bracket. Thus, higher-income households benefit more from tax deductions than do lower-income taxpayers. Low-income families generally lack the resources to save for retirement, but when they do try to save, they benefit less from current tax policy than higher-income families.

The alternative is a tax credit, which can be designed to offset the amount of total tax due rather than just reducing the amount of income subject to tax. Generally, tax credits can only be applied to the extent that they reduce the tax due to zero; that is, they are not refundable. Hence, standard tax credits may be of little value to low-income taxpayers, who often owe little in taxes, and may qualify for other credits as well. Tax credits can be made refundable, meaning that a taxpayer with little or no taxes due can receive a refund. However, refundable credits face significant opposition by policymakers due to concerns about fraud and abuse.

There are much smaller direct-subsidy programs that offer lower-income families matched savings, but these are generally restricted to savings for buying a home or starting a business. There are no major federal savings policies that facilitate unrestricted savings and are targeted at low-income families (see Lopez-Fernandini, 2010 for a discussion). This gap represents an opportunity for community-based organizations, private businesses, and entrepreneurial policymakers to develop new approaches to encouraging emergency savings and increasing access to liquidity. Small-scale pilot programs and carefully designed models have the potential to both aid individual clients and provide replicable models that can be expanded on a state or national level.

Conclusions

Everyone faces some probability of a cash-flow shortfall in the future, but preparedness for a financial shock is uneven by socioeconomic status. People who do not have short-term savings reserved for such emergencies have limited choices when they need liquidity. In the absence of assets that can be accessed to ease the impact of a financial shock, there are only a finite set of avenues to provide the needed funds: decrease consumption, increase borrowing, or increase income. Having emergency savings extends the time a household can weather a negative financial shock. Not having such support to backstop the household budget could result in material hardship and exacerbate economic instability.

Especially for low-income households, the solution must extend beyond traditional savings accounts. Increasing saving behavior is not as simple as teaching people to save. Emergency savings is only one part of how households manage liquidity, in combination with credit, changes in employment, and resources provided through social networks. Prior studies suggest that the need for liquidity is growing, as volatility in both the incomes and consumption of low-income households has increased over time. New approaches are needed.

Often, discussions of financial literacy focus on savings for retirement or major financial decisions, such as taking out a mortgage. But for many households, the knowledge most needed is daily cash flow management—making ends meet given unpredictable patterns of income and expenses. Managing the timing of payments, especially without a sufficient liquidity cushion, is difficult and likely to be stressful for consumers. Savings for emergencies or contingencies lacks the gravity of large-scale, long-term savings, but accumulating assets that could be used to provide liquidity on a day-to-day basis may be just as important for economic security. Some observers may argue that low-income people should not save, since they need to spend income on important immediate consumption. But emergency savings is a different and more essential form of savings than longer-term savings. It is a way to smooth consumption and avoid expenditure deficiencies, reducing the risk of hardships and distress.

Any new program needs to be evaluated in terms of its ability to (1) reach an impactful scale, (2) utilize an effective delivery system, (3) accommodate regulatory constraints, (4) leverage insights from research to address behavioral biases, and (5) show evidence of effectiveness.

This volume provides descriptions of ten models for consideration. The approaches include programs integrated into housing, tax filing, and public assistance programs, as well as new financial products. Technology plays a key role in many of these models, as does the incorporation of intentional behavioral mechanisms designed to enhance cooperation and adherence. These programs are not the only innovations in the marketplace, but they are illustrative of the breadth of approaches possible. Low-income families can potentially benefit from well-designed approaches to facilitate savings. The hope of this volume is to generate interest in this topic and inspire new ideas that improve the well-being of families.

References

Abbi, Sarika. 2012. "A Need for Product Innovation to Help LMI Consumers Manage Financial Emergencies." January. D2D Fund. Allston, MA.

Acs, Gregory, Pamela J. Loprest, and Austin Nichols. 2009. "Risk and Recovery: Documenting the Changing Risks to Family Incomes." Perspectives on Low-Income Working Families, Brief 8. The Urban Institute, Washington, DC.

Ando, Albert, and Franco Modigliani. 1963. "The 'Life Cycle' Hypothesis of Saving: Aggregate Implications and Tests." *The American Economic Review* 53 (1): 55–84.

Babiarz, Patryk, and Cliff A. Robb. 2014. "Financial Literacy and Emergency Saving." *Journal of Family and Economic Issues* 35 (1): 40–50.

Babiarz, Patryk, Richard Widdows, and Tansel Yilmazer. 2013. "Borrowing to Cope with Adverse Health Events: Liquidity Constraints, Insurance Coverage, and Unsecured Debt." *Health Economics* 22 (10): 1177–1198.

Ben-Shalom, Yonatan, Robert A. Moffitt, and John Karl Scholz. 2011. "An Assessment of the Effectiveness of Anti-Poverty Programs in the United States." National Bureau of Economic Research Working Paper Series, No. 17042.

Bhargava, Vibha, and Jean M. Lown. 2006. "Preparedness for Financial Emergencies: Evidence from the Survey of Consumer Finances." *Journal of Financial Counseling & Planning* 17 (2): 17–26.

Brobeck, Stephen. 2008. "Understanding the Emergency Savings Needs of Low- and Moderate-Income Households: A Survey-Based Analysis of Impacts, Causes, and Remedies." Working Paper. Consumer Federation of America, November. Washington, DC.

Browning, Martin, and Annamaria Lusardi. 1996. "Household Saving: Micro Theories and Micro Facts." *Journal of Economic Literature* 34 (4): 1797–1855.

Carrell, Scott, and Jonathan Zinman. 2014. "In Harm's Way? Payday Loan Access and Military Personnel Performance" *Review of Financial Studies*. Published electronically May 28. doi: 10.1093/rfs/hhu034.

Carter, Michael R., and Christopher B. Barrett. 2006. "The Economics of Poverty Traps and Persistent Poverty: An Asset-Based Approach." *The Journal of Development Studies* 42 (2): 178–199.

Chang, Y. Regina, Sherman Hanna, and Jessie X. Fan. 1997. "Emergency Fund Levels: Is Household Behavior Rational?" *Financial Counseling and Planning* 8 (1): 47–55.

Chase, Stephanie, Leah Gjertson, and J. Michael Collins. 2011. "Coming Up with Cash in a Pinch: Emergency Savings and Its Alternatives." Working Paper, June. Center for Financial Security, University of Wisconsin-Madison.

Chetty, Raj. 2012. "Bounds on Elasticities with Optimization Frictions: A Synthesis of Micro and Macro Evidence on Labor Supply." *Econometrica* 80 (3): 969–1018.

Dynan, Karen E., Douglas W. Elmendorf, and Daniel E. Sichel. 2012. "The Evolution of Household Income Volatility." *The B.E. Journal of Economic Analysis & Policy*. 12 (2): 1935–1682.

Feigenbaum, James. 2008. "Information Shocks and Precautionary Saving." *Journal of Economic Dynamics and Control* 32 (12): 3917–3938.

Fernandes, Daniel, John G. Lynch, and Richard G. Netemeyer. 2014. "Financial Literacy, Financial Education, and Downstream Financial Behaviors." *Management Science* 60 (8): 1861–1883.

Gorbachev, Olga. 2011. "Did Household Consumption Become More Volatile?" *The American Economic Review* 101 (5): 2248–2270.

Gottschalk, Peter, and Robert Moffitt. 2009. "The Rising Instability of US Earnings." *The Journal of Economic Perspectives* 23 (4): 3–24.

Guiso, Luigi, Tullio Jappelli, and Daniele Terlizzese. 1992. "Earnings Uncertainty and Precautionary Saving." *Journal of Monetary Economics* 30 (2): 307–337.

Hubbard, R. Glenn, Jonathan Skinner, and Stephen P. Zeldes. 1994a. "Expanding the Life-Cycle Model: Precautionary Saving and Public Policy." *The American Economic Review* 84 (2): 174–179.

———. 1994b. "Precautionary Saving and Social Insurance." National Bureau of Economic Research Working Paper Series, No. 4884.

Hurst, Erik, and James P. Ziliak. 2006. "Do Welfare Asset Limits Affect Household Saving?: Evidence from Welfare Reform." *Journal of Human Resources* 41 (1): 46–71.

Karlan, Dean, Aishwarya Lakshmi Ratan, and Jonathan Zinman. 2014. "Savings by and for the Poor: A Research Review and Agenda." *Review of Income and Wealth* 60 (1): 36–78.

Kennickell, Arthur, and Annamaria Lusardi. 2004. "Disentangling the Importance of the Precautionary Saving Mode." National Bureau of Economic Research Working Paper Series, No. 10888.

Laibson, David. 1997. "Golden Eggs and Hyperbolic Discounting." *The Quarterly Journal of Economics* 112 (2): 443–477.

Lise, Jeremy. 2013. "On-the-Job Search and Precautionary Savings." *Review of Economic Studies* 80 (3): 1086–1113.

Lopez-Fernandini, Alejandra. 2010. "Unrestricted Savings: Their Role in Household Economic Security and the Case for Policy Action." Working Paper, February 15. New America Foundation, Washington, DC.

Lusardi, Annamaria. 1998. "On the Importance of the Precautionary Saving Motive." *The American Economic Review* 88 (2): 449–453.

Lusardi, Annamaria, and Olivia S. Mitchell. 2007. "Financial Literacy and Retirement Preparedness: Evidence and Implications for Financial Education." *Business Economics* 42 (1): 35–44.

Lusardi, Annamaria, Daniel J. Schneider, and Peter Tufano. 2011. "Financially Fragile Households: Evidence and Implications." National Bureau of Economic Research Working Paper Series, No. 17072.

McKernan, Signe-Mary, Caroline Ratcliffe, and Katie Vinopal. 2009. "Do Assets Help Families Cope with Adverse Events?" Perspectives on Low-Income Working Families, Brief 10. The Urban Institute, Washington, DC.

Melzer, Brian T. 2011. "The Real Costs of Credit Access: Evidence from the Payday Lending Market." *The Quarterly Journal of Economics* 126 (1): 517–555.

Mills, Gregory, and Joe Amick. 2010. "Can Savings Help Overcome Income Instability?" Perspectives on Low-Income Working Families, Brief 18. The Urban Institute, Washington, DC.

Mullainathan, Sendhil, and Eldar Shafir. 2009. "Savings Policy and Decisionmaking in Low-Income Households." In *Insufficient Funds: Savings, Assets, Credit, and Banking Among Low-Income Households*, ed. Rebecca M. Blank and Michael S. Barr, 121–145. New York: Russell Sage Foundation.

Nocetti, Diego, and William T. Smith. 2010. "Uncertainty, the Demand for Health Care, and Precautionary Saving." *The B.E. Journal of Economic Analysis & Policy* 10 (1): 1935–1682.

O'Brien, Rourke. 2008. "Ineligible to Save? Asset Limits and the Saving Behavior of Welfare Recipients." *Journal of Community Practice* 16 (2): 183–199.

O'Donoghue, Ted, and Matthew Rabin. 1999. "Doing It Now or Later." *The American Economic Review* 89 (1): 103–124.

Rhine, Sherrie L. W., and William H. Greene. 2013. "Factors That Contribute to Becoming Unbanked." *Journal of Consumer Affairs* 47 (1): 27–45.

Scholz, John Karl, Ananth Seshadri, and Surachai Khitatrakun. 2006. "Are Americans Saving 'Optimally' for Retirement?" *Journal of Political Economy* 114 (4): 607–643.

Stango, Victor, and Jonathan Zinman. 2014. "Limited and Varying Consumer Attention Evidence from Shocks to the Salience of Bank Overdraft Fees." *Review of Financial Studies* 27 (4): 990–1030.

Telyukova, Irina A. 2013. "Household Need for Liquidity and the Credit Card Debt Puzzle." *Review of Economic Studies* 80 (3): 1148–1177.

Wilson, Bradley K. 1998. "The Aggregate Existence of Precautionary Saving: Time-Series Evidence from Expenditures on Nondurable and Durable Goods." *Journal of Macroeconomics* 20 (2): 309–323.

Xiao, Jing Jian. 2013. "Family Economic Well-Being." In *Handbook of Marriage and the Family*, 3rd ed., ed. Gary W. Peterson and Kevin R. Bush, 573–611. New York: Springer.

Chapter 2

Liquid Savings Patterns and Credit Usage among the Poor

Leah Gjertson

Introduction

People who lack reserve funds are financially vulnerable, one lost paycheck or unexpected expense away from financial hardship. Emergency savings can provide a cushion, so the households facing a financial shock can continue to function in the event of a significant income or expense shock, such as unemployment or a major car repair.

Households without liquid savings are sometimes classified as "liquid-asset poor" (Haveman and Wolff 2005; Caner and Wolff 2004). There is evidence that liquid assets have protective effects with regard to financial well-being. For example, low-income households with modest liquid assets are less likely to experience material hardships or miss housing or utility payments, and more likely to stave off deprivation when faced with an economic shock (Mills and Amick 2010; McKernan, Ratcliffe, and Vinopal 2009). However, research on emergency savings and liquid assets consistently finds that only a minority of households, and very few lower-income households, have sufficient emergency funds; the finding holds across a range of measurement strategies (Key 2014; Ratcliffe and Vinopal 2009; Lown 2005).

Measuring Emergency Savings

Prior studies often suggest that three months of funds is the appropriate emergency savings benchmark, although there is some variation around whether to use monthly income or monthly expenses in calculating the target amount (Greninger et al. 1996; DeVaney 1995; Hanna and Wang 1995). The income measure is more frequently used, largely due to the limited expenditure data available in existing data sets, although efforts have been made to develop a ratio-based expenditure measure derived from income data (Hong, Hanna, and Kim 2013; Kim and Hanna 2013). Similar metrics have also been used to measure asset poverty, typically defined as holding total financial assets less than the value of three months of income at the federal poverty threshold (Brandolini, Magri, and Smeeding 2010; Gornick, Sierminska, and Smeeding 2009; Haveman and Wolff 2005). As a result of the multiple measurement strategies, studies of emergency savings show a range of estimates for who has "adequate" savings levels.

There is also variability with respect to the liquidity level that is regarded as emergency savings—in other words, what kinds of financial assets count as emergency savings (Bi and Montalto 2004). Funds held in cash, checking or savings accounts, and money market accounts are always included, while highly illiquid assets such as those tied up in real estate are not. But decisions must be made about assets between these two extremes of liquidity. A classification scheme suggested by Johnson and Widdows (1985) is illustrative. The authors label the most highly liquid funds—like savings accounts and money market accounts—"quick assets." Other assets that are relatively liquid, such as certificates of deposit and savings certificates, are combined with the quick assets in the intermediate classification of emergency funds. The most inclusive measure, called the comprehensive measure, adds stocks and bonds to intermediate assets when counting emergency funds holdings. In general, the most restrictive measure of highly liquid assets has the lowest rates of households meeting the emergency funds benchmark, with slightly higher rates when more inclusive measures are used.

The Survey of Consumer Finances (SCF) has served as a prime data source for documenting savings in the United States. The SCF, which is fielded by the Federal Reserve Board of Governors on a triennial basis, provides extensive information regarding the financial status and balance sheets of households. Lown (2005), reviewing research on emergency funds holdings from 1977 to 2003, finds consistently low numbers of Americans meeting the standard benchmark: approximately one third or fewer households have three months' income as reserved savings over the three decades of the survey. This low rate continues in more recent data, with estimates suggesting that less than a quarter of households have emergency savings at the three-month threshold amount (Hong, Hanna, and Kim 2013). In fact, using alternate measures with lower thresholds does not substantially improve the picture. About 31 percent of all households in the 2007 SCF are classified as liquid-asset poor, but within the bottom income quintile, over two-thirds fall into this category (Ratcliffe and Vinopal 2009). When the threshold amount for adequate emergency funds is set at 75 percent of one month's income, only half of households in the 2010 SCF satisfy the condition; among households below the poverty line, only 37 percent have these funds available (Key 2014).

Correlates of Emergency Savings

While average rates of savings are somewhat low, there is a body of research showing notable variation between characteristics of households that do and do not have emergengcy savings. Predictably, higher income, greater wealth, and characteristics associated with human capital development are related to a higher likelihood of having emergency savings (Huston and Chang 1997). For example, higher education attainment, full-time employment, and older age have all been associated with having emergency savings (Hong, Hanna, and Kim 2013; Bhargava and Lown 2006; Bi and Montalto 2004; Huston and Chang 1997; DeVaney 1995). The majority of studies examining family structure find single-parent and divorced households and households with young children are less likely to meet emergency saving benchmarks (Bhargava and Lown 2006; Chen and Devaney 2001; Huston and Chang 1997). There is also evidence that rates of having three months of savings are lower among racial minority groups, with the exception of Asian Americans, whose rates of emergency fund holding surpass those of whites (Key 2014; Hong, Hanna, and Kim 2013; Chen and DeVaney 2001; Hong and Kao 1997; Chang and Huston 1995).

Some studies show that having clear precautionary and emergency savings motives, such as an expectation of an income drop, may contribute to meeting emergency saving benchmarks, although the results are not consistent across all studies (Bi and Montalto 2004; Kennickell and Lusardi 2004; Chen and DeVaney 2001; Huston and Chang 1997). Chang, Hanna, and Fan (1997) find empirical evidence in the 1983–1986 SCF that households with greater income uncertainty are more likely to hold emergency funds; they suggest that it may only be optimal for households to hold three or more months of income if they anticipate a sizable drop in income. Factors such as financial risk tolerance and length of planning horizon may also contribute to the likelihood of having savings (DeVaney, Anong, and Whirl 2007). However, there is little evidence that specific attitudes about emergency savings play a meaningful role in building emergency savings, leading some researchers to conclude that ability to save, rather than need or motive to save, is the more influential factor (Bi and Montalto 2004; Ding and Devaney 2000).

Measuring Emergency Liquidity

There is an alternative way to think about a household's ability to access liquidity in the event of a financial emergency. Access to liquidity includes savings on hand and the household's ability to borrow from and tap social networks for financial assistance. Whether the credit comes through informal loans from friends or family or through formal avenues such as a traditional bank or credit union or an alternative financial service provider, these funds are potentially accessible when the need arises. In some ways, this type of measure paints the most realistic picture of how households cope with unexpected financial shocks. However, it is worth noting that the use of credit and social network borrowing has costs. Formal credit charges fees and interest and imposes the burden of incurred debt. Even if friends and family do not charge interest, a social loan often comes with other costs, such as strained relationships or the expectation of future reciprocal lending.

Lusardi, Schneider, and Tufano (2011), using data from the 2009 TNS Global Economic Crisis survey, offer one measure that captures this expanded definition of emergency liquidity. They examine households' confidence in their capacity to come up with $2,000 within a month in order to meet an emergency expense. In such an event, households may plan to use savings or formal credit, borrow informally from family or friends, increase income with additional labor, sell possessions, or invoke a combination of these strategies. Unlike the three-month threshold, the amount needed to meet this benchmark—$2,000—does not vary regardless of the household's income or expense level. Those unable to cope with a $2,000 shock are considered financially fragile (Lusardi, Schneider, and Tufano 2011). Lusardi, Schneider, and Tufano's results indicate about half of US households could not come up with $2,000 in one month. Among households with income below $20,000, less than one-quarter (23 percent) could do so, and only one-third of those with incomes between $20,000 and $30,000 could find the funds.

Households that could come up with $2,000 reported a range of sources for funds. Reliance on social networks for financial assistance was a key strategy for coping with an unexpected expense, second only to using savings (Lusardi, Schneider, and Tufano 2011). Research using other data suggests that the importance of getting help from friends and family may be greatest for low-income households, which typically have limited access to other sources of credit. For example, in a sample of African American households in an urban neighborhood, families in the lowest income quartile were more likely than other households to seek financial assistance through social networks to cope with a financial emergency (Rhine and Toussaint-Comeau 1999). Finally, although Lusardi, Schneider, and Tufano find that just over one-tenth of households in the United States would turn to alternative credit to cope with an unexpected expense, it is likely the rate of alternative credit usage is notably higher among low-income households, as they have limited access to traditional credit cards and bank loans (McKay and Atkinson 2014; Lee et al. 2006).

Descriptive Statistics of Emergency Savings

The prior studies raise the question of how much of a problem a lack of emergency savings is for low-income households today, and whether it is a problem worthy of attention from policymakers. To address these questions, estimates of emergency savings are derived from two recent, national data sets: the 2010 SCF and the 2012 National Financial Capability Study (NFCS). In addition to describing which households lack savings, these data also illustrate relationships between emergency liquidity and financial satisfaction.

Survey of Consumer Finances

The 2010 SCF is a cross-sectional sample of US households capturing financial characteristics as the nation was emerging from the official end of the Great Recession. Table 2.1 uses these data to document five measures related to emergency saving by household income level: amount of emergency savings needed, total value of savings accounts, total value of financial assets, whether households have saved in the last 12 months, and whether households could get $3,000 in financial assistance from a friend or relative in an emergency. Note that the SCF question differs somewhat from the TNS Global Economic Crisis survey question, which asks

Table 2.1 SCF Household Emergency Saving by Income

Income	**<$20,000 mean/p50**	**$20,000–$35,000 mean/p50**	**$35,000–$60,000 mean/p50**	**$60,000–$95,000 mean/p50**	**>$95,000 mean/p50**
Saving measures					
Emergency savings needed ($)	11,388	9,801	13,957	14,627	53,884
	(2,000)	(3,000)	(5,000)	(6,000)	(17,000)
Total savings accounts ($)	5,135	5,065	5,047	8,886	46,883
	(450)	(600)	(1,500)	(3,000)	(9,000)
Total financial assets ($)	38,189	26,937	57,441	92,791	695,828
	(860)	(3,300)	(11,240)	(31,150)	(199,900)
Saved in last 12 months (proportion)	0.328	0.415	0.456	0.586	0.736
Get $3,000 in emergency (proportion)	0.412	0.493	0.618	0.757	0.837

Note: Observations (n = 26,530) comprised of adult respondents under age 65 including implicates, the five multiply imputed data files within the SCF that contain estimates for missing item values. Means and medians using population weights. Median (p50) in parentheses.

Source: Author's calculations using SCF 2010.

about confidence in the ability to acquire $2,000 from any source within 30 days—the SCF uses a larger amount and does not impose a set time period.[1]

Table 2.1 shows that the average low-income respondent in the SCF (defined as income below $20,000) perceives a need for $11,388 in emergency savings, with the median (middle of the distribution) saying they need $2,000.[2] This compares to an *actual* average savings amount of $5,135 and total financial assets of any kind of $38,189. Median savings account balances among households with annual incomes below $20,000 are less than $500, and median measures of financial assets are only $860. Only 32 percent of low-income households saved in the last year, and just 41 percent feel they could obtain $3,000 in an emergency—less than half the level of high-income households.

As expected, the rate of households who saved in the past year increases steadily as income increases, suggesting income is a strong driver of savings. The measure of whether households could acquire $3,000 in an emergency follows a similar pattern, as households with the lowest income also report the lowest ability to tap family or friends to cope with a financial emergency. Overall, these data support the notion that low-income households are especially constrained for emergency savings or liquidity, even using broader measures of sources of funds. In fact, even the majority of households making $20,000 to $35,000 cannot come up with $3,000 in an emergency. Higher-income households are much less constrained, suggesting that focusing emergency savings initiatives on lower-income households could be a useful strategy.

National Financial Capability Study

The Financial Industry Regulatory Authority (FINRA) Investor Education Foundation's NFCS was designed in consultation with the US Department of the Treasury and the President's Advisory Council on Financial Capability. The 2012 NFSC sample includes about 25,000 responses collected through an Internet-based panel with approximately 500 respondents in each state and the District of Columbia.

Table 2.2 displays the sample demographics and financial characteristics for the total sample (column 1), including gender, race, education, income, and financial knowledge and behaviors. Note that about 43 percent of respondents report having an emergency fund of three months' expenses, while 61 percent feel confident they could find $2,000 within 30 days to cover an unexpected expense. The following columns divide the total sample by whether the respondent household had an emergency fund

Table 2.2 NFCS Selected Metrics, by Emergency Fund and Liquidity

	Total mean/sd	No emergency fund mean/sd	Have emergency fund mean/sd	Not confident to find $2,000 mean/sd	Confident to find $2,000 mean/sd
	(1)	(2)	(3)	(4)	(5)
Demographics					
Male	0.45 (0.50)	0.41 (0.49)	0.50*** (0.50)	0.37 (0.48)	0.50*** (0.50)
White race	0.74 (0.44)	0.71 (0.45)	0.77*** (0.42)	0.68 (0.47)	0.77*** (0.42)
High school	0.33 (0.47)	0.40 (0.49)	0.23*** (0.42)	0.45 (0.50)	0.24**** (0.43)
Some college	0.33 (0.47)	0.34 (0.48)	0.31*** (0.46)	0.34 (0.47)	0.33* (0.47)
College/advanced degree	0.34 (0.47)	0.25 (0.43)	0.46*** (0.50)	0.21 (0.41)	0.43*** (0.50)
Financial characteristics					
Income < $15,000	0.13 (0.34)	0.19 (0.39)	0.051*** (0.22)	0.25 (0.44)	0.048*** (0.21)
Income $15,000–$35,000	0.23 (0.42)	0.30 (0.46)	0.13*** (0.34)	0.35 (0.48)	0.15*** (0.36)
Income $35,000–$50,000	0.15 (0.35)	0.16 (0.37)	0.13*** (0.33)	0.16 (0.37)	0.14*** (0.35)

Income $50,000–$75,000	0.19 (0.39)	0.17 (0.38)	0.21*** (0.41)	0.14 (0.35)	0.23*** (0.42)
Income > $75,000	0.30 (0.46)	0.17 (0.38)	0.48*** (0.50)	0.097 (0.30)	0.44*** (0.50)
Use of overdraft	0.21 (0.41)	0.32 (0.46)	0.095*** (0.29)	0.36 (0.48)	0.13*** (0.34)
Use of AFS borrowing	0.28 (0.45)	0.38 (0.49)	0.15*** (0.36)	0.45 (0.50)	0.18*** (0.38)
Financial knowledge	0.66 (0.47)	0.59 (0.49)	0.76** (0.43)	0.51 (0.50)	0.76*** (0.43)
Financial risk tolerance	4.74 (2.64)	4.29 (2.64)	5.33*** (2.52)	4.03 (2.67)	5.19*** (2.51)
Financial satisfaction	6.46 (11.3)	5.61 (12.9)	7.60*** (8.45)	5.35 (13.5)	7.09*** (8.93)
Have emergency fund	0.43 (0.49)			0.088 (0.28)	0.65*** (0.48)
Confident to find $2,000	0.61 (0.49)	0.37 (0.48)	0.92** (0.27)		

Note: Observations (n = 22,970), after (n = 2,039) cases with missing values for variables of interest were excluded. Calculations performed using NFCS-provided weights. AFS = alternative financial services, including products such as payday loans, auto title loans, and pawn. Financial knowledge is a binary variable indicating that at least three of five financial literacy questions were answered correctly. Financial risk tolerance is a ten-point scale with higher values indicating a greater tolerance for financial risk. Financial satisfaction is a ten-point scale with higher values indicating greater financial satisfaction. Have an emergency fund is a binary variable indicating savings sufficient to cover expenses for three months. Confident to find $2,000 is a binary variable indicating respondent household is confident they could "certainly" or "probably" find $2,000 in the next month for an unexpected need. T-tests of mean differences between respondents who have an emergency fund and those who do not and between respondents who are confident to find $2,000 and those who are not. Standard deviations in parentheses.

* $p < .05$, ** $p < .01$, *** $p < .001$

Source: Author's calculations using NFCS 2012.

Table 2.3 NFCS Emergency Fund, Liquidity, and Financial Satisfaction

	Have emergency fund b/se	**Confident to find $2,000 b/se**	**Financial satisfaction b/se**	**Financial satisfaction b/se**
	(1)	**(2)**	**(3)**	**(4)**
Demographics				
Male	0.00 (0.01)	0.03*** (0.01)	0.09 (0.14)	0.09 (0.15)
White race	0.03*** (0.01)	0.06*** (0.01)	0.06 (0.15)	–0.02 (0.17)
High school[i]	–0.09*** (0.01)	–0.07*** (0.01)	0.45** (0.15)	0.44** (0.17)
Some college	–0.07*** (0.01)	–0.05*** (0.01)	–0.07 (0.13)	–0.05 (0.15)
Income <$15,000[ii]	–0.33*** (0.01)	–0.45*** (0.01)	–0.66* (0.28)	–0.69* (0.30)
Income $15,000–$35,000	–0.28*** (0.01)	–0.31*** (0.01)	–0.51* (0.20)	–0.49* (0.24)
Income $35,000–$50,000	–0.20*** (0.01)	–0.18*** (0.01)	–0.34 (0.20)	–0.24 (0.21)
Income $50,000–$75,000	–0.12*** (0.01)	–0.09*** (0.01)	–0.42** (0.16)	–0.38* (0.17)
Use of overdraft	–0.21*** (0.01)	–0.17*** (0.01)	–0.92*** (0.16)	–1.13*** (0.17)

Use of AFS borrowing	–0.11*** (0.01)	–0.13*** (0.01)	–0.02 (0.17)	–0.14 (0.19)
Financial knowledge	0.01 (0.01)	0.07*** (0.01)	–1.15*** (0.18)	–1.07*** (0.19)
Financial risk tolerance	0.02*** (0.00)	0.02*** (0.00)	0.12*** (0.03)	0.11** (0.03)
Have emergency fund			1.62*** (0.15)	
Confident to find $2,000			1.32*** (0.19)	
Neither liquidity				–2.37*** (0.16)
Constant	0.60*** (0.02)	0.70*** (0.01)	4.80*** (0.29)	7.94*** (0.32)
Observations	20135	20212	19718	20718
R^2	0.19	0.27	0.04	0.03

[i] College or advanced degree is the education attainment reference group.

[ii] Income of more than $75,000 is the income reference group.

Note: OLS regression with robust standard errors using NFCS-provided weights. AFS = alternative financial services, including products such as payday loans, auto title loans, and pawn. Financial knowledge is a binary variable indicating that at least three of five financial literacy questions were answered correctly. Financial risk tolerance is a ten-point scale with higher values indicating a greater tolerance for financial risk. Financial satisfaction is a ten-point scale with higher values indicating greater financial satisfaction. Have an emergency fund is a binary variable indicating savings sufficient to cover expenses for three months. Confident to find $2,000 is a binary variable indicating respondent household could "certainly" or "probably" find $2,000 in the next month for an unexpected need. Neither liquidity is binary variable indicating households that do not have three months of emergency funds and are not confident they could come up with $2,000 within 30 days.

* $p < .05$, ** $p < .01$, *** $p < .001$

Source: Author's calculations using NFCS 2012.

and whether the household could probably find $2,000 in an emergency. Comparing those without an emergency fund (column 2) with those who do have one (column 3) highlights the differences between the two groups. Further comparisons are highlighted between those who probably could not find $2,000 (column 4) and those who probably could (column 5). While a larger proportion of the sample can acquire $2,000 than has an emergency fund, the demographics patterns and financial characteristics of these two groups are quite similar. As one might expect, many of those with emergency funds are also represented in the group able to find $2,000.

Examining column 2 versus column 3 in table 2.2 shows that males are more likely to have an emergency fund and more likely to feel they can acquire $2,000 in an emergency. Consistent with previous research, white households and households with higher education attainment and income have higher rates of preparedness for financial emergencies by both measures.

Among those prepared for a financial emergency, either through holding emergency savings or through an ability to find $2,000, reported usage of overdraft protection and borrowing through alternative financial services (such as payday loans, auto title loans, and pawn loans) is lower; people who lack liquidity as savings appear likely to turn to credit as a substitute. In addition, financial knowledge and tolerance of financial risk are higher among those with accessible emergency liquidity, suggesting a greater level of financial sophistication in those groups. These results are similar to those of Babiarz and Robb (2014), who find that among households in the NFCS, greater financial knowledge and financial ability are related to an increased likelihood of having emergency funds. Consistent with the higher financial status of those with emergency savings or a perceived ability to find $2,000 in an emergency, households with savings are more satisfied with their finances. All of these comparisons suggest that there are differences in access to emergency savings by personal characteristics and behaviors. But these pairwise comparisons could be confounded since income, education, and other factors are correlated.

Table 2.3 provides estimates of having emergency funds, being able to find $2,000, and reported financial satisfaction using a regression framework. An ordinary least squares (OLS) regression analysis was conducted on the demographic and financial characteristics associated with having an emergency fund (column 1), being confident in the ability to find $2,000 (column 2), and reported financial satisfaction (columns 3 and 4). Controlling for other factors, being white and having a college education, higher income, and higher risk tolerance are all associated with having an emergency fund in column 1. Income is a very strong predictor of having emergency funds, with the lowest income groups showing as much as a 33 percentage point lower rate of having an emergency fund, controlling for other factors. Financial risk-taking has a smaller effect, but using overdrafts and alternative financial service borrowing have large and negative effects. This emphasizes that credit and savings are often substitutes for each other; without savings, people likely turn to credit alternatives.

The estimates in column 2 are similar to those in column 1, although the effects among lower-income households are even more profound. While having an emergency fund is not associated with financial knowledge level, it does have a modest association with being confident in being able to find $2,000 in an emergency. This suggests that the ability to find liquidity may be related to the strength of social networks and the ability to liquidate assets and access credit.

Overall, these regression results largely mirror the sample means reported in table 2.2. In column 3, the results for financial satisfaction, which is measured on a self-reported ten-point scale, show that having emergency funds and confidence in the ability to find $2,000 are associated with large estimates of increased financial satisfaction. In fact, these two variables could explain up to three of the ten points of financial satisfaction. Given the average satisfaction score was around 6.5, emergency funds appear strongly associated with financial satisfaction, controlling for income, education, and other factors. In column 4, estimates from an alternate specification for financial satisfaction show that having both no emergency savings and low confidence in the ability to find $2,000 is related to a substantial reduction in financial satisfaction. Overall, the regression results affirm that income is a major factor in the lack of emergency savings, and that access to liquidity in the form of savings, as opposed to credit, may help people feel more financially secure or satisfied with their financial life.

Emergency Liquidity and Financial Wellness

The NFCS data related to financial satisfaction is perhaps most provocative. Having emergency savings and access to $2,000 in an emergency have large and statistically significant effects on satisfaction. Figure 2.1 displays data from the NFCS that shows financial satisfaction decreasing as access to emergency liquidity decreases, a result consistent with the associations between emergency savings and financial satisfaction and the ability to find $2,000 and financial satisfaction shown in table 2.3. This might be predictable since people lacking resources may face hardships and stress in the event of an emergency, or worry about making ends meet (Mills and

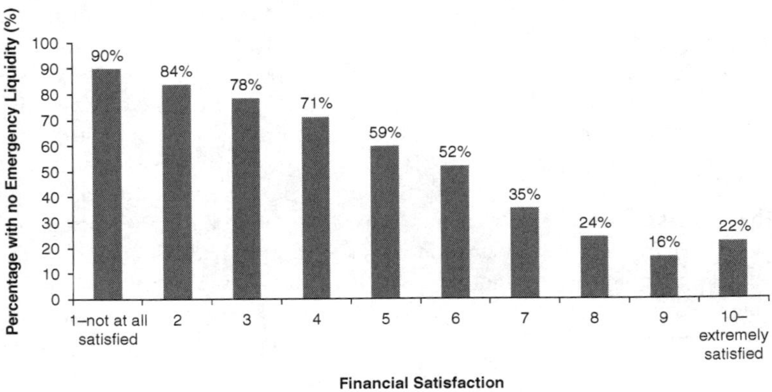

Figure 2.1 Percentage of Families with No Emergency Liquidity by Financial Satisfaction.

Note: *n* = 22,970. Calculations performed using NFCS-provided weights. Having no emergency liquidity is defined as not having three months of emergency funds and not being confident about one's ability to come up with $2,000 within 30 days.

Source: Author's calculations using data from the NFCS 2012.

Amick 2010; McKernan, Ratcliffe, and Vinopal 2009). Access to liquidity via savings may provide some sense of financial control or security for the future that reduces worry and contributes to financial satisfaction, whereas households without sufficient liquidity have little capacity to absorb an economic shock (Hira and Mugenda 1998; Sumarwan and Hira 1993; Davis and Helmick 1985; Liang and Fairchild 1979).

This is consistent with the idea that having emergency savings supports broader household well-being. Financial stress has been associated with negative impacts on health (Keese and Schmitz 2013; Choi 2009), adult relationship quality, parenting, and child and adolescent development (Conger et al. 2002; Conger, Rueter, and Elder 1999; Elder et al. 1992). While emergency savings are only one component of a household's financial circumstances, the existence of adequate emergency savings may contribute to reductions in financial stress that negatively impacts families. Policies and programs that facilitate unrestricted savings for unexpected needs may therefore help households not only smooth consumption but also achieve a greater sense of well-being.

It is important to note that the correlation shown in figure 2.1 does not identify causal mechanisms; simply giving low-income households $1,000 or $2,000 in emergency savings funds may not make households better off.

It is likely financial satisfaction is determined jointly by income, wealth, and access to credit—and these same factors facilitate the accumulation of emergency funds. However, there may be some unique factors that contribute to satisfaction beyond household income and net worth (Davis and Helmick 1985). Access to liquidity could be one of these factors. The ideal study would randomly assign families to receive emergency savings, but the correlations here provoke questions about the potential of liquid accounts to play a unique role for families.

Limitations of Existing Measures

There is a need to continue examining and validating measures of emergency savings and liquidity, especially for low-income households. The current landscape includes a variety of measures that are not fully standardized and are difficult to compare across studies. Existing measures of emergency savings essentially rely on two factors: How much? (months of current income or current expenses—typically three, $2,000, or $3,000, among other variations) What counts? (financial assets, liquid savings, credit from traditional and alternative sources, and borrowing from social networks). The measures, determined by somewhat arbitrary thresholds for sufficient savings, change who is considered unprepared. Further, some measures, such as the ability to find $2,000 within 30 days, include a specified time component while others, such as the ability to acquire $3,000 from social networks in an emergency, do not.

Many of these measures are least useful when applied to lower-income households. For example, the most frequently used threshold (three months of income) does not make sense for many low-income households. The income and expenses of low-income households are often characterized by significant volatility (Morduch and Schneider 2013). These households must deal with irregular work hours, seasonal employment, unreliable transportation, and other factors. In this context, three months of income or expenses may be difficult to calculate, let alone actually accumulate in the context of basic expenses that absorb most or all of—or even exceed—the available income. The three-month threshold is also likely inappropriate for highly leveraged households; it may not be realistic to expect households to set aside emergency funds when they are carrying substantial debt.

An alternative to the three months' income measure could be fixed-cost measures, such as the average cost of one month's housing or a car repair. A measure of the average cost of one month's rent or mortgage may be the most promising strategy. Missed housing payments can have dramatic consequences on housing stability, consequences that are especially swift for renters. A reserve fund that at a minimum prepares households to maintain their housing for another month has tangible value while being a realistic target for lower-income households.

Geographic variation in cost of living has important implications for the amount households need to meet basic needs, including housing. Researchers and practitioners must take this variation into account. Rules of thumb like three months earnings are arbitrary but potentially have the benefit of reflecting geographic variation in wages. For fixed-cost measures such as one month's housing, the threshold needs to account for regional differences.

Still another approach could borrow from the asset poverty framework and set a threshold based on income at the federal poverty level for a specified time period, such as one month. In addition, when calculating a household's ability to meet fixed costs, it may be beneficial to consider measures that account for access to public supports such as unemployment benefits (Shapiro, Oliver, and Meschede 2009). In general, when designing measures to elicit information about amounts of money over periods of time, researchers can gain insights from survey methods used in consumption studies by varying the form and approaches used in asking questions (Angrisani, Kapteyn, and Schuh, forthcoming; Crossley and Winter, forthcoming).

It is important to think holistically and reach beyond balance sheet-based measures of emergency liquidity, as these metrics may miss potentially important variety in the capacity of households to weather financial shocks. Measures that account for the ability to borrow (formally or informally) and the ability to generate additional income are a valuable addition. However, work is needed to determine the optimal level of emergency liquidity for lower-income households. The ability to acquire $2,000 in 30 days is a useful measure, but there may be other meaningful amounts of accessible liquidity that would provide families the capacity to avert hardship and reduce financial stress.

There may also be value in understanding the ability to come up with funds in a shorter period of time. In the absence of credit, many unexpected expenses must be paid within a few days. The work of the US Financial Diaries highlights the granularity of cash-flow management among lower-income households, driven by the irregularity of income and expenses; this finding accentuates the need for liquidity to smooth consumption in the short term (Morduch and Schneider 2013). Assessing access to funds over very short time frames, such as five days, can capture the capacity of a household to respond quickly to an immediate economic shock. Measures that align with weekly or biweekly payroll cycles may also have value.

There is a need to better understand how various metrics of emergency savings and liquidity interact with each other to capture a meaningful assessment of households' capacity to cope with financial shock. There are likely substitution effects between savings and credit. Comprehensive measures of emergency savings should aim to identify and unpack the interaction between these liquidity mechanisms among lower-income households.

Finally, researchers must carefully consider issues of well-being. Lack of liquidity and resulting financial stress might directly lead to declines in physical and mental health, child welfare, and relationship quality. As a result, interventions that improve access to emergency savings and liquidity have the potential to improve family circumstances beyond household balance sheets. Additional research is needed to document the relationship between lack of liquidity and the well-being of lower-income households as well as to capture the extent to which efforts that increase liquidity influence family well-being outcomes.

Conclusion

Households with the lowest income are least prepared to cope with a financial emergency by any measure. Half of households with incomes under $20,000 have less than $450 in saving accounts and only 41 percent of these households could get $3,000 of financial assistance from their social networks. Households without emergency savings utilize such high-cost alternatives as bank overdrafts and alternative financial services at notably higher rates than households with emergency savings. There is also a strong negative relationship between having no source of emergency liquidity and financial satisfaction, which suggest that increasing the ability to smooth consumption via emergency liquidity may increase financial satisfaction and reduce financial stress. Considering the established relationship between financial strain and adult and child outcomes, an important next step for emergency savings research is to understand whether increases in emergency savings or liquidity can influence broader family well-being. Research that tests the capacity of emergency savings interventions to decrease financial strain and positively affect adult and child well-being may be of particular value. More focused studies are needed to test variations in measures, including variations in savings levels and the time required to tap funds, differentiation of the credit and social forms of liquidity, and consumption-based benchmarks such as housing costs. Studies that evaluate the impact of emergency funds as a specific, unrestricted form of liquidity are also needed, including longitudinal randomized experiments that can assess the impacts of savings on child and family hardships and wellbeing.

While the tight budgets of lower-income households undoubtedly make saving difficult, there may be interventions that can promote modest savings or increase access to safe and affordable credit. If policy, programs, and research are to be focused on shoring up the financial stability of low-income households, then there is a clear need for improved benchmarks of emergency saving and liquidity that can serve as standards by which to measure the effects of programmatic or policy interventions. Such innovations have the potential to increase economic stability, reduce financial stress and hardship, and improve outcomes for low-income families.

Notes

1. SCF question: "In an emergency could you (or your husband/wife/partner) get financial assistance of $3,000 or more from any friends or relatives who do not live with you?"
2. SCF question: "About how much do you think you (and your family) need to have in savings for emergencies and other unexpected things that may come up?"

References

Angrisani, Marco, Arie Kapteyn, and Scott Schuh. Forthcoming. "Measuring Household Spending and Payment Habits: The Role of 'Typical' and 'Specific' Time Frames in Survey Questions." In *Improving the Measurement of Consumer Expenditures*, ed. Christopher Carroll, Thomas Crossley, and John Sabelhaus. Chicago, IL: University of Chicago Press.

Babiarz, Patryk, and Cliff A. Robb. 2014. "Financial Literacy and Emergency Saving." *Journal of Family and Economic Issues* 35 (1): 40–50.

Bhargava, Vibha, and Jean M. Lown. 2006. "Preparedness for Financial Emergencies: Evidence from the Survey of Consumer Finances." *Financial Counseling and Planning* 17 (2): 17–26.

Bi, Lan, and Catherine P. Montalto. 2004. "Emergency Funds and Alternative Forms of Saving." *Financial Services Review* 13 (2): 93–109.

Brandolini, Andrea, Silvia Magri, and Timothy M. Smeeding. 2010. "Asset-based Measurement of Poverty." *Journal of Policy Analysis and Management* 29 (2): 267–284.

Caner, Asena, and Edward N. Wolff. 2004. "Asset Poverty in the United States, 1984–99: Evidence from the Panel Study of Income Dynamics." *Review of Income and Wealth* 50 (4): 493–518.

Chang, Y. Regina, Sherman Hanna, and Jessie X. Fan. 1997. "Emergency Fund Levels: Is Household Behavior Rational?" *Financial Counseling and Planning* 8 (1): 47–55.

Chang, Y. Regina, and Sandra J. Huston. 1995. "Patterns of Adequate Household Emergency Fund Holdings: A Comparison of Households in 1983 and 1986." *Financial Counseling and Planning* 6:119–128.

Chen, Chiu, and Sharon A. DeVaney. 2001. "The Effect of Life Cycle Stages and Saving Motives on The Probability Of Emergency Fund Adequacy." In *Proceedings of the Association for Financial Counseling and Planning Education*, ed. J. M. Hogarth, 176–185. Columbus OH: AFCPE.

Choi, Laura. 2009. "Financial Stress and Its Physical Effects on Individuals and Communities." *Community Development Investment Review* 5 (3): 120–122.

Conger, Rand D., Martha A. Rueter, and Glen H. Elder Jr. 1999. "Couple Resilience to Economic Pressure." *Journal of Personality and Social Psychology* 76 (1): 54–71.

Conger, Rand D., Lora Ebert Wallace, Yumei Sun, Ronald L. Simons, Vonnie C. McLoyd, and Gene H. Brody. 2002. "Economic Pressure in African American Families: A Replication and Extension of the Family Stress Model." *Developmental Psychology* 38 (2): 179–193.

Crossley, Thomas F., and Joachim K. Winter. Forthcoming. "Asking Households About Expenditures: What Have We Learned?" In *Improving the Measurement of Consumer Expenditures*, ed. Christopher Carroll, Thomas Crossley, and John Sabelhaus. Chicago, IL: University of Chicago Press.

Davis, Elizabeth P., and Sandra A. Helmick. 1985. "Family Financial Satisfaction: The Impact of Reference Points." *Home Economics Research Journal* 14 (1): 123–131.

DeVaney, S. A. 1995. "Emergency Fund Adequacy Among US Households in 1977 and 1989." *Consumer Interests Annual* 41:222–223.

DeVaney, Sharon A., Sophia T. Anong, and Stacy E. Whirl. 2007. "Household Savings Motives." *Journal of Consumer Affairs* 41 (1): 174–186.

Ding, J., and S. A. DeVaney. 2000. "Predictors of Emergency Funds Adequacy." In *Proceedings of Association for Financial Counseling and Planning Education*, ed. J. E. Morris and C. R. Hayhoe, 56–65. Columbus, OH: AFCPE.

Elder, Glen H., Rand D. Conger, E. Michael Foster, and Monika Ardelt. 1992. "Families Under Economic Pressure." *Journal of Family Issues* 13 (1): 5–37.

Gornick, Janet C., Eva Sierminska, and Timothy M. Smeeding. 2009. "The Income and Wealth Packages of Older Women in Cross-National Perspective." *The Journals of Gerontology Series B: Psychological Sciences and Social Sciences* 64 (3): 402–414.

Greninger, Sue A., Vickie L. Hampton, Karrol A. Kitt, and Joseph A. Achacoso. 1996. "Ratios and Benchmarks for Measuring the Financial Well-Being of Families and Individuals." *Financial Services Review* 5 (1): 57–70.

Hanna, Sherman, and Hui Wang. 1995. "The Adequacy of Emergency Funds to Cover Household Expenditures." In *Proceedings of the 41st Annual Conference of the American Council on Consumer Interests*, ed. Karen F. Folk, 224–225. Columbia, MO: American Council of Consumer Interests.

Haveman, Robert, and Edward N. Wolff. 2005. "The Concept and Measurement of Asset Poverty: Levels, Trends and Composition for the US, 1983–2001." *The Journal of Economic Inequality* 2 (2): 145–169.

Hira, Tahira K., and Olive M. Mugenda. 1998. "Predictors of Financial Satisfaction: Differences Between Retirees and Non-Retirees." *Financial Counseling and Planning* 9 (2): 75–83.

Hong, Eunice O., Sherman D. Hanna, and Kyoung Tae Kim. 2013. "Which Households Have Adequate Emergency Funds After the Great Recession? Estimate Based on an Income Measure and a Spending Measure." Paper presented at the Annual Meeting of the Academy of Financial Services, October 17, 2013, Chicago, IL.

Hong, Gong-Soog, and Y. Emily Kao. 1997. "Emergency Fund Adequacy of Asian Americans." *Journal of Family and Economic Issues* 18 (2): 127–145.

Huston, Sandra J., and Y. Regina Chang. 1997. "Adequate Emergency Fund Holdings and Household Type." *Financial Counseling and Planning* 8 (1): 37–46.

Johnson, D., and R. Widdows. 1985. "Emergency Fund Levels of Households." In *The Proceedings of the American Council on Consumer Interests 31st Annual Conference*, ed. K. Schnittgrund, 235–241. Columbia, MO: American Council of Consumer Interests.

Keese, Matthias, and Hendrik Schmitz. 2013. "Broke, Ill, and Obese: Is There an Effect of Household Debt on Health?" *Review of Income and Wealth* 60 (3): 525–541.

Kennickell, Arthur, and Annamaria Lusardi. 2004. "Disentangling the Importance of the Precautionary Saving Mode." National Bureau of Economic Research Working Paper Series, No. 10888.

Key, Clinton. 2014. "The Finances of Typical Households After the Great Recession." In *The Assets Perspective*, ed. Reid Cramer and Trina R. Williams Shanks, 33–66. New York: Palgrave Macmillian.

Kim, KyoungTae, and Sherman D. Hanna. 2013. "Does Financial Sophistication Matter in Retirement Preparedness of US Households? Evidence from the 2010 Survey of Consumer Finances." *Consumer Interests Annual* 59. http://www.consumerinterests.org/cia2013.

Lee, Alyssa Stewart, Ann Schnare, Michael A. Turner, Patrick D. Walker, and Robin Varghese. 2006. "Give Credit Where Credit Is Due: Increasing Access to Affordable Mainstream Credit Using Alternative Data." Report, December. Brookings Institution, Washington, DC.

Liang, Jersey, and Thomas J. Fairchild. 1979. "Relative Deprivation and Perception of Financial Adequacy Among the Aged." *Journal of Gerontology* 34 (5): 746–759.

Lown, Jean M. 2005. "Emergency Fund Essentials." *The Journal of Consumer Education* 22:27–34.

Lusardi, Annamaria, Daniel J. Schneider, and Peter Tufano. 2011. "Financially Fragile Households: Evidence and Implications." National Bureau of Economic Research Working Paper Series, No. 17072.

McKay, Katherine Lucas, and Alicia Atkinson. 2014. "Alternative Data Helps Families Build Credit and Wealth." Federal Policy Brief, April. CFED, Washington, DC.

McKernan, Signe-Mary, Caroline Ratcliffe, and Katie Vinopal. 2009. "Do Assets Help Families Cope with Adverse Events?" Perspectives on Low-Income Working Families, Brief 10. Urban Institute, Washington, DC.

Mills, Gregory, and Joe Amick. 2010. "Can Savings Help Overcome Income Instability?" Perspectives on Low-Income Working Families, Brief 18. Urban Institute, Washington, DC.

Morduch, Jonathan, and Rachel Schneider. 2013. "Spikes and Dips: How Income Uncertainty Affects Households." Issue Brief, December. US Financial Diaries, New York.

Ratcliffe, Caroline, and Katie Vinopal. 2009. "Are Families Prepared for Financial Emergencies?" *Opportunity and Ownership Facts* 16, September. Urban Institute, Washington, DC.

Rhine, Sherrie L. W., and Maude Toussaint-Comeau. 1999. "The Use Of Formal and Informal Financial Markets Among Black Households." *Consumer Interest Annual* 45:146–151.

Shapiro, Thomas M., Melvin L. Oliver, and Tatjana Meschede. 2009. "The Asset Security and Opportunity Index." Research and Policy Brief, November. Institute on Assets and Social Policy, Brandeis University, Waltham, MA.

Sumarwan, Ujang, and Tahira K. Hira. 1993. "The Effects of Perceived Locus of Control and Perceived Income Adequacy on Satisfaction with Financial Status of Rural Households." *Journal of Family and Economic Issues* 14 (4): 343–364.

Chapter 3

Upside Down: The Failure of Federal Tax Policies to Support Emergency Savings

Ezra Levin

Introduction

Nearly all families experience fluctuations in income, and low- and moderate-income (LMI) families appear increasingly likely to experience significant income interruptions (see Collins, this volume). Almost half of Americans are "liquid asset poor," meaning they lack even a modest amount of accessible savings to tap into in the case of an emergency (Brooks et al. 2014). Liquid savings and long-term savings or assets are quite different forms of financial resources. Using long-term savings as liquid savings can have serious consequences. For example, withdrawals from retirement or education savings accounts often come with significant financial penalties. Likewise, borrowing against home equity can be difficult, especially in the short term. In the case of an emergency, households without accessible savings must rely on family, friends, high-cost credit, or the high costs of missing payments.

Families build savings in two general ways: saving and investing their own income, or receiving someone else's savings and investments as a gift or an inheritance. The federal government is an active participant when it comes to these strategies. In 2014 alone, the federal government spent more than $175 billion on tax programs, also known as "tax expenditures," related to investments and inheritances.[1] Yet, these tax programs are "upside down" because they almost entirely benefit the highest-income households, while doing little for most LMI households.

This need not be the case. Federal policy can provide savings opportunities for a broader set of households. Policymakers can expand financial security and economic opportunity for millions of Americans simply by turning these tax programs "right-side up." This chapter provides a brief overview of the size and distribution of investment and inheritance tax programs, an analysis of which households benefit from these programs, and a review of several potential policy reforms.

Tax Benefits to Incentivize Household Savings

Tax programs, often called tax expenditures, take the form of tax credits, deductions, exclusions, exemptions, deferrals, and reduced tax rates. Stanley Surrey, assistant secretary for tax policy at the US Treasury in the 1960s, coined the term tax expenditure (Burman, Toder, and Geissler 2008), which Surrey later defined with McDaniel (1985) as "government spending for favored activities or groups, effected through the tax system" (3). Both sides of the political aisle largely agree that tax programs are simply federal spending programs by a different name. Donald Marron, a member of President George W. Bush's council of economic advisors, described tax programs as "spending in disguise" (Marron 2011). Leonard Burman and Eric Toder, who each served as President Clinton's deputy assistant secretary for tax analysis, took the same view (Burman, Toder, and Geissler 2008). So too does Senator Tom Coburn, the Republican conservative stalwart (Coburn 2011).

The fact that tax programs are effectively spending programs should inform debates around social policy and economic opportunity. The Earned Income Tax Credit (EITC)—one of the largest "antipoverty" programs in the country—is often seen as an anomalous tax program in the economic opportunity policy space. The reality is that the EITC is just one of several social policy programs run through the tax code.

Combined, the major tax programs to boost savings and investment cost the federal government over $175 billion in 2014 according to data from the Congressional Joint Committee on Taxation (JCT) and Tax Policy Center. Identifying tax programs that specifically boost savings through investments and inheritances is a subjective process, and the analysis in this chapter takes a conservative approach. In other words, this analysis understates the total cost of these types of tax programs.[2] The remainder of this section reviews the largest of these tax programs individually.

Preferential Rate on Capital Gains and Dividends

The largest savings and investment tax incentive in 2014 was the $96.5 billion reduction in taxes on long-term capital gains and dividends for individual taxpayers (JCT 2014). When an investor buys a stock and later sells it for more than the purchase price, it is classified as a capital gain and subject to federal and (usually) state taxes. Similarly, when a corporation issues a dividend to stockholders, this dividend is taxable. Both capital gains and dividends are types of investment income, which can be distinguished from "earned" income received through salaries or wages. When the federal income tax was originally enacted, investment income and earned income were taxed at the same rate. The marginal tax rates on earned income currently range from 10 percent to 39.6 percent. Income from long-term capital gains now receives preferential tax treatment, with a top tax rate of only 20 percent, roughly half the top tax rate for earned income. Capital gains for an investment held for less than a year are classified as short-term capital gains and taxed at a higher rate. Dividends were taxed at the same rate as earned income until 2003 (Leiserson and Rohaly 2008), but today dividends receive the same preferential tax rate as capital gains.

Exclusion of Inherited Investments ("Stepped-Up Basis at Death")

The next largest tax program in 2014 is the $31.5 billion exclusion of inherited investments from capital gains taxes (JCT 2014). Often called the "Stepped-Up Basis at Death," this program reduces taxes on inherited investments. As an example, imagine that Mary's grandfather buys $1,000 worth of stock in 2004. The $1,000 purchase price is known as the "basis." In his will, he leaves Mary the stock, which by the time of his death had increased in value to $2,500. Had Mary's grandfather been able to sell the stock then, he would have owed tax on the $1,500 increase in value. This $1,500 increase over the $1,000 basis is his "capital gain." When Mary inherits the stock, however, the basis is "stepped up" to $2,500, the stock value at the time of her grandfather's passing. This means that Mary can sell the stock when she inherits it and record only the capital gain from the stepped up basis value. If she does so, her capital gain is the new basis ($2,500) minus the sale price ($2,500), which is zero. Alternatively, Mary can sell the stock at a later date, again with the capital gain calculated based on the stepped up basis value of $2,500. Regardless, the estate and Mary effectively avoid paying taxes on the original $1,500 capital gain.

Reduced Estate Tax Rate and Increased Estate Tax Exemption

Related to this exclusion is the $23.5 billion estate tax cut, a figure that reflects the reduction in federal revenue for 2013 that occurred as a result of the most recent cut to the estate tax (Tax Policy Center 2013). Unlike the other items in this list, the reduced tax rate on estates is not a traditional tax program (or "income tax expenditure") because it applies to assets rather than income. For the 2014 tax year, estates can exclude the first $5.34 million in taxable value ($10.68 million for couples). The taxable value is the total value of the estate minus deductions, such as costs of administering the estate and the cost of debt. Any portion of the estate passed on to a surviving spouse is also deductible. Any taxable value over the $5.34 million exemption is taxed at a flat 40 percent rate.

Exclusion of Interest on State and Local Bonds

Roughly the same size as the estate tax reduction, the exclusion of interest on state and local bonds is estimated to cost the federal government $23.8 billion for individuals in 2014 (JCT 2014). Almost all state and local governments issue debt in the form of bonds to pay for investments, such as road construction, municipal buildings, hospitals, schools, and sewage treatment facilities. This tax program makes these bonds tax-exempt, meaning that the interest earned on these bonds is tax free. In contrast, an investor who purchases a corporate bond is required to pay tax on bond interest. As the size of this tax program indicates, these state and local bonds are very popular with investors largely due to the tax benefits they receive.

Deferral of Interest on US Treasury Savings Bonds

Finally, the deferral of interest on savings bonds cost $1.2 billion in 2014 (JCT 2014). When a taxpayer buys a savings bond, she earns interest on the bond. For instance, given the current interest rate of 0.5 percent, $1,000 in Series EE US Treasury savings bonds will earn $5 in interest over the course of a year. Bond holders have the option of paying income tax on this $5 when it accrues, or they can defer tax payment until they cash in the bond (often years or decades later). The deferral of taxes on interest costs the federal government tax revenue each year taxes are deferred.

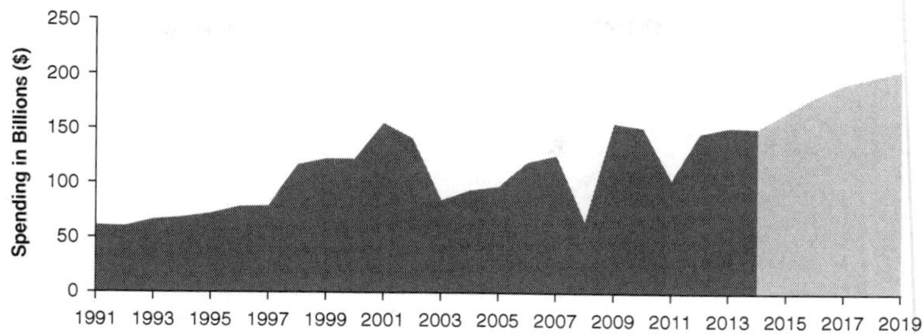

Figure 3.1 Annual Federal Spending on Investment and Inheritance Tax Programs in Constant Dollars.

Note: All values in constant 2015 dollars. 2014–2019 is projected spending. Tax expenditures include: preferential rate on capital gains and dividends, stepped-up basis at death, exclusion of interest on state and local bonds, carryover basis of capital gains on gifts, and deferral of interest on US savings bonds.

Source: Office of Management and Budget data compiled by the National Priorities Project (2014).

Historical and Projected Growth of Tax Expenditures

The total cost of these programs has increased greatly in the last several years, and it is projected to grow rapidly in the next few years. Figure 3.1 shows that between 1991 and 2014, the cost of these tax programs for individuals and corporations nearly tripled in size, from just over $50 billion to slightly over $150 billion (in constant 2015 dollars). These programs are estimated to cost about $205 billion in 2019, again in constant 2015 dollars (National Priorities Project 2014). This analysis actually understates to the total growth in cost, as it does not count the forgone revenue from cuts to the estate tax.

Distributional Effects

Tax programs that boost savings through investments and inheritances benefit the highest-income households—the same households least in need of support to build savings. These tax programs are "upside down" in the sense that the LMI households who need the most support building savings receive the least amount of support.

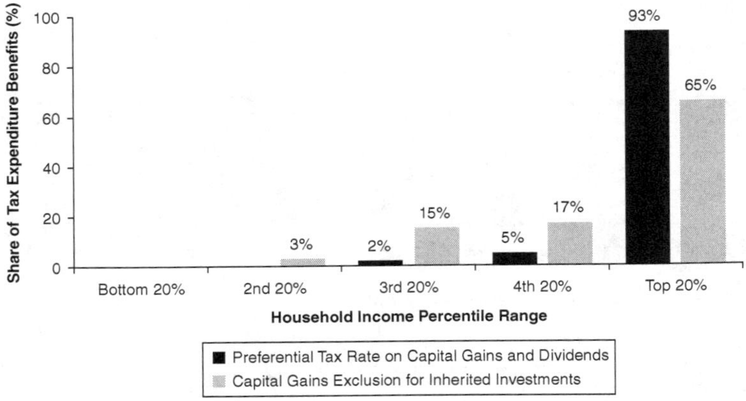

Figure 3.2 Share of Tax Expenditure Benefits Received by Income Group.

Source: CBO (2013).

Data from the Congressional Budget Office (CBO) illustrate exactly how much these tax programs concentrate benefits on the top-income earners. Figure 3.2 shows CBO distributional estimates of the reduced tax rate on investment income (capital gains and dividends) and the capital gains exclusion on inherited investments (the "stepped-up basis"). The data reveal a set of programs that are extremely tilted toward boosting the wealth of the already-wealthy. Further analysis of the CBO (2013) data reveals that the bottom 40 percent of households receive less than 1 percent of the total tax benefit from these programs. Furthermore, the top 1 percent of households receive more than the entire bottom 99 percent combined.

A Tax Policy Center analysis paints a similar picture of the federal spending on state and local bonds (Galper et al. 2013). While these bonds help state and local governments finance needed expenditures, federal tax spending on these bonds gives high-income investors a large tax break. The Tax Policy Center analyzed several scenarios, and under the one that is least-friendly to high-income households, the top 5 percent of households receive more than half of the total benefit from this tax program (Galper et al. 2013). In short, tax-exempt bonds offer savings incentives that mainly benefit high-income households.

To illustrate the extent to which tax programs focus benefits on high-income households, it is helpful to compare the EITC, the main targeted tax benefit for low-income workers, and the preferential tax rates on capital gains and dividends. The EITC is commonly accepted to focus benefits on low-income households. The bottom 60 percent of households by income receive 91 percent of the EITC's benefits, as expected for an antipoverty program (CBO 2013). By comparison, the top 20 percent of households by income receive 93 percent of the share of tax expenditures from the preferential tax rates for capital gains and dividends (CBO 2013). In other words, preferential rates on capital gains and dividends concentrate benefits on high-income households more than the EITC concentrates benefits on low-income households. And the cost of the preferential rates on capital gains and dividends far outweights the cost of the EITC. The EITC cost $61 billion in 2013 (CBO 2013), only about two-thirds as much as the preferential tax rates for capital gains and dividends.

Discussion

As the EITC demonstrates, it is possible to structure a tax program to benefit LMI households. But most existing investment and inheritance tax programs fail to support these households. This section reviews three reasons for the large size and inequitable distribution of benefits from these tax programs.

First, high-income households are much more likely to have significant income from investments and large estates. According to Tax Policy Center estimates, less than one in ten households in the bottom 60 percent of the income distribution will report any tax-preferred investment income from capital gains or dividends in 2014. By comparison, 95 percent of the taxpayers in the top 0.1 percent will report investment income (Tax Policy Center 2013). Needless to say, the investment income that higher-income households have is also much greater than the investment income of LMI households, as shown in figure 3.3. In 2013, the average investment income for someone in the top 0.1 percent of household incomes was $2.7 million. By comparison, households in the bottom 90 percent had average investment incomes of less than $5,000. The bottom 60 percent of taxpayers claimed less than 3 percent of all investment income in 2013 (Tax Policy Center 2013).

A similar story emerges for estates. In 2011, the top 1 percent of taxpayers accounted for roughly half of all estates that were large enough to be taxable. The highest-income 10 percent of taxpayers accounted for more than 9 in 10 taxable estates (Rohaly and Lim 2011). There is a significant racial element to the estate tax as well. Whites are more likely to inherit

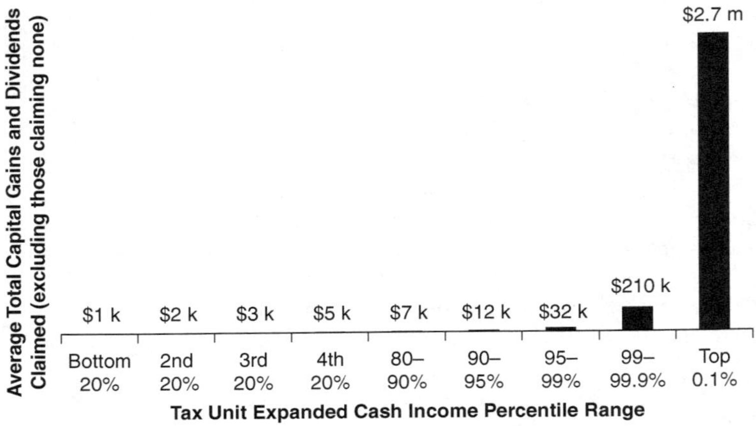

Figure 3.3 Average Income from Capital Gains and Dividends by Income Group.

Source: TPC (2013)

than blacks, and white households' inheritances are much larger than black households' inheritances (Thomas et al. 2014).

Second, while the estate tax is inherently a progressive tax, it has been cut significantly in recent years. Estate taxes are only applied to estates after the value of the estate is reduced through deductions, and then after a large portion of the estate is exempted. Since the modern estate tax was created in 1916, the federal government has allowed for an estate tax exemption. Nonetheless, policy changes in recent years have made the estate exemption more generous to large estates (Tax Foundation 2014). Between 1916 and 2001, the exemption was almost always below $1 million in 2013 inflation-adjusted dollars. Starting in 2002, the exemption began to increase rapidly. For 2014, the exemption is $5.34 million, about 8 times the median inflation-adjusted exemption for the first 85 years of the estate tax. This exemption is far greater than the median inheritance, which in 2007 was just under $74,000 (Wolff and Gittleman 2013).

Just as the size of the exemption began growing in 2002, the estate tax rate began decreasing. Between 1916 and 2001 the median maximum estate tax was 70 percent, and it never dropped below 60 percent between 1934 and 1983 (Tax Foundation 2014). In 2014, the tax rate was 40 percent, which is lower than any point in history since 1931 (save for a three-year span from 2010 to 2012). Figure 3.4 displays estate tax exemption levels and rates over time.

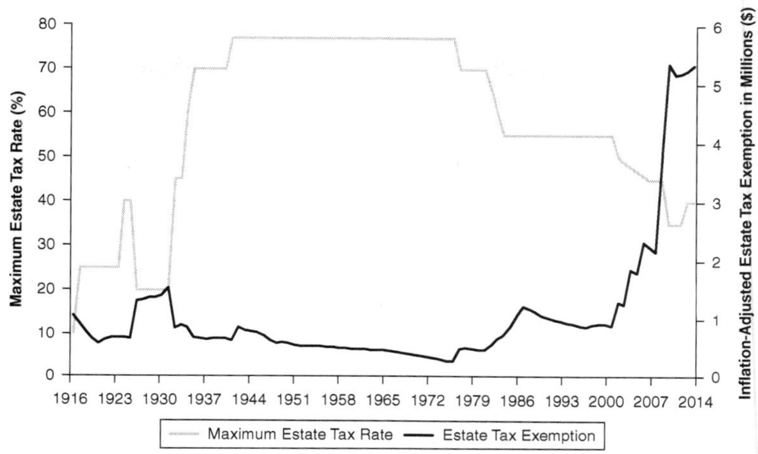

Figure 3.4 Maximum Estate Tax Rate and Inflation-Adjusted Estate Tax Exemption Levels: 1916–2014.

Source: Tax Foundation (2014). Tax exemption levels adjusted for inflation in 2013 dollars.

Consider the combined effect of these features. Suppose an estate is worth $20 million. Ten million dollars is left to a surviving spouse, $3 million is given to charities, $1 million is used to pay off debt, and $700,000 is used to pay accountants and lawyers who administer the estate. All of these amounts are deductible, leaving $5.3 million in "taxable" value from the $20 million estate. Because this amount is less than $5.34 million exemption, the estate is not taxable.

The Tax Policy Center has calculated the impact of these recent policy changes. The 2010 "current law" set an exemption of $1 million. Reforms enacted that year increased the exemption to $5 million. As a result of this change, the number of taxable estates dropped about 90 percent, from 43,540 to 3,600 (Tax Policy Center 2010). The exemption was later indexed to inflation, resulting in a $5.34 million exemption for 2014.

Finally, the third reason these tax programs are upside down is that they often combine to create significant tax loopholes, allowing particularly high-income individuals to avoid paying taxes on large amount of income and inherited wealth. Consider the exclusion for inheritances and the enlarged estate tax exclusion. The combined effect of these programs is to allow a large amount of investment income to avoid taxes entirely. Imagine that granddad George bought $500,000 of stock, and it increased in value to $5 million. If granddad George sells the stock, he'll owe tax on the investment income—$4.5 million. But instead imagine that granddad George bequeaths the stock to his son, Sonny. Because the value of the estate ($5 million) is less than $5.34 million, no estate tax is owed. And because of the exclusion for inheritances ("stepped-up basis"), the son doesn't have to pay any tax on the inheritance. As result of these two programs in the tax code, $4.5 million in investment income avoids taxes altogether. This is not an uncommon occurrence. The Center on Budget and Policy Priorities has estimated that these unrealized and untaxed capital gains account for more than half of the value of the largest estates (those worth more than $10 million) (Huang and Frentz 2013).

Three Tax Policy Alternatives to Boost Savings

For a policymaker who believes the federal tax code should encourage all families to save, new policies that go beyond the highest-income families are needed. The right-side up reforms discussed below would help more Americans build accessible savings.

An Economic Opportunity Fund for Children's Savings Funded with Estate and Inheritance Tax Reforms.

Currently, revenue from estate and inheritance taxes goes into the federal government's general revenue fund to pay for all types of federal expenses. A reform of these tax programs could create a new guaranteed source of annual funding to create a permanent Economic Opportunity Fund. Such a system would be built on the principle of creating a link between successive generations—a portion of the wealth of one generation would go directly toward investing in economic opportunity for the next generation.

A similar reform has been proposed as a funding mechanism for early childhood programs (Bell, Bernstein, and Greenberg 2008), and indeed, there are several ways to structure an Economic Opportunity Fund. One laudable goal would be to provide a Children's Savings Account to every one of the four million children born in America every year. While Children's Savings Accounts are often restricted-use accounts for education or other long-term assets, several proposals would provide flexible accounts for use once children reach adulthood (Zichawo, Farber, and Mensah 2014).

Reforms to two existing tax programs could provide the annual funding for the Fund. First, eliminate the capital gains exclusion for inherited investments (the step-up in basis). Two recent bipartisan commissions, the Bowles-Simpson debt commission and the Domenici-Rivlin Debt Reduction Task Force, recommended repealing this program.[3] Second, revise the estate tax rate and exclusion closer to historical standards. Historically, the estate tax has had a median exclusion of about $666,000 in 2013 dollars and a maximum tax rate of about 70 percent. Returning the estate tax to a $1 million exemption and a 55 percent tax rate would raise billions of dollars in annual federal revenue.

Reforming these tax programs would raise tens of billions of dollars on an annual basis—more than enough to generously support an Economic Opportunity Fund, create universal Children's Savings Accounts, and invest in a number of other evidence-based policies to expand economic opportunity.

Two EITC Reforms to Support Wealth-Building for Low- and Moderate-Income Workers

The EITC was not created to directly support wealth-building. Workers become eligible for an EITC tax refund, but they cannot access that resource until they file their taxes. The EITC effectively forces low-income workers to use the US Treasury as a safe but zero-interest savings account to build up savings once per year (Mendenhall et al. 2012). For most EITC recipients, this forced savings is a valued feature of the program, not a bug. Several scholarly studies and anecdotes from the field reveal that the vast majority of EITC recipients prefer the forced savings mechanism of the EITC to an alternative monthly wage boost (Greene 2013; Romich and Wiesner 2012; Jones 2010). For low-income families who are unbanked, a zero-interest "savings account" with Treasury Department may be the best option they have. In fact, in addition to the EITC, many low-income workers routinely increase the amount of withholdings from their paycheck in order to boost their eventual lump-sum tax refund check (Edin, Tach, and Halpern-Meekin 2014). But while the EITC is often used as a makeshift savings tool, it was not built to function as one. Congress needs to make reforms to ensure that LMI households are able to build accessible savings. Two laudable reforms—one an expansion of the EITC, and another the creation of a new type of credit—would accomplish this goal.

The first option would be to reform the EITC with an add-on feature to support accessible savings. Greene (2013) proposed such a reform in the form of a Savings and Emergency Fund (SAEF) account. For this program,

20 percent of the existing EITC (or an additional amount paid for by the reforms above), would be deposited automatically into an interest-bearing savings account held by the Internal Revenue Service (IRS). Workers could choose to withhold additional amounts and would receive a match for doing so. Access to the funds would be provided with a fee-free debit card, presented as an "emergency" card. To discourage nonemergency use of the card, additional savings matches would be available annually based on the amount of savings left in the SAEF account at the end of each year. This program would ensure that LMI workers do not simply receive a lump sum at tax time through the EITC, but are actually supported in building a source of safe, accessible wealth. A 20 percent increase in the EITC would cost around $12 billion annually.

Second, Congress could create new credit, separate from the EITC. Recent proposals for a Financial Security Credit have been inspired by the work of SaveUSA, a pilot program that has been implemented in the last few years in New York City and other communities. The SaveUSA program incentivizes EITC-eligible workers to save a portion of their EITC refund for several months. Rigorous evaluation of the program has found that the LMI workers do indeed deposit savings into accessible accounts through the program (Azurdia et al. 2014). The Financial Security Credit legislation would cost $4 billion a year. (New America Foundation 2012).

Either of these programs could be paid for by taxing investment income at the same rate as earned income. The tax break for dividend income alone cost nearly $24 billion in 2013 (National Priorities Project 2014). This is double the cost of the most expensive version of the proposed reforms above.

Conclusion

Emergency savings is a crucial component of financial security. Most families—and especially LMI families—experience sudden declines in income. Parents lose their jobs, children get sick, cars break down—life events interrupt income. Accessible savings helps families avoid the material hardship that often follows these economic shocks.

Families build accessible savings in two ways, by saving and investing their own money, or by receiving the savings and investments of others through gifts and bequests. The federal government actively boosts these investments and inheritances through tax programs that cost over $175 billion in 2014. The problem with these programs is that they increase the wealth of high-income families while providing little or no support to LMI families.

But there are ways to correct this policy failure. Congress cannot guarantee that every American will earn a livable income from investments or inherit millions of dollars from relatives. But policymakers can help millions of Americans build savings and wealth by turning upside-down tax policies right-side up.

Acknowledgments

For their invaluable edits, comments, and guidance, I thank Alicia Atkinson, J. Michael Collins, Leah Gjertson, Sara Sternberg Greene, Jeremie Greer, and Collin O'Rourke. All remaining errors are my own.

Notes

1. There are several sources of tax expenditure estimates including the Joint Committee on Taxation (JCT), Congressional Budget Office (CBO), Office of Management and Budget (OMB), and Urban-Brookings Tax Policy Center (TPC). The estimates from each source vary slightly.
2. In particular, this analysis does not include the tax program supporting life insurance "inside buildup," which some convincingly argue subsidizes similar types of savings at a cost to the federal government of $27.4 billion in 2014 according to the JCT (2014). For an overview of this tax expenditure, see Hanlon and Eizenga 2011.
3. For a more in-depth review of the stepped-up in basis at death, see Stein 2014.

References

Azurdia, Gilda, Stephen Freedman, Gayle Hamilton, and Caroline Schultz. 2014. "Encouraging Low- and Moderate-Income Tax Filers to Save: Implementation and Interim Impact Findings from the SaveUSA Evaluation." Report, April. MDRC, New York, NY.

Bell, Kate, Jared Bernstein, and Mark Greenberg. 2008. "Lessons for the United Sates from Other Advanced Economies in Tackling Child Poverty." In *Big Ideas for Children: Investing in Our Nation's Future,* 81–92. Washington, DC: First Focus.

Brooks, Jennifer, Kasey Wiedrich, Lebaron Sims Jr., and Jennifer Medina. 2014. "Treading Water in the Deep End: Findings from the 2014 Assets & Opportunity Scorecard." Report, January. CFED, Washington, DC.

Burman, Leonard, Eric Toder, and Christopher Geissler. 2008 "How Big Are Total Individual Income Tax Expenditures, and Who Benefits from Them?" Discussion Paper No. 31, December. Urban Institute, Washington, DC.

CBO, Congressional Budget Office. 2013. "The Distribution of Major Tax Expenditures in the Individual Income Tax System." Publication No. 4308, May. Congress of the United States, Congressional Budget Office, Washington, DC.

Coburn, Tom. 2011. "Back in Black: A Deficit Reduction Plan," 558–561. *Legislation & Issues*, July.

Edin, Kathryn, Laura Tach, and Sarah Halpern-Meekin. 2014. "Tax Code Knowledge and Behavioral Responses Among EITC Recipients: Policy Insights from Qualitative Data." *Journal of Policy Analysis and Management* 33 (2): 413–439.

Galper, Harvey, Joseph Rosenberg, Kim Rueben, and Eric Toder. 2013. "Who Benefits from Tax-Exempt Bonds? An Application of the Theory of Tax Incidence." Working Paper, September 27. Tax Policy Center, Urban Institute and Brookings Institution, Washington, DC.

Greene, Sara Sternberg. 2013. "The Broken Safety Net: A Study of Earned Income Tax Credit Recipients and a Proposal for Repair." *New York University Law Review* 88 (2): 515–588.

Hanlon, Seth, and Jordan Eizenga. 2011. "Tax Expenditure of the Week: Tax-Free 'Inside Buildup' of Life Insurance." *Counting Down the Country's Biggest Tax Breaks, Week by Week*, March 30. Center for American Progress, Washington, DC. http://www.americanprogress.org/issues/open-government/news/2011/03/30/9220/tax-expenditure-of-the-week-tax-free-inside-buildup-of-life-insurance/.

Huang, Chye-Ching, and Nathaniel Frentz. 2013. "Myths and Realities About the Estate Tax." Revised August 29. Center on Budget and Policy Priorities, Washington, DC.

JCT, Joint Committee on Taxation. 2014. "Estimates of Federal Tax Expenditures for Fiscal Years 2014–2018." Prepared for the House Committee on Ways and Means and the Senate Committee on Finance, August 5. Washington, DC.

Jones, Damon. 2010. "Information, Preferences, and Public Benefit Participation: Experimental Evidence from the Advance EITC and 401(k) Savings." *American Economic Journal: Applied Economics* 2 (April): 147–163.

Leiserson, Greg, and Jeffrey Rohaly. 2008. "Distribution of the 2001–2006 Tax Cuts: Updated Projections, July 2008." Report. Tax Policy Center, Urban Institute and Brookings Institution, Washington, DC.

Marron, Donald B. 2011. "Spending in Disguise." *National Affairs* 8 (Summer). http://www.nationalaffairs.com/publications/detail/spending-in-disguise.

Mendenhall, Ruby, Kathryn Edin, Susan Crowley, Jennifer Sykes, Laura Tach, Katrin Kriz, and Jeffrey R. Kling. 2012. "The Role of Earned Income Tax Credit in the Budgets of Low-Income Families." *Social Service Review* 86 (3): 367–400.

National Priorities Project. 2014. Tax Break Costs: 1974–Present. https://www.nationalpriorities.org/analysis/2014/big-money-tax-breaks/complete-data-on-tax-breaks/

New America Foundation. 2012. "The Financial Security Credit: Tax Reform That Supports Savings for Hard-Working Americans." Asset-Building Program, September. New America Foundation, Washington, DC.

Rohaly, Jeffrey, and Katherine Lim. 2011. "Wealth Transfer Taxes: Who Pays the Estate Tax?" *The Tax Policy Briefing Book*. Tax Policy Center, Urban Institute and Brookings Institution, Washington, DC. http://www.taxpolicycenter.org/briefing-book/key-elements/estate/who.cfm.

Romich, Jennifer L., and Thomas S. Weisner. 2002. "How Families View and Use the Earned Income Tax Credit: Advance Payment Versus Lump-Sum Delivery." In *Making Work Pay*, ed. Bruce Meyer and Douglas Holtz-Eakin, 399–392. New York: Russell Sage Foundation.

Stein, Harry. 2014. "How the Government Subsidizes Wealth Inequality." Issue Brief, June 25. Center for American Progress, Washington, DC.

Surrey, Stanley S., and Paul R. McDaniel. 1985. *Tax Expenditures*. Cambridge, MA: Harvard University Press.

Tax Foundation. 2014. "Federal Estate and Gift Tax Rates, Exemptions, and Exclusions, 1916–2014." February 4. Tax Foundation, Washington, DC. http://taxfoundation.org/article/federal-estate-and-gift-tax-rates-exemptions-and-exclusions-1916-2014.

Tax Policy Center. 2010. "Taxable Estates, Estate Tax Liability, and Average Estate Tax Rate, by Size of Gross Estate, Multiple Baselines, 2011." *The Numbers*. December 8. Tax Policy Center, Urban Institute and Brookings Institution, Washington, DC. http://www.taxpolicycenter.org/numbers/displayatab.cfm?Docid=2868.

Tax Policy Center. 2013. "Estate Tax Returns and Liability Under Current Law and Various Reform Proposals, 2011–2022." *The Numbers*, January 9. Tax Policy Center, Urban Institute and Brookings Institution, Washington, DC. http://www.taxpolicycenter.org/numbers/displayatab.cfm?DocID=3775

Thomas, Hannah, Tatjana Meschede, Alexis Mann, Janet Boguslaw, and Thomas Shapiro. 2014. "The Web of Wealth: Resiliency and Opportunity or Driver of Inequality?" Leveraging Mobility Series, No. 4. Institute on Assets and Social Policy, Brandeis University, Waltham, MA.

Wolff, Edward N., and Maury Gittleman. 2013. "Inheritances and the Distribution of Wealth, Or Whatever Happened to the Great Inheritance Boom?" *The Journal of Economic Inequality*. Published electronically November 7.

Zichawo, William, Colby Farber, and Lisa Mensah. 2014. "Child Trust Funds: Renewing the Debate for Long-Term Savings Policies." Issue Brief, March. Initiative on Financial Security, The Aspen Institute, Washington, DC.

Chapter 4

Save at Home: Building Emergency Savings One Mortgage Payment at a Time

Stephanie Moulton, Anya Samek, and Cäzilia Loibl

Introduction

This chapter explores the potential of behaviorally motivated "mortgage reserve accounts" as an automated tool to build emergency savings for otherwise vulnerable low- and moderate-income (LMI) households purchasing their first homes. Financial shocks, such as involuntary unemployment or reduction in wages, and unexpected expenses, such as emergency furnace replacement or roof repairs, within the first few years of homeownership can derail the fragile financial foundation of LMI households and put them at risk of losing their homes through foreclosure. Most LMI households enter homeownership with little equity or residual savings—holding on average only $2,000 in liquid assets, including cash on hand and savings and checking accounts (Moulton et al. 2011; Van Zandt and Rohe 2011). Although homeowners are building equity through their monthly mortgage payments, that equity is not accessible for consumption until the loan balance falls below a leverageable threshold (typically, 80 percent of the value of the home). To the extent that extending homeownership to LMI households remains a policy goal, scalable strategies to offset the higher default risk of such mortgages become a critical, yet challenging, objective.

Mortgage Reserve Accounts (MRAs) combine mortgage financing for LMI first-time homebuyers with a mechanism to build accessible emergency savings, thereby buffering income and expense shocks in the first few years after home purchase. The key feature of the MRA model is the post-purchase emergency savings mechanism integrated with the monthly mortgage payment. From a behavioral perspective, the MRA targets specific consumer vulnerabilities through automation, incentives, and monitoring. Furthermore, MRAs take advantage of existing infrastructure, as they can be readily incorporated into existing first-time homebuyer programs, such as those administered through state housing finance agencies (HFAs). State HFAs serve an average of 100,000 first-time homebuyers nationwide each year, providing affordable mortgages to LMI households. A recent pilot study conducted by researchers with the Ohio Housing Finance Agency demonstrates the potential to combine the HFA financing structure with savings interventions for LMI homebuyers (Moulton et al. 2011).

This chapter proceeds as follows. First, the financial and behavioral challenges facing LMI homebuyers are described, indicating the need for emergency reserves. Second, possible MRA models are described in detail, highlighting the target population, key implementation components, and costs and benefits of different implementation strategies. Finally, the chapter concludes by noting the importance of field experimentation to determine the best implementation strategy and its effect on key outcomes.

Financial Vulnerabilities of LMI Homebuyers

The recent financial crisis provides an extreme example of the link between economic stability and housing stability for individuals, communities, and the macro-economy. Even prior to the crisis, however, it was understood that financial shocks (often referred to in the literature as "triggering events") are a primary cause of mortgage delinquency for homeowners, and that financial shocks combined with high leverage increase the risk of default (Avery et al. 1996;

Quercia and Stegman 1992). These shocks include events such as loss of income, unexpected medical expenses, divorce, or loss of wage earners in the household (Getter 2003). For new homeowners, these shocks could also include expenses related to unanticipated home repairs.

While no household is immune to financial shocks, homeowners with a sufficient cushion have more options to draw on to avoid defaulting on their mortgage payments. This cushion could be held in the form of equity; sufficient equity can increase the ability of a homeowner to sell and move or to borrow against the home (such as through a home equity loan), and access to equity may also help cushion income or expense shocks over time. However, most homeowners have very little equity to draw on in the first few years after purchase (Belsky 2010). The cushion may also be in the form of savings: homeowners could draw from existing savings to cover emergency expenses or to tide over unexpected loss of income. Recent survey data from FINRA's National Financial Capability Study reveal that homeowners facing an income shock who did not have emergency savings were significantly more likely to make a late mortgage payment or experience foreclosure than were similar homeowners who did have emergency savings (Mottola 2013).

LMI first-time homebuyers are particularly vulnerable to financial shocks. The majority of LMI families enter homeownership with very small emergency reserves (Mottola 2013; Moulton et al. 2011; Van Zandt and Rohe 2011). For example, in a survey of new LMI homebuyers, Van Zandt and Rohe (2011) find that the average amount participants had in savings at the time of purchase was $3,500, and that amount decreased in the first two years after purchase. They also report that nearly half of new LMI homeowners experience major unexpected home repairs, and more than one-third report major unexpected increases in utility costs, property taxes, or homeowner's insurance in the first two years after purchase. As a result, rather than building emergency reserves, new homeowners often increase their level of debt. Van Zandt and Rohe (2011) find that non-mortgage consumer debt payments increased by an average 48 percent (nearly $200 per month) in the first two years after home purchase.

Behavioral Challenges Facing First-Time Homebuyers

Strategies to address the financial vulnerabilities of LMI consumers focus primarily on education and counseling provided prior to home purchase, often referred to as "homebuyer education and counseling," or counseling when a homeowner enters into default (Moulton 2012; Collins 2007). There is some evidence that borrowers who receive education and counseling prior to purchase have a lower risk of mortgage default (Agarwal et al. 2010a, 2010b; Quercia and Spader 2008; Hirad and Zorn 2002). However, current approaches to homebuyer education and counseling often overlook the behavioral challenges facing new LMI homeowners. In contrast, the concept of MRAs begins with an identification of such challenges.

LMI first-time homebuyers may experience common behavioral biases that impede their ability to accumulate emergency savings, both during and after home purchase. The emotional stress of purchasing a home may overwhelm decision-making capabilities, causing homeowners to focus on the actual purchase in the short term while blocking out the potential for post-purchase emergencies in the long term (Payne, Bettman, and Schkade 1999). Similar behavioral challenges impede the ability of LMI first-time homebuyers to prepare for and build sufficient financial reserves to buffer financial shocks after the purchase of a home. We focus on three relevant behavioral challenges that homeowners encounter on a daily basis: (1) present bias, (2) excessive focus on short-term horizons, and (3) mental accounting.

Present bias in this context refers to the tendency to prefer consumption over saving today, while maintaining the belief that saving will be preferable tomorrow. Present bias would predict that homeowners would not choose to save for a financial cushion in the present, but may demand a commitment device (or a savings vehicle) for the future. Yet, when the future arrives, present-biased homeowners will again procrastinate, putting off saving. Present-biased individuals may also face more intense financial challenges, such as higher credit card debt, than individuals who are more future-oriented (Meier and Sprenger 2010). Thus, present bias provides an explanation for the lack of savings habits or saving accumulation among households in general, and LMI households in particular.

A second common tendency is an excessive focus on short-term horizons. Individuals who focus on the short term have difficulty considering the consequences of today's actions over longer-time horizons. Short-term horizons may explain why LMI homeowners fail to adequately prepare for financial emergencies post-purchase, as they do not anticipate the probability of negative shocks such as emergency home repairs—even though these types of expenses are relatively common. Incentives or external monitoring systems associated with savings may provide a mechanism to help individuals focused on short-time horizons to begin saving.

The third behavioral challenge is mental accounting (Thaler 2008). Mental accounting describes the tendency of individuals to treat money differently depending on what account it is in. That is, individuals earmark different streams of money for different types of activities, and due to present bias and excessive focus on the short term, may not earmark any funds for savings. This may explain low savings rates of new LMI homebuyers, who may not be thinking about setting aside additional funds for home-related expenses when they purchase their home. These households may benefit from an opportunity to commit some portion of their income to a savings account set aside for emergencies.

Proposed Intervention: Mortgage Reserve Accounts

MRAs are an innovative mechanism to address the vulnerabilities and challenges of LMI homebuyers. While MRAs may be implemented under a variety of models and strategies, the basic concept seeks to accomplish three primary objectives:

1. To integrate an automatic savings component into the monthly mortgage payment for LMI first-time homebuyers, providing an emergency savings cushion for unexpected expenses or financial shocks.
2. To incentivize targeted homebuyers to participate in the automated savings program, through underwriting flexibility (overlays), financial incentives (such as matched deposits), or program requirements.
3. To provide evidence-based, low-touch monitoring (via external reminders and accountability mechanisms) during the first few years after home purchase to encourage timely mortgage payments and other positive financial behaviors.

These objectives incorporate behaviorally targeted mechanisms grounded in research from behavioral economics, psychology, and consumer financial decision making.

Automated Savings

The foundation of the MRA design is an automated savings component built into the monthly mortgage payment and held in a reserve account similar to the escrow account commonly held for property taxes and homeowners insurance. Mortgage escrow accounts were first created after the Great Depression, when many homeowners faced foreclosure for failure to pay property taxes. While taxes and insurance are typically due one or two times per year, borrowers with escrow accounts pay the lender a prorated portion of the taxes and insurance each month, and the lender pays the tax and insurance bill on behalf of the borrower. This system reduces the probability that a borrower will default on property taxes and homeowners insurance (Anderson and Dokko 2009).

Automating savings by integrating it into the mortgage payment helps address the behavioral challenges of present bias and mental accounting. Researchers have called for more opportunities for automated savings

(Bertrand, Mullainathan, and Shafir 2004). Integrated reserve savings accounts can overcome present bias by acting as a commitment device—an automated arrangement that helps individuals meet the difficult goal of increasing savings (Bryan, Karlan, and Nelson 2010). Commitment devices have been shown to be effective in both laboratory and field data, with the level of commitment directly related to the size of the penalty for failing to meet the commitment (see Bryan, Karlan, and Nelson 2010 for an overview). The reserve account can also take advantage of mental accounting. Mental accounting theory predicts that money that is not restricted in any way (such as money retained as cash or in a checking account) may be more quickly spent without intent than money that is earmarked for another purpose. The MRA integrates savings with the mortgage payment, making it an earmarked money flow.

Incentives

Incentives are important at different stages of the MRA, as they provide an external motivation to save for households that may be excessively focused on the short term. First, an up-front incentive encourages homebuyers to enroll in an MRA program. The incentive could be operationalized by requiring the establishment of an MRA in conjunction with an affordable loan product that offers additional subsidies (for instance, a reduced interest rate or down-payment assistance), or by requiring an MRA to qualify under relaxed underwriting criteria for homebuyers who would otherwise be ineligible for conventional mortgage financing. To the extent that regulatory changes to the mortgage market restrict certain loan characteristics (e.g., high loan-to-value [LTV] mortgages), MRAs could be incorporated with certain exempt mortgage channels (including mortgages originated by state HFAs) as a compensating factor to offset the higher risk of these mortgages. The ability to qualify for additional subsidies or financing may be sufficient incentive to elicit participation.

Aside from initial participation, an incentive or restriction is likely needed to encourage compliance with the MRA payments and ensure accumulation of funds for emergency use. For example, research on retirement savings demonstrates the effectiveness of employer-provided matching in increasing employee contributions (Choi, Laibson, and Madrian 2004). Rewards are also effective across many domains outside of financial planning, encouraging such desirable behavior as improved exercise habits (Charness and Gneezy 2009), smoking cessation (Volpp et al. 2009), and healthier food choices (List and Samek 2014). Penalties may be more effective than rewards at inducing cooperation in some environments, but when given the choice, individuals are more likely to choose rewards over penalties (Sutter, Haigner, and Kocher 2010). Thus, penalties may work better to enforce compliance but rewards are likely to encourage participation, and the MRA designer must weigh the costs and benefits of each of these options.

One additional consideration with incentives is framing. Prospect theory would suggest that individuals value an equivalent unit *loss* more than an equivalent unit *gain*—economists refer to this concept as loss aversion (Tversky and Kahneman 1991). Thus, an incentive amount may be more effective if it is deposited in the account and then taken away if the MRA goal is not met, than if it is added to the account incrementally as payments are made. Further, recent experiments show that loss-framed incentives are not any less preferred than gain-framed incentives (Imas, Sadoff, and Samek 2014).

External Monitoring

In addition to automating and incentivizing desired behaviors, external monitoring also encourages the development of healthy financial behaviors. Research finds that external monitoring may prove more effective than self-monitoring in increasing participant adherence to their goals (Ariely and Wertenbroch 2002). Monitoring increases the salience of accountability on four dimensions: expectation of being observed, identifiability, expectation that performance will be assessed, and expectation that one will have to give reasons for actions (Lerner and Tetlock 1999). Further, external monitoring can lead to increased impulse control.

The application of external monitoring to financial behaviors is relatively new; however, preliminary evidence suggests that a program that incorporates external monitoring and modeling, such as financial coaching, may lead to sustained behavioral change and increased goal attainment (Collins, Baker, and Gorey 2007; Baumeister 2002). With regard to emergency savings decisions, academic studies have shown the positive effects of reminder calls for engaging LMI consumers with their financial goals (Kast, Meier, and Pomeranz 2011).

Homebuyers can be encouraged to set specific financial goals related to their debt or savings prior to the home purchase, for example, during an initial intake session over the phone or as a part of online mortgage eligibility screening. Once these goals are set, external monitoring of progress toward goals can be integrated into the MRA program and communicated through monthly account statements or regularly scheduled follow-up calls or emails. Missed mortgage payments or associated deposits into the reserve account can trigger early intervention from a financial coach or counselor by phone, email, or mail.

Putting It all Together: Design Considerations

Automation, incentive, and monitoring mechanisms can be integrated into MRA programs in a variety of ways. There is likely no one best way to structure an MRA. Rather, implementers will need to select strategies that best fit the opportunities and constraints within a given context. Several critical questions will need to be addressed: Is enrollment in the MRA program voluntary or required? If it is voluntary, what steps will be taken to increase participation? What is the appropriate savings target for each month, and is that target tied to the mortgage payment amount or to the household's overall income and budget? Does the account require an initial deposit? How long will the account remain active, and what happens when a participant wishes to close the account? What is the process for authorized withdrawals, and what are the penalties for unauthorized withdrawals? Table 4.1 summarizes design considerations for automation, incentives, and monitoring processes at three key stages in the MRA process, including account enrollment, monthly deposits, and withdrawals.

Account Enrollment

Ideally, MRAs would be linked to affordable loan products and thus be required in order to receive the product. However, there may be situations where the account is offered but not required, thus necessitating strategies to increase participation. Individuals are more likely to participate in accounts that have low time costs for set-up; thus, framing the account as an opt-out program rather than opt-in program can increase participation rates. However, as Choi, Laibson, and Madrian (2004) note, opt-out policies are not neutral; they are prescriptive in that they nudge individuals to engage with programs they may have otherwise not taken up.

A second consideration would be the amount and nature of initial deposits. Although the core of the MRA design consists of automated monthly deposits, there are strong rationales for requiring an initial deposit at closing to seed the account. This initial deposit can serve as an immediate cushion for hardships within the first year after purchase, and it can also provide an incentive for homeowners to enroll in and maintain their accounts. Furthermore, given the tendency of debt balances to rise and savings balances to fall in the first years after a home purchase, households may be in a position to deposit a larger amount in the MRA at the time of

Table 4.1 MRA Design Considerations by Stage and Mechanism

Stage	Automation	Incentives	Monitoring
Account enrollment	Voluntary versus required	Required or optional up-front deposit; use of third-party funds as up-front incentive	Mode of initial participant goal setting and implementation planning (online, telephone, letter); self-directed versus third-party feedback; Frequency, mode, and content of account updates and monitoring
Monthly deposits	Program determined versus participant determined; fixed versus variable amount	Penalties for missed deposits versus incentives for regular deposits	Mode, content, and frequency of monitoring; additional monitoring and penalties triggered by missed deposits
Withdrawals	Unrestricted versus restricted (and restriction period); if restricted, nature of restrictions (i.e., only for mortgage payments or demonstrated hardships); Set MRA duration (e.g., three years) versus ongoing	Penalties for withdrawals versus incentives for no withdrawals	Processes for reviewing documentation for withdrawal requests

Source: Authors' own.

the purchase than they will in later years, particularly if the initial deposit can be lumped in with the other costs associated with the mortgage. Third-party providers could also contribute toward the initial deposit, similar to down-payment assistance programs. A portion of the financial assistance typically structured as down-payment assistance could be set aside in the MRA as an incentive to create and maintain the account.

At the time of enrollment, participants should be provided the opportunity to set financial goals that will serve as the basis for post-purchase monitoring. Ideally, goal setting will be self-directed with aid from a third party to help ensure that goals are specific and supported by explicit implementation intentions. Several studies have shown that establishing specific implementation intentions can improve the likelihood of goal attainment. Implementation plans establish links between specific situations and the desired behavioral responses (Gollwitzer 1999). A variety of modes could be employed for guiding participants to set goals and implementation steps, such as online instruction modules or telephone sessions with a financial coach.

Monthly Deposits

The amount to be deposited into the account each month, whether it is a set dollar amount determined programmatically or a customized amount determined in cooperation with the participant, should be defined prior to loan closing. A number of approaches can be taken to determine the deposit amount. For instance, "top up" strategies, in which mortgage payments are rounded up to the nearest $100 and the difference deposited in the MRA, can be particularly effective. How the deposit amount is presented also makes a difference; for instance, displaying the required monthly deposit amount together with the larger mortgage payment will make the MRA feel less intimidating and more achievable than if it is presented as a stand-alone number.

Decisions will also have to be made about the consequences of failing to make the monthly deposit. The reserve deposit could be missed either because the participant fails to make the entire mortgage payment (of which the reserve payment is a part) or because the participant makes only the mortgage portion of the payment. In the first case, the missed mortgage payment will trigger consequences from the servicer (such as late payment fees), and no additional financial penalties may be necessary. In the second case, the consequences will vary based on the structure of the payment. At one extreme, failure to make the reserve portion could trigger the same delinquency consequences as failing to make a full mortgage payment. At the other extreme, there could be no financial consequence for failure to make the reserve payment; instead, the missed reserve payment could trigger monitoring contact. Alternatively, participants could receive an incentive for making the reserve deposits with their mortgage each month (such as a reduced interest rate on the mortgage over time, or matched deposits into the reserve account after a set number of deposits).

Withdrawals

The structure of the MRA withdrawal process and account duration has significant behavioral implications. If the account is too illiquid, potential participants may be wary of the program, resulting in reduced participation rates, and the account may not provide the intended cushion, as participants will be unable to access the money in times of need. However, if the account is too liquid, participants may not build up meaningful emergency savings, reducing the effectiveness of the MRA as a tool to build a cushion against financial shock.

These considerations must be balanced against the costs associated with monitoring account activity. One solution is to determine a specified waiting period of up to three years during which withdrawals can be made for any reason, but incur a set penalty (for instance, forfeiture of interest or loss of some portion of the initial deposit or up-front incentive). After the waiting period, the account and periodic deposits may remain active but withdrawals can be made at any time for any reason. The benefit of this approach is that borrowers have direct control over their accounts, reducing administrative burden. The downside is that participants may not accumulate sufficient funds without some meaningful restrictions on withdrawals.

Another option is to make account withdrawals contingent on hardship as observed based on timely mortgage payments. For instance, the account holder could specify that in the event a mortgage payment is missed, the reserve account could be used to make the payment with no penalty. This is a more customized approach than the waiting period, which is a positive, but there is a risk that it could be overused, as individuals come to rely on the cushion in lieu of making timely payments on their own. Alternatively, a wider definition of hardship could be employed; in this model, households needing to withdraw funds from the MRA would submit receipts for acceptable household expenses and documentation of hardship, such as loss of income, in order to access the reserve account. The tradeoff here is the higher cost associated with reviewing documentation and approving withdrawals, likely involving a third party in addition to the loan servicer.

Regardless of the level and nature of restrictions, the duration of the account must be considered. Ideally, the individual should have the ability to continue with the MRA throughout the lifetime of the mortgage. Alternatively, the borrower may receive the emergency savings in a lump sum at some defined endpoint—for instance, after a predetermined number of years or when the equity in the home reaches a particular threshold.

Implementation

The MRA relies for its effectiveness on structured, repeated interactions with homebuyers both during and after purchase. Given this need, state HFAs provide a scalable delivery channel for the proposed model. Most HFA first-time homebuyer programs meet the criteria for the MRA model, and HFA programs provide a structure within which key elements of the MRA program can easily be implemented. For instance, about 82 percent of state HFAs already require homebuyer education and counseling for at least some of their funded borrowers at the time of home purchase (Dylla and Caldwell-Tautges 2012); MRA counseling could be included in these existing education tools.

In addition to having extensive contact with homebuyers prior to purchase, many HFAs collect or monitor the loan payments of funded borrowers after purchase. According to a recent survey of state HFAs (Moulton and Quercia 2014), about one-third directly service their own mortgages, one-third contract with a single lender (known as a "master servicer"), and the remainder rely on a network of servicers to collect payments in accordance with agency-specified guidelines. Beyond monitoring the performance of monthly borrower payments, about half of HFAs (49 percent) intervene with delinquent borrowers post-purchase, above and beyond what would be provided through conventional servicing, thus meeting the design goals of MRAs.

MRAs may also offer HFAs and servicers incentives to administer the program, in the form of reduced default risk. Most LMI borrowers purchasing homes through affordable mortgage programs such as those administered by state HFAs have high LTV ratios at the time of purchase, and consequently little up-front equity. Any equity accumulated through timely mortgage payments during the first several years is highly illiquid, inaccessible to the borrower until the LTV is reduced to 80 percent or lower. MRAs allow high-LTV borrowers to build assets in a more liquid form during the first few years as a homeowner. The MRA can then be used in the case of a missed mortgage payment, thereby mitigating a portion of the default risk to the lender (and HFA). This reduced default risk can in turn serve as an incentive for HFAs and their servicers to administer MRAs.

Comparisons of MRA Models with State HFAs

There are multiple strategies for structuring MRAs, which can be chosen to match state HFA structures for origination, servicing, and funding of mortgages through first-time homebuyer programs. Thus, rather than proposing one model for state HFAs, table 4.2 provides an overview of four different MRA implementation models based on different entities that may: (1) collect the monthly MRA deposit; (2) hold the MRA; and (3) control the disbursement of funds from the MRA.

These four models are prototypes of the different structural options available. Certain aspects of different models may be combined to tailor a particular program to the circumstances of the particular HFA. Evaluation of different model components is necessary to identify which mechanisms are most likely to lead to positive outcomes for borrowers. A carefully designed evaluation plan is thus a critical component of any MRA program design.

Model 1: The Servicer Model

Model 1 is referred to as the Servicer Model because the servicer collects the reserve deposit, holds the account, and controls the disbursement of funds (at least for a restricted period of time). This model is most beneficial for HFAs that seek to use the MFA to reduce mortgage default risk, potentially pricing the reserve account as an insurance against risk, thereby allowing the agency to lend to riskier borrowers. From a behavioral perspective, the account can be easily automated with the mortgage payment, and the servicer may even trigger default proceedings if the borrower fails to make the full payment, including the mortgage reserve, thus incentivizing compliance through severe penalties for noncompliance. Ongoing monitoring outside of the servicing channel is less likely under this model, as the servicer retains control of the account. It is likely that the account would be restricted for the first two to three years, with withdrawals allowed only to cover mortgage payments, and then released to borrowers thereafter. Simple reminders on mortgage statements could be used to provide some contact with borrowers about their accounts; however, this would likely need to be highly programmed.

From a cost-benefit perspective, the costs of this model for both participants and administering programs are very low once the reserve account is established with the servicer, thus allowing for significant scalability. However, there could be significant regulatory challenges for the servicer if the account falls under the same regulations that govern escrow accounts (Bone 2008; Mills 1994). Accounts must be structured so they are not simply cushioning servicers' risk without providing tangible benefits to the borrowers. In terms of effectiveness, this structure would be most beneficial for protecting against mortgage payment default risk, but would be

Table 4.2 Comparison of Models for Mortgage Reserve Savings Accounts with HFAs

	Model 1 (servicer model)	**Model 2 (hybrid model)**	**Model 3 (borrower model)**	**Model 4 (nonprofit model)**
Collects	Servicer	Servicer/HFA	Servicer/HFA	NP/CDFI
Holds	Servicer	HFA/NP/CDFI	Servicer/HFA/NP/CDFI	NP/CDFI
Controls	Servicer	HFA/NP/CDFI	Borrower	NP/CDFI
Behavioral mechanisms	Automated (+) Incentives (+/–) Monitoring (–)	Automated (+) Incentives (+) Monitoring (+)	Automated (+) Incentives (+) Monitoring (+/–)	Automated (–) Incentives (+) Monitoring (+)
Cost considerations	Participant costs (–) Administrative costs (–) Regulative costs (+) Scale (+)	Participant costs (–) Administrative costs (+) Regulative Costs (+/–) Scale (+/–)	Participant costs (–) Administrative costs (–) Regulative costs (–) Scale (+)	Participant costs (+) Administrative costs (+) Regulative costs (–) Scale (–)
Effectiveness	Mortgage payment (+) Financial shocks (–)	Mortgage payment (+) Financial shocks (+)	Mortgage payment (+/–) Financial shocks (+/–)	Mortgage payment (+/–) Financial shocks (+/–)

Primary advantage	Automated deposits; insures against default risk; servicer can price reduced risk, similar to mortgage insurance; reserve account can be required for underwriting	Automated deposits; insures against default risk and can restrict approved withdrawals; more opportunity for monitoring	Automated deposits; low administrative and regulatory burden; gives borrower full access to funds; can incentivize (but not control) positive behavior	Can restrict approved withdrawals; opportunity for monitoring; can incentivize (but not control) positive behavior
Primary disadvantage	Less accessible to borrower; could encourage strategic default; potential regulatory challenges	More administrative burden to screen eligible withdrawals; more difficult to price into underwriting without servicer control	Little insurance against default risk, as funds are controlled by borrower; not likely to be priced into underwriting; incentives for deposits/not withdrawing may need to be significant	Not automated, relies on participant deposits which may be less effective; high administrative burden to collect and manage deposits; incentives for deposits would have to be significant

Notes: HFA—Housing finance agency; NP—Nonprofit organization; CDFI—Community development financial institution or third-party bank. A plus sign indicates the model scores high on the criterion, a minus sign indicates a low score, and a plus-minus sign indicates a moderate score.

Source: Authors' own.

less effective at covering borrowers against other emergency expenses or shocks, as the funds would be relatively illiquid.

Model 2: The Hybrid Model

Model 2, the Hybrid Model, incorporates some of the benefits of the Servicer Model while addressing some of its deficiencies. The primary difference in this model is that while the servicer collects the reserve deposit as part of the monthly mortgage payment, the reserve account is held and controlled by a third party. This third party could be the state HFA (if the HFA has the capacity to serve as a bank), a nonprofit organization, a community development financial institution (CDFI), a separate bank partner or credit union, or some combination of these entities. The addition of the third-party partner increases the capacity for monitoring and for screening withdrawal requests for eligible uses outside of missed mortgage payments.

From a cost-benefit perspective, the automated nature of the deposits reduces transaction costs for participants, and third-party administration of the MRA potentially avoids some regulatory constraints faced by mortgage servicers. However, third-party administration of the account increases administrative costs, potentially reducing scalability. In terms of effectiveness, this model is likely beneficial for both reducing default risk (as the account can be restricted) and for buffering against other emergency shocks.

Model 3: The Borrower Model

Model 3 places control of the account with the borrower, and is thus called the Borrower Model. This model has potentially the lowest cost of all of the models, as there is little administrative burden beyond the initial set-up of the account. This model relies heavily on behavioral mechanisms to build reserve savings, as borrowers have unlimited access to funds accumulated in the account without third-party control of disbursements. The account may be held by the servicer or a third party; however, the borrower retains ownership of it and can access funds at any time for any reason. Incentives may be offered for retaining funds in the account or for continuing to make reserve deposits as part of monthly mortgage payments, or penalties (such as loss of the initial deposit) may be incurred for lack of compliance.

Because of the low costs associated with this model, scalability is high. The effectiveness of protecting against mortgage default risk or emergency expenses is largely dependent on the strength of the behavioral mechanisms; to the extent that automation, incentives, and monitoring work together to encourage deposits and restrict access to funds to emergencies, then the effectiveness could be high. However, if the behavioral mechanisms are not well designed or implemented, this account will function as little more than a regular savings account.

Model 4: The Nonprofit Model

Model 4, the Nonprofit Model, is included more for comparison than as a realistic option. This model does not include the automated component of the MRA that is central to its effectiveness, but rather relies on participant deposits into an account that can be used for emergency expenses associated with the home purchase. Similar to Individual Development Accounts (IDAs), the accounts are managed by a nonprofit provider who provides some incentive or monitoring, or both, to encourage deposits and restrict withdrawals. In fact, some IDA programs offer post-purchase home-repair IDAs.

The drawbacks of this model are that it places high demands on participants to make regular deposits, and high administrative costs on the third-party organization to collect and track deposits. From a behavioral perspective, the lack of automation may reduce the propensity for borrowers to accumulate savings without incentive. Thus, incentives have to be significant to ensure compliance, further increasing the cost of this model. Because of the costs associated with the account, scalability is relatively difficult. While there are likely fewer regulatory constraints and barriers to entry, the effectiveness of the model is questionable without strong behavioral mechanisms that may be costly to enforce.

Conclusion

LMI homebuyers are particularly vulnerable to financial shocks. Not only do they often lack savings, but home equity is highly illiquid for these homebuyers, as most enter homeownership with little money down and high LTVs. In addition to these financial vulnerabilities, LMI homebuyers face common behavioral biases that influence their financial decisions and decrease their likelihood of accumulating emergency savings. Unexpected shocks to income or unplanned expenses can have serious consequences for vulnerable homebuyers who lack a reserve cushion.

MRAs offer an innovative mechanism for building accessible emergency savings. MRAs incorporate automation, incentives, and monitoring as behaviorally targeted commitment devices to incite saving. Rather than a one-size-fits-all strategy, there are several variations that implementers should consider to design a program that best fits the constraints and opportunities of a given context. The outcomes of MRAs can be evaluated through field experiments with program participants, isolating components of the model that lead to reduced mortgage delinquency and financial stability.

In order for MRAs to be successful, implementation must be efficient and scalable. State HFAs provide a scalable delivery channel because of their structured, repeated interactions with homebuyers before and after purchase. Regulatory constraints, such as those governing escrow accounts, should be explored in more detail. Policy changes may be necessary to reduce servicer risk in administering or servicing mortgages with MRAs. To the extent that the MRA model can demonstrate decreased default risk, MRAs may offer a viable strategy to support the extension of mortgages to borrowers who fall outside tighter underwriting criteria.

REFERENCES

Agarwal, Sumit, Gene Amromin, Itzhak Ben-David, Souphala Chomsisengphet, and Douglas D. Evanoff. 2010a. "Financial Counseling, Financial Literacy, and Household Decision Making." Working Paper 2010–34, November 11. Pension Research Council.

———. 2010b. "Learning to Cope: Voluntary Financial Education and Loan Performance During a Housing Crisis." *The American Economic Review* 100 (2): 495–500.

Anderson, Nathan B., and Jane K. Dokko. 2009. "Mortgage Delinquency and Property Taxes." *State Tax Notes* 52 (1): 49–57.

Ariely, Dan, and Klaus Wertenbroch. 2002. "Procrastination, Deadlines, and Performance: Self-Control by Precommitment." *Psychological Science* 13 (3): 219–224.

Avery, Robert B., Raphael W. Bostic, Paul S. Calem, and Glenn B. Canner. 1996. "Credit Risk, Credit Scoring, and the Performance of Home Mortgages." *Federal Reserve Bulletin* 82 (July): 621–648.

Baumeister, Roy F. 2002. "Yielding to Temptation: Self-Control Failure, Impulsive Purchasing, and Consumer Behavior." *Journal of Consumer Research* 28 (March): 670–676.

Belsky, Eric. S. 2010. "Housing Wealth Effects and Course of the U.S. Economy: Theory, Evidence, and Policy Implications." In *The Blackwell Companion to the Economics of Housing: The Housing Wealth of Nations*, ed. Susan J. Smith and Beverley A. Searle, 82–104. Oxford: Wiley-Blackwell.

Bertrand, Marianne, Sendhil Mullainathan, and Eldar Shafir. 2004. "A Behavioral-Economics View of Poverty." *American Economic Review* 94 (2): 419–423.

Bone, Paula Fitzgerald. 2008. "Toward a General Model of Consumer Empowerment and Welfare in Financial Markets with an Application to Mortgage Servicers." *Journal of Consumer Affairs* 42 (2): 165–188.

Bryan, Gharad, Dean Karlan, and Scott Nelson. 2010. "Commitment Devices." *Annual Review of Economics* 2 (1): 671–698.

Charness, Gary, and Uri Gneezy. 2009. "Incentives to Exercise." *Econometrica* 77 (3): 909–931.

Choi, James J., David Laibson, and Brigitte C. Madrian. 2004. "Plan Design and 401(K) Savings Outcomes." *National Tax Journal* 57 (2): 275–298.

Collins, J. Michael. 2007. "Exploring the Design of Financial Counseling for Mortgage Borrowers in Default." *Journal of Family and Economic Issues* 28 (2): 207–225.

Collins, J. Michael, Christi Baker, and Rochelle Gorey. 2007. "Financial Coaching: A New Approach for Asset Building? A Report for the Annie E. Casey Foundation." November 20. PolicyLab Consulting Group.

Dylla, Doug, and Dean Caldwell-Tautges. 2012. "Winning Strategies: An Analysis of Housing Finance Agency Support for Homeownership Education and Counseling Services: HFA HEC Report, March 2012." Doug Dylla Consulting, Ithaca, NY.

Getter, Darryl E. 2003. "Contributing to the Delinquency of Borrowers." *Journal of Consumer Affairs* 37 (1): 86–100.

Gollwitzer, Peter M. 1999. "Implementation Intentions: Strong Effects on Simple Plans." *American Psychologist* 54 (7): 493–503.

Hirad, Abdighani, and Peter Zorn. 2002. "A Little Knowledge Is a Good Thing: Empirical Evidence of the Effectiveness of Pre-Purchase Homeownership Counseling." In *Low-Income Homeownership: Examining the Unexamined Goal*, ed. Nicolas P. Retsinas and Eric S. Belsky, 146–174. Washington, DC: The Brookings Institution Press.

Imas, Alex, Sally Sadoff, and Anya Savikhin Samek. 2014. "Do People Anticipate Loss Aversion?" Working Paper, March 18. Social Science Research Network (SSRN).

Kast, Felipe, Stephan Meier, and Dina Pomeranz. 2011. "Under-Savers Anonymous: Evidence on Self-Help Groups and Peer Pressure as a Savings Commitment Device" Working Paper. Columbia Business School, New York.

Lerner, Jennifer S., and Philip E. Tetlock. 1999. "Accounting for the Effects of Accountability." *Psychological Bulletin* 125 (2): 255–275.

List, John A., and Anya Savikhin Samek. 2014. "The Behavioralist as Nutritionist: Leveraging Behavioral Economics to Improve Child Food Choice and Consumption." National Bureau of Economic Research Working Paper Series, No. 20132.

Meier, Stephan, and Charles Sprenger. 2010. "Present-Biased Preferences and Credit Card Borrowing." *American Economic Journal: Applied Economics* 2 (1): 193–210.

Mills, Edwin S. 1994. "The Functioning and Regulation of Escrow Accounts." *Housing Policy Debate* 5 (2): 203–218.

Mottola, Gary. 2013. "Softening the Blow: Income Shocks, Mortgage Payment and Emergency Savings." *Insights: American Financial Capability*, March. FINRA Investor Education Foundation, Washington, DC.

Moulton, Stephanie. 2012. "Pre-Purchase Homebuyer Education and Counseling: Diverse Strategies for Diverse Homebuyers." In *Consumer Knowledge and Financial Decisions*, ed. Douglas Lamdin, 145–164. New York: Springer.

Moulton, Stephanie, Cäzilia Loibl, J. Michael Collins, and Anya Savakhin. 2011. "Field Experiments on the Impact of Financial Planning Interventions for Recent Homebuyers." Working Paper 2011-Cfs.5. Center for Financial Security, University of Wisconsin-Madison.

Moulton, Stephanie, and Roberto Quercia. 2014. "Access and Sustainability for First Time Homebuyers: The Evolving Role of State Housing Finance Agencies." In *Homeownership Built to Last: Balancing Access, Affordability, and Risk after the Housing Crisis*, ed. Eric S. Belsky, Christopher E. Herbert, and Jennifer H. Molinsky, 267–289. Washington, DC: The Brookings Institution Press.

Payne, John W., James R. Bettman, and David A. Schkade. 1999. "Measuring Constructed Preferences: Towards a Building Code." *Journal of Risk and Uncertainty* 19 (1–3): 243–270.

Quercia, Roberto G., and Jonathan S. Spader. 2008. "Does Homeownership Counseling Affect the Prepayment and Default Behavior of Affordable Mortgage Borrowers?" *Journal of Policy Analysis and Management* 27 (2): 304–325.

Quercia, Roberto G., and Michael A. Stegman. 1992. "Residential Mortgage Default: A Review of the Literature." *Journal of Housing Research* 3 (2): 341–379.

Sutter, Matthias, Stefan Haigner, and Martin G. Kocher. 2010. "Choosing the Carrot or the Stick? Endogenous Institutional Choice in Social Dilemma Situations." *The Review of Economic Studies* 77 (4): 1540–1566.

Thaler, Richard H. 2008. "Mental Accounting and Consumer Choice." *Marketing Science* 27 (1): 15–25.

Tversky, Amos, and Daniel Kahneman. 1991. "Loss Aversion in Riskless Choice: A Reference Dependent Model." *Quarterly Journal of Economics* 106:1039–1061.

Van Zandt, Shannon, and William M. Rohe. 2011. "The Sustainability of Low-Income Homeownership: The Incidence of Unexpected Costs and Needed Repairs among Low-Income Home Buyers." *Housing Policy Debate* 21 (2): 317–341.

Volpp, Kevin G., Andrea B. Troxel, Mark V. Pauly, Henry A. Glick, Andrea Puig, David A. Asch, Robert Galvin, Jingsan Zhu, Fei Wan, Jill DeGuzman, Elizabeth Corbett, Janet Weiner, and Janet Audrain-McGovern. 2009. "A Randomized, Controlled Trial of Financial Incentives for Smoking Cessation." *New England Journal of Medicine* 360 (7): 699–709.

Chapter 5

The SaveUSA Coalition: Using Behavioral Economics to Build Unrestricted Savings at Tax Time

Jonathan Mintz

Introduction

In most cities, low- to moderate-income (LMI) households are the primary users of municipal social services, including workforce development and homelessness prevention programs, among others. But the progress gained through a social service intervention can be wiped out by the lack of fundamental financial stability. For example, a lack of funds to pay for a car repair could make it impossible to get to work, resulting in the loss of a day's pay—or of a job. Access to emergency savings could bolster families' ability to withstand such setbacks. For this reason, improving the financial stability of these families is a high priority for cities.

The SaveUSA Coalition, managed by the Cities for Financial Empowerment Fund (CFE Fund), offers a powerful tool to help families accumulate the first building block of financial security—emergency savings. By teaming with tax preparation services to provide an opportunity and incentive for saving at tax filing time, the SaveUSA model offers LMI families an opportunity to save at the moment when they have extra money coming in and makes it easy for them to do so.

Emergency Savings and Tax Refunds

The SaveUSA model targets LMI tax filers because these households are among those most affected by a lack of emergency savings. Increasing the financial stability of LMI households is a high priority because these households are the primary users of municipal social services. Financial instability can not only increase their reliance on such services but also prevent them from successfully completing or sustaining their service goals. Helping these families achieve financial stability could have real effects for the families and for the city as a whole: LMI households with greater emergency savings reserves should develop greater financial stability, and consequently lessen their use of some social services. Added stability should also allow these families to reap greater or more sustained benefit from other services. Taken together, these effects should produce greater efficiency in municipal social service budgets, allowing more people to be served at a lower cost. The New York City Department of Consumer Affairs Office of Financial Empowerment (OFE) coined this theory of change the "supervitamin effect" (Department of Consumer Affairs 2013).

Emergency savings are a critical building block in achieving financial stability, particularly in households living paycheck-to-paycheck. However, these families find it difficult to save for a number of reasons. A lack of sufficient funds is one important reason; the lack of simple, safe, and appropriate opportunities to save is also an important factor. SaveUSA addresses both factors with a simple strategy: approach consumers with a savings opportunity with a readily accessible savings product at tax filing, when they have a windfall in the form of a tax refund.

SaveUSA builds on the hugely successful Earned Income Tax Credit (EITC). The EITC creates a relatively large, one-time cash infusion for LMI households, often the largest lump sum of money they will receive all year. The EITC also represents a windfall for cities. In fact, it has been shown to generate a larger cash infusion for cities than many other federal programs designed to support urban economic development; in 2004 the EITC brought $20.2 billion to cities, while the Community Development Block Grant and HOME grants combined brought only $3.1 billion (Berube 2007). And because EITC recipients typically spend their funds quickly and buy locally, the program has a large multiplier effect that stimulates city economies. In 2004, according to one report, each additional $1.00 in EITC claimed in San Antonio would generate $1.58 in local economic activity (Texas Perspectives 2004).

However, to receive the credit, families must file a tax return. Recognizing the power of the EITC, many cities have active campaigns to help eligible families file taxes. Offering free tax-preparation services is typically a central element of these campaigns. Many cities work with the Volunteer Income Tax Assistance (VITA) program, through which Internal Revenue Service–certified volunteers provide free tax preparation and electronic filing to LMI households (typically earnings of $52,000 or less), persons with disabilities, the elderly, and limited English speaking taxpayers (IRS 2014). Thus, the tax-filing moment is a once-a-year opportunity to encourage people to save when they can realistically anticipate having enough funds to do so, and a moment when they have contact with those who can help them do so. As a result, tax-time-savings pilots have gained popularity with a diverse group of practitioners who are leveraging the filing infrastructure to facilitate personal savings decisions at a critical moment.

The SaveUSA Model

The SaveUSA model builds on early lessons from three notable pilots: the Extra Credit Saving Program, tested by a community development bank in Chicago in 2000; a 2005 study carried out in St. Louis in cooperation with H&R Block; and New York City's $aveNYC pilot, launched in 2008. The Extra Credit Saving Program offered EITC-eligible filers the opportunity to open a no-fee, no-minimum balance savings account into which they could directly deposit their federal tax refund (Beverly, Romich, and Tescher 2003). Participants were eligible to receive a 10 percent bonus (up to $100) on funds remaining in the account at the end of the year. Of eligible filers offered the opportunity, 20 percent opened an account and 86 percent of those participants received the bonus; 61 percent of participants had been unbanked at enrollment.

In a study by Duflo et al. (2005), tax filers at select H&R Block offices in the St. Louis metropolitan area were offered the opportunity to open an Express Individual Retirement Account (IRA) and deposit a portion of their tax refund into it. Those who elected to participate were randomly assigned to one of three groups: a control group that was invited to open an IRA but offered no match incentive, a group offered a 20 percent match incentive on contributions up to $1,000, and a group offered a 50 percent match on contributions up to $1,000. The study concluded that a combination of financial incentives, involvement of a tax professional, and ease of participation had a significant effect both on the willingness of individuals to participate and on the amount they were willing to contribute.

$aveNYC

Building on these and other promising results (Beverly, Romich, and Tescher 2003 and Madrian 2012), the OFE launched its $aveNYC Account pilot, which offered tax filers the opportunity to deposit tax refunds in a savings account, in 2008 and expanded it in 2009; the pilot ran through 2010, for a total of three years. Through the program, select VITA sites in New York City offered savings matches for deposits into branded $aveNYC accounts. For the first two years, deposits of at least $100 into the accounts were eligible to receive a 50 percent match up to $250 if the initial deposits were held in the account for at least one year.[1]

Results from the $aveNYC Account pilot program demonstrate that adults with low incomes will save at tax time when presented with the right opportunity and incentive. From 2008–2010, 2,165 people, roughly 9 percent of those eligible, chose to open a $aveNYC account and saved a total of nearly $1.4 million. The majority of participants (79 percent) saved for the full program term and received matching funds; 71 percent of participants who received the match in 2008 or 2009 chose to keep the account open for another year. In addition, participants were found to avoid incurring debt as a way to maintain their $aveNYC account balance (Department of Consumer Affairs 2010).

A program evaluation of $aveNYC conducted by the Center for Community Capital (CCC) at the University of North Carolina at Chapel Hill with support from the Ford Foundation showed that participation in the program was positively associated with an increased savings level and, thus, improved financial stability (Key et al. 2013). $aveNYC participants held more savings relative to a comparison group, and participants were found to be saving for the short term and withdrawing funds to pay household expenses, reduce debt, or cover emergencies. The research also suggested that, in the face of very low household income and unstable employment, participants appeared to have used their savings to meet shortfalls instead of incurring new debt (Key et al. 2013). Of particular importance was the finding that $aveNYC participants were better equipped to deal with emergencies or a loss of income. Program participants increased their odds of having one month's worth of savings to cover expenses and, over the course of the study period, increased their savings, while comparison group members experienced reductions in their savings (Key et al. 2013).

Piloting SaveUSA

The well-documented success of $aveNYC attracted wide attention. In 2010, the Obama administration's Social Innovation Fund awarded a grant to the Mayor's Fund for New York City and NYC Center for Economic Opportunity (CEO), to replicate $aveNYC as SaveUSA, which launched in New York City, Tulsa, Oklahoma, San Antonio, Texas, and Newark, New Jersey, in 2011. The research firm MDRC is conducting a full-scale evaluation of the implementation in all four cities, as well as the comparative outcomes for participants and nonparticipants in New York City and Tulsa, where potential participants were randomized so that only half were offered the incentive match. To date, MDRC has issued interim reports (Azurdia et al. 2013, 2014). The final report, planned for late 2015, will assess SaveUSA's effects over four years.

The program design, modelled after $aveNYC, offers tax filers at VITA sites the ability to direct deposit some or all of their refunds into special savings accounts using the IRS split-refund mechanism (documented in Form 8888, Allocation of Refund). Participants can make withdrawals at any time for any reason, and they can make additional deposits, but they must pledge to save $200 to $1,000. If they maintain their pledged amount in the account for approximately one year, they earn matching funds worth 50 percent of the pledged amount (up to $500). If they withdraw an amount that reduces their initial deposit, they are ineligible for the match, although they can still access all of the money in the account, including accrued interest with no fees. After successful savers receive their match, they may withdraw funds from their SaveUSA account or keep the account and continue to accrue interest. Even if they do not earn the match in a given year, they can keep the account and repeat the deposit, pledge, and match process in future years.

The SaveUSA model does not mandate or attach a goal to participant savings; without monitoring around goal verification the program is easier to administer, and non-goal savings is a more realistic first step for participants. Participants are encouraged to continue making deposits each tax season to foster a savings habit. Both are key ingredients to achieving scale.

About 9 percent of tax filers who were eligible for SaveUSA at the select VITA sites chose to sign up; site staffing, ease of setting up accounts, and marketing were significant factors affecting uptake (Azurdia 2014). This program participation rate is comparable to, if not slightly better than, similar tax-time savings programs for LMI individuals. Participants' average gross income was less than $18,000; half of the participants were single filers with children, and 66 percent were EITC recipients. Despite low household incomes, 29 percent of participants pledged to save $1,000, the maximum amount eligible for a match (Azurdia et al. 2013).

Nearly two-thirds of first-year participants earned the savings match, receiving an average of $291. Receiving the match increased the likelihood that participants would save again—nearly half of all match recipients pledged again. For participants who decided not to save again the second year, 31 percent said "they needed to use their refund to pay debts or bills or to make expenditures" (Azurdia et al. 2014, ES-7). This further emphasizes the urgency of having access to savings to cover income-expense gaps and emergencies. The early results of the randomized control trial aspect of the evaluation in New York City and Tulsa show that SaveUSA increased short-term, non-retirement savings for participants, both in terms of the incidence of having non-retirement savings and in terms of total dollars saved. In addition, SaveUSA led to more frequent savings-oriented attitudes among participants than nonparticipants (Azurdia 2014).

Most significantly, with regard to the theory of change behind municipalities' focus on financial empowerment and emergency savings, MDRC found that most participants and nonparticipants experienced financial instability, including suffering financial shocks and owing more in nonhousing debt than they held in savings. The increased savings achieved by participants gave them a "financial cushion" through access to cash that could cover up to one month's expenses (Azurdia 2014, 82).

The SaveUSA Coalition: Working to Scale SaveUSA

The SaveUSA Coalition was created to support the expansion of SaveUSA, because this model has proven effective and cities are an appropriate venue for bringing it to scale and to prioritize efforts to help LMI households build short-term savings. Another key driver of the coalition is to bring about changes in the tax code to better incentivize LMI households to save. The coalition is housed at the CFE Fund, whose mission is to help families build financial security by embedding financial empowerment strategies into local government infrastructures. The organization's approach combines technical and adaptive work to enable cities to embrace financial empowerment strategies, consider the most appropriate large-scale services within which to embed these strategies, and boost outcomes for individuals and families in the most cost-effective manner. The coalition's objectives are to provide technical assistance to member cities, to expand enrollment through new service providers, to test program elements that may maximize savings, to conduct rigorous evaluations that provide credible evidence of program effectiveness, and to build momentum for institutionalizing the model in federal tax policy.

Providing Technical Assistance

A primary goal of the SaveUSA Coalition is to assist coalition cities in designing programs that fit the city's programmatic goals while adhering to a number of foundational features of the model. Local modifications may be designed to reach a broader audience and demonstrate that savings cushions can help people be successful in a range of social service interventions, providing an opportunity to test program features such as match rates, match thresholds, and program eligibility. The degree to which programs can be customized should ensure that program design accounts for local challenges.

Cities could use any free or affordable tax preparation service to deliver the program and the match. Some cities could serve roughly the same population as is currently served, while others could integrate the program into tax preparation models outside of VITA to offer the savings opportunity to tax filers with moderate incomes. Including moderate-income consumers in the program will better reflect the full population of interest to federal policy makers. Tax preparation sites serve large volumes of clients who are focused on tax preparation and may not be interested in taking the time to learn about additional services. Integrating the SaveUSA enrollment process at these sites can be challenging and requires time and resources from all levels of staffing. The experience of overcoming similar operational challenges in New York City and in the pilot replication cities will inform the CFE Fund's technical assistance, enhancing the feasibility of launching programs in new coalition cities.

The CFE Fund is raising funds to seed additional pilots as well as to provide in-depth technical assistance. Together with experienced SaveUSA cities, the CFE Fund can also offer fundraising guidance to municipal entities, service providers, and tax preparation organizations so they can fully support their local programs.

Working with More Service Providers

Replication efforts under the SaveUSA Coalition will be focused on identifying social service providers who can embed tax-time savings in their program model and develop a savings on-ramp for their clients. To date, the SaveUSA model has focused solely on VITA sites, which provided an easy-to-access infrastructure for this type of tax-related intervention. However, the IRS has reported that less than 1 percent of EITC returns are prepared at a VITA site. After a number of years focused on the current implementation model through the VITAs, the time is right to build on this foundation and identify other target audiences for which tax-time savings would be effective.

Expanding the range of partners beyond VITA will increase opportunities for eligible families to participate in the program by making it available through a range of providers who recognize the value of short-term savings for their clients and are willing to embed such an opportunity into their own approach. Providers will still leverage the infrastructure of tax preparation services, through partnerships, but will introduce this powerful emergency savings model within their own service context. Replication partners will need to work with financial institutions that are able to provide an account that offers the necessary terms, provide data reports, and distribute match funds to successful savers.

These may be the most challenging of the SaveUSA Coalition's objectives. Other types of providers may not yet see the relevance of tax-time savings to their clients, especially compared to other pressing needs, and the ways in which such access to a savings vehicle could benefit their own programmatic outcomes (the supervitamin effect). The model is based on participants having access to a safe and affordable bank account and the need to monitor accounts in order to provide the match.

However, involving more service providers is crucial for both the short- and long-term success of SaveUSA. In the short run, cities and their diverse local partners offer significant opportunities to reach a large number of people. Channeling the program opportunity through service providers that are integrated with municipal social services offers a way to reach scale and make this savings on-ramp available to more of the families who need its benefits. In the long run, involving more providers will engage new stakeholders and present opportunities to test the effectiveness of various programmatic options—both vital factors in building momentum toward federal policy action.

Testing Program Elements

Scalability will also hinge on the cost implications and participation rates of the model; data on these elements will come from further tests around the match rate and savings threshold. In the current SaveUSA implementation cities, the match rate is 50 percent and the match threshold is $1,000. As an increasing number of cities and service providers partner with the CFE Fund to create their own version of a matched tax-time savings program for LMI earners, the SaveUSA Coalition will be able to evaluate the optimal match rate and match threshold to maximize participation rates and savings levels while minimizing costs. These variations in match rates and savings thresholds will help to identify the "sweet spot" where savings participation and level are incentivized while keeping the match rate as low as possible to minimize cost and allow for scale. As cities work with service providers that serve a broader income range than VITA sites, the CFE Fund will also be able to compare the effects of participant income levels on take-up rates, savings rates, costs, saving for the entire year to earn the match, and other outcomes.

Conducting Rigorous Evaluations

Evidence regarding the optimal program design that maximizes savings amounts and participation rates while minimizing costs will be invaluable for policy makers, funders, and other stakeholders. Rigorous evaluation of program impact in a variety of contexts is critical to build the political will to create a nationally available incentive structure for flexible emergency savings. Findings from evaluations in additional municipalities can provide evidence-based learning on the impact of matched tax-time savings on participating families and the program terms necessary to hone in on appropriate policy parameters and realistic cost projections. The SaveUSA Coalition's evaluation approach will further examine the super-vitamin effect of integrating financial stability programming into other programs, by asking how and to what extent building clients' emergency savings boosts the efficiency and improves the outcomes of social service programs.

Laying Groundwork for Federal Policy Change

The creation of the SaveUSA Coalition and the proliferation of local programs to encourage savings at tax time through the SaveUSA model will have meaningful impacts, especially in replication cities. However, to achieve national scale, an incentive for emergency savings must be universally implemented as a refundable credit for LMI tax filers through the federal tax code. This structure will leverage the existing infrastructure of the tax filing and reporting process to ensure universal access to the savings incentive.

The tax code already contains a number of incentives for households to build retirement savings, including the Savers Credit. However, retirement savings may not be the right first step for many households whose most immediate concern is having a cushion for emergencies or shorter-term savings needs. Further, since it is not refundable, the current Savers Credit provides no benefit to those filers who do not have a tax liability. For incentives to truly shape savings behavior, current policy must be expanded to provide on-ramps to savings that provide a buffer when emergencies occur and jumpstart recipients on the path to longer-term savings.

Legislation has already been introduced to incorporate the SaveUSA model into the tax code. The Financial Security Credit Act of 2013 (H.R. 2917) was introduced by José Serrano (D-NY) on August 1, 2013; the bill had 30 Democratic cosponsors as of August 2014. The bill, whose full title is "To promote savings by providing a tax credit for eligible taxpayers who contribute to savings products and to facilitate taxpayers receiving this credit and open a designated savings product when they file their Federal income tax returns," would allow a tax credit of $500 or 50 percent of the total amount deposited in or contributed to a designated savings product; the credit itself must be deposited into the same savings product. The amount of the credit depends on adjusted gross income and on the filer keeping the funds in the account for at least eight continuous months. Savings products may include a qualified retirement plan, qualified tuition program, Coverdell education savings account, US savings bond, certificate of deposit (or similar class of deposit) with a duration of at least eight months, or a savings account.

Implementation guidelines are required to ensure the successful functioning of the Financial Security Credit Act and provide for saver support and verification. Ideally, income-eligible filers should be able to simply designate on their tax form the amount of their refund to deposit in an approved savings account for one year, and then present documentation that the account was open and funded for the previous year with their tax return to claim the credit. Tax filers who do not have an account should be able to open one via the federal income tax form and deposit all or part of the refund directly into the newly opened account. The size and duration of deposits in savings products could be verified via enhanced 1099 reporting for eligible savings vehicles, and additional safeguards should be provided to ensure requirements are met.

The Findings section of the bill specifically cites the successful pilots in Houston, Texas, Newark, New Jersey, New York City, San Antonio, Texas, and Tulsa, Oklahoma. Additional local replications and evaluations will further support the bill since they will build the evidence base needed to support the expansion of federal policy.

The SaveUSA Coalition will work with partner organizations and champions to secure additional cosponsors and ensure the passage of the Financial Security Credit. The amplified voice of multiple cities working together to implement the model can be a powerful impetus for change in the federal tax code. Building legislative buy-in to enact this model through the tax code will hinge upon building a network of supporters through the growth of the SaveUSA Coalition.

Conclusion

SaveUSA has grown from a one-city pilot to a federally supported national model. The model's innovative approach to coupling the tax refund windfall moment with a significant savings incentive provides a realistic on-ramp to encourage short-term savings and help filers along the road to greater financial stability. In coming years, the SaveUSA Coalition and the CFE Fund will guide various iterations of the model in diverse contexts and provide additional evidence on optimal program design. Ultimately, the coalition and the evidence it provides can midwife the passage of a Financial Security Credit Act that will enable millions of Americans with low incomes to leverage their tax refunds to begin saving.

NOTE

1. After observing that participants from the first year who made smaller deposits were more likely to withdraw their funds before the one-year match, OFE increased the minimum deposit to $200 and increased the available matching funds to $500, or 50 percent of the first $1,000 saved.

REFERENCES

Azurdia, Gilda, Stephen Freedman, Gayle Hamilton, and Caroline Schultz. 2013. "Encouraging Savings for Low- And Moderate-Income Individuals: Preliminary Implementation Findings from the SaveUSA Evaluation." Policy Brief 14, April MDRC, New York, NY.

———. 2014. "Encouraging Low- And Moderate-Income Tax Filers to Save: Implementation and Interim Impact Findings from the SaveUSA Evaluation." Report, April. MDRC, New York, NY.

Berube, Alan. 2007. "The Importance of the EITC to Urban Economies." Staff briefing given at the Congressional Former Mayors Caucus, July 13, Washington, DC..

Beverly, Sondra G., Jennifer L. Romich, and Jennifer Tescher. 2003. "Linking Tax Refunds and Low-Cost Bank Accounts: A Social Development Strategy for

Low-Income Families?" Working Paper No. 03–17. Washington University at St. Louis, Center for Social Development, St. Louis, MO.

Department of Consumer Affairs. 2010. "The $aveNYC Account: Innovation in Asset Building." Research Update, December. Department of Consumer Affairs, Office of Financial Empowerment, New York City.

Department of Consumer Affairs. 2013. "Strategy #1: Integrating Professional Financial Counseling." Municipal Financial Empowerment: A Supervitamin for Public Programs Report Series. Department of Consumer Affairs, Office of Financial Empowerment, New York City.

Duflo, Esther, William Gale, Jeffrey Liebman, Peter Orszag, and Emmanuel Saez. 2005. "Saving Incentives for Low- and Middle-Income Families: Evidence from a Field Experiment with H&R Block." National Bureau of Economic Research Working Paper Series, No. 11680.

IRS, Internal Revenue Service. 2014. "Free Tax Return Preparation for Qualifying Taxpayers." Internal Revenue Service. Last updated June 11. http://www.irs.gov/Individuals/Free-Tax-Return-Preparation-for-You-by-Volunteers.

Key, Clinton C., Michal Grinstein-Weiss, Jenna N. Tucker, and Krista Holub. 2013. "Savings at Tax Time: The Effect of $aveNYC on Savings in Low-Income Households." Working Paper, September. Center for Community Capital at University of Northern Carolina Chapel Hill, Chapel Hill, NC.

Madrian, Brigitte C. 2012. "Matching Contributions and Savings Outcomes: A Behavioral Economics Perspective." National Bureau of Economic Research Working Paper Series, No. 18220.

Texas Perspectives, Inc. 2004. "2004 Update: Increased Participation in the Earned Income Tax Credit in San Antonio." Report prepared for the City of San Antonio, November 23. Austin, Texas, Texas Perspectives, Inc.

Chapter 6

Refund to Savings: Creating Contingency Savings at Tax Time

Michal Grinstein-Weiss, Krista Comer, Blair Russell, Clinton Key, Dana Perantie, and Dan Ariely

Introduction

The Refund to Savings (R2S) initiative aims to help low- and moderate-income (LMI) households build short-term contingency savings by providing motivation and opportunity to save their tax refunds, the largest single sum many households receive all year. Other research on tax-time interventions has yielded promising findings (Key et al. 2012; Tufano 2010; Beverly, Tescher, and Romich 2004), but R2S expands the potential of such interventions by using a scalable delivery system (online tax-preparation software) and incorporating motivational mechanisms grounded in behavioral economics theory. The delivery of the intervention is seamlessly integrated within an existing infrastructure, ensures high fidelity between the intervention's design and its implementation, and minimizes the cost of the intervention. The intervention mechanisms are designed to help tax filers overcome psychological and behavioral barriers that limit the accumulation of savings.

The R2S initiative is the product of a unique collaboration among researchers at Washington University in St. Louis, Duke University, and Intuit, Inc., the makers of TurboTax. Focusing on LMI households that use the TurboTax Freedom Edition to prepare their returns online, the intervention was implemented as a randomized controlled experiment to enable the R2S team to rigorously evaluate its impact. With a sample of approximately 680,000 tax filers, it is one of the largest savings experiments ever conducted in the United States. Because of the unique partnership supporting it and the innovative design of the intervention, R2S offers substantial promise as an effort to increase contingency savings among economically vulnerable LMI households.

This chapter will discuss the barriers to and opportunities for saving at tax time. It also will describe an innovative intervention designed to help LMI households build savings at tax time and offer a critical evaluation of the costs and benefits of the intervention. The first section discusses barriers to saving, considering why and how tax time affords an ideal opportunity to help households build savings. In the second section, the authors discuss R2S, presenting the intervention's goals, target audience, mechanisms, evaluation, and limitations. The third and final section of the chapter discusses ideas for new testing and future directions.

Barriers to Saving and the Promise of Tax-Time Savings Interventions

The lack of contingency savings is a salient problem in the United States. It exposes households to economic, social, psychological, and physical consequences. Helping households make financial preparations for the unexpected is not easy. LMI households in particular face very real material constraints on saving; many have sufficient income only to meet consumption needs. Even when households have some slack in the budget, they may fall short of savings goals for a number of reasons—many of them not rational. Ariely's (2011, 2010) work on choice and behavior demonstrates that people are irrational in all areas of their lives, but this irrationality arises in ways that are predictable and can be overcome with smart program design. This perspective helps explain why economic insecurity remains high even though people know that they will be better off if they have contingency savings. Tax time may be the ideal moment to circumvent some of the psychological and logistical barriers that perpetuate low emergency savings rates among LMI households.

Psychological and Behavioral Influences on Savings Decisions and Actions

An array of psychological and behavioral factors limits the ability of LMI households to accumulate savings. These factors include present bias, procrastination, inertia, limited attention, and inaccurate or distorted perceptions of savings needs. Numerous studies demonstrate that individuals are present biased—that is, they strongly favor current and near-term spending and consumption over saving for future consumption (Meier and Sprenger 2010; Stango and Zinman 2007; Frederick, Loewenstein, and O'Donoghue 2002; Angeletos et al. 2001; Harris and Laibson 2001; Laibson 1997). For instance, the average person may require the promise of a 50 percent or greater return on investment before he or she will consider it worthwhile to forgo consumption and save. In other words, many people would rather have $100 to spend today than $150 to spend a year from now (Frederick, Loewenstein, and O'Donoghue 2002).

Procrastination, inertia, and limited attention also play roles in financial decision making. Individuals who intend to save often procrastinate instead of taking action (O'Donoghue and Rabin 1999). Households embrace financial inertia, continuing whatever habits, accounts, and transactions they have in place, even if those are not optimal (Barr 2007; Benartzi and Thaler 2007; Madrian and Shea 2001). When facing multiple savings options, households tend to accept defaults in order to avoid exerting mental effort (Bronchetti et al. 2011; Beshears et al. 2009) and to avoid difficult decisions (Ariely et al. 2009; Mullainathan and Shafir 2009; Ariely and Norton 2008; Choi et al. 2006).

Finally, the accumulation of emergency savings is impeded by distorted perceptions concerning emergency savings needs and the costs of not having emergency savings. Households may underestimate the incidence and costs of financial emergencies (Brobeck 2008). They also often underestimate the true costs of using credit, debt, and alternative financial services, choosing these options instead of less expensive alternatives like saving in advance (Zinman 2009; Desmond and Sprenger 2007; Stegman and Faris 2003).

Using Tax Time to Encourage Saving

Several factors make tax time an ideal opportunity to encourage households to build contingency savings. These include the availability of lump-sum payments, the options to directly deposit the tax refund and split the deposit among multiple accounts, the opportunity to implement behavioral techniques at key financial decision points, and the promise of scalability.

Lump-Sum Payments and Mental Accounting

Over 75 percent of filers receive a tax refund. Because of excessive withholding, tax credits, and deductions, the Treasury owes many households money and pays that debt in a sizable lump sum. The Internal Revenue Service (IRS) estimates that the average household received a $2,883 refund in tax year 2011 (IRS 2012). This suggests that many households already accomplish what is often considered the hardest part of saving: deferring consumption and accumulating funds. Because households receive the tax refund as a lump-sum payment, encouragement to save for contingencies may be particularly effective at tax time. Thaler and Shefrin's (1981) behavioral life-cycle theory suggests that people view lump-sum payments differently than payroll income. Saving a lump sum may be easier than saving income because the lump sum is not considered part of the flow of funds used for current consumption. Tax refunds, which tend to be relatively large and come only once a year, fall into this category. Many tax filers view their refunds as a windfall and use them for normally unaffordable priorities, including setting some funds aside in savings (Mammen and Lawrence 2006; Schreiner et al. 2001; Romich and Weisner 2000).

However, saving a lump sum can also be challenging. Filers may use mental accounting (Thaler 1985), prespending their anticipated refund. As tax season approaches, anticipation of a refund may lead them to incur debt, delay necessary expenditures, or plan for additional spending (Barr 2012; Mendenhall et al. 2012; Bronchetti et al. 2011). Other research confirms a general desire to save the tax refund: 60 percent of filers express an intention to save at least part of their refund, as do 55 percent of filers with adjusted gross incomes below $35,000. The average respondent plans to save about 40 percent of the refund (Grinstein-Weiss et al. 2012).

Despite the opportunities presented by lump-sum tax refunds, a contingency savings intervention must channel the refund into a savings account or other short-term liquid savings product in order to succeed. The intervention must also influence the mental accounting that some filers employ to plan for and manage refunds.

Opportunity for Direct Deposit and Split Tax Refunds

Reducing the steps required to execute the savings decision is fundamental to creating effective and scalable savings programs. Direct deposit is a crucial element in efforts to build emergency reserves, because many filers intend to transfer some of their refund to savings, but few act on this desire and actually move the money. Recent innovations enable tax filers to save all or part of their refund. Since 2007, the IRS has allowed taxpayers to split refunds. Using IRS form 8888, filers can deposit them into as many as three existing accounts. In 2011, over 842,000 taxpayers used this mechanism to split more than $3.4 billion in refunds (Treasury Inspector General for Tax Administration 2012). This option enables filers to build dedicated savings in a vehicle of the tax filer's choosing (such as a traditional savings account or a prepaid card account). The same IRS form enables filers to use part or all of their refund to buy Series-I US Savings Bonds. Savings bonds are a safe, interest-bearing product available to everyone—even those who lack a connection to the mainstream banking system.

Using Behavioral Techniques to Convert the Tax Refund to Contingency Savings

Tax-filing software presents an opportunity to use behavioral techniques to help individuals overcome limited attention, lack of self-control, and biases toward present orientation. Countless behavioral experiments show that small changes in choice architecture (i.e., the way a choice is presented) can have dramatic effects on behavior (Choi et al. 2012; Thaler and Sunstein 2008; Ashraf, Karlan, and Yin 2006; Thaler and Benartzi 2004). Notably, altering the default presentation of options and introducing context-specific motivational language can nudge consumers toward desired behavioral outcomes.

Early research from the R2S initiative has identified specific motivational messages that significantly increase respondents' hypothetical allocation to savings. For instance, the initiative shows low-income respondents a message encouraging them to form a picture of their life after retirement. Compared with counterparts in the control group, treatment-group members shown the message indicated that they would allocate 13 percent more of their refund to savings (Grinstein-Weiss et al. 2012). Likewise, a subsequent randomized controlled trial using TurboTax software finds that treatment-group members shown motivational prompts and default savings amounts were significantly more likely than those in the control group to split a portion of their refund into a savings account (Grinstein-Weiss et al. 2012). Participants in the treatment group also allocated significantly more money to savings accounts. However, the effects of the intervention are heavily concentrated on the small proportion of users who split their refund.

Some evidence suggests that a precommitment to saving the tax refund or future income is effective in increasing the likelihood of saving and the amount of money saved (Jones and Mahajan 2011; Thaler and Benartzi 2004). Jones and Mahajan (2012) find that it can be beneficial to offer tax filers a modest incentive to make a nonbinding precommitment to save a portion of the refund; they find that filers offered such an incentive save up to 50 percent more than do those offered the incentive when they file their tax return.

Promise of Scalability

Tax filing is a nearly universal experience, and tax day is a part of the American experience: each year, about 143 million US households file income tax returns; the IRS refunded about $338 billion to taxpayers in the 2011 tax year (IRS 2012). The filing process is thus an exciting site for an intervention to address the widespread shortage of contingency saving in households across the income distribution, but particularly in low-income households. During the 2011 tax year, the Earned Income Tax Credit (EITC) provided 26.5 million low-income households with nearly $60.7 billion in refunds.

Building a contingency savings intervention into a widely used delivery channel offers a clearly advantageous pathway to scale. However, the effort must control costs, provide a means to serve large numbers of users, and ensure consistency in delivery. These obligations pose several daunting challenges. Face-to-face intervention with filers is costly and time consuming; it would be difficult to bring such an effort to scale. Conversely, using software to deliver an intervention fundamentally changes the intervention's cost structure and execution. Design (programming) and delivery drive intervention costs and so are realized before implementation. Once the software is programmed, the unit cost to deliver the intervention to each additional user is effectively zero. If the intervention is successful and replicated, ongoing costs diminish year over year. The pathway also scales to the number of users who enter it. Intuit's systems, for example, have the capacity to serve hundreds of thousands of simultaneous users.

In addition to low delivery costs, the software platform offers the advantage of uniformity and fidelity in delivery. Researchers observe that, in tax-time savings programs delivered face-to-face, substantial program success depends on where, when, and by whom the intervention is delivered (Tufano 2010; Duflo et al. 2006). In the TurboTax platform, the delivery of the intervention is consistent across the tax season, across the country, and around the clock. It shows each participant precisely the intended message at precisely the intended time. This allows for a clean evaluation of program elements and for easy expansion of successful features.

R2S: Putting Ideas to Action

The overall goal of the R2S initiative is to transform tax season into saving season. The 2013 intervention attempted to help LMI households choose to convert part of their refund into short-term contingency savings. Likewise, the design sought to demonstrate the programmatic benefit of building contingency savings programs into existing infrastructure and the promise of public-private partnerships to promote economic well-being. Finally, the intervention rigorously tested theoretical propositions from behavioral economics and sought evidence generated through real economic decisions. Insights from these efforts are meant to inform the design and implementation of programs and policies aimed at increasing financial security for economically vulnerable households.

Target Population

The 2013 R2S intervention focused on LMI tax filers who use Intuit's TurboTax Freedom Edition software, a free online platform offered as part of the IRS's Free File Alliance program (http://www.freefilealliance.org). In 2013, taxpayers filing 2012 returns qualified to file with the Freedom Edition if they (1) had an adjusted gross income of less than $31,000, (2) qualified for the EITC, or (3) were an active duty member of the military with an adjusted gross income of less than $58,000. Participants accessed the TurboTax Freedom Edition via the IRS website, the Freedom Edition website, or a local community-based tax-preparation center.

The mode of delivery does constrain the intervention's ability to reach the full target population. To see the intervention, a person must have a computer and Internet access. Because filers can only access the Freedom Edition platform online (the software cannot be downloaded), they must also have sufficient familiarity with and trust in that platform to prepare their taxes using a web-based interface. Although this may limit the intervention's ability to reach target-population members who have low levels of computer literacy or are not comfortable preparing their own tax returns, some community tax-preparation sites use the TurboTax Freedom Edition, and consumers can get assistance from volunteers at such sites.

Mechanisms

The R2S intervention design uniquely employs two mechanisms to promote emergency savings. The first is the use of software technology through the TurboTax platform. The second is the use of a combination of behavioral techniques designed to elicit the desired response.

The TurboTax Platform

The Freedom Edition software guides users who meet the program criteria through the preparation of their tax returns. It includes a series of modules on income, credits, deductions, and other tax-relevant aspects of users' social and financial lives. The process takes the form of a guided interview. The software socializes users to receive tips and suggestions.

After entering all information and completing the preparation process, the participant must decide how and where to receive the tax refund. At this point in the TurboTax process, the R2S intervention prompts people to save some of the refund windfall in a dedicated contingency-savings vehicle of their choice.

The Behavioral Mechanisms

The presentation of the stimulus to save is grounded in the principles of behavioral economics. In 2013, the R2S intervention tested three types of behavioral mechanisms: an automatic savings opportunity, motivational messages (*prompts*), and suggested savings amounts set by default (*anchors*). Filers experienced the first mechanism when TurboTax asked them to indicate where to send the refund: the intervention suggested that filers save a portion of it by exercising the IRS's split-refund option to divide their refund or purchase US savings bonds directly at the time of filing. If a filer opted to receive a paper check, TurboTax suggested saving some of the refund and showed how the refund would be allocated automatically if it were split between the paper check and a Series-I US Savings Bond (figure 6.1). Filers who chose direct deposit were presented a similar option, with a choice between purchasing savings bonds and depositing a portion of the funds into an existing savings account (figure 6.2). Participants could use any account that has conforming routing and account numbers and that is held in the name of the tax filer or his or her spouse. In both situations, the user could choose not to save by clicking a button labeled "No thanks," or, "I don't need to save."

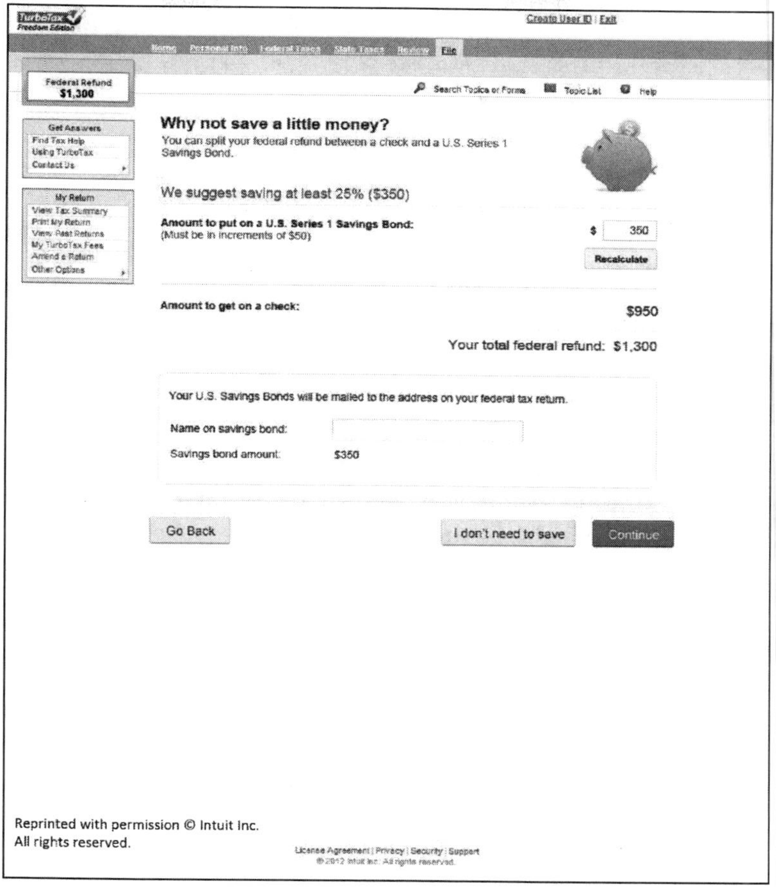

Figure 6.1 Paper Check Intervention Experience.

Source: TurboTax Freedom Edition, 2013.

The second behavioral mechanism involved messages designed to motivate saving. TurboTax showed filers a generic prompt (control condition) or one of three behavioral prompts designed to increase savings desire (treatment condition). In developing the prompts, the R2S team employed lessons learned from previous phases of the initiative (Grinstein-Weiss, Gale, et al. 2014; Grinstein-Weiss et al. 2013; Key et al. 2013). All prompts encouraged filers to save (see table 6.1 for prompts). The generic

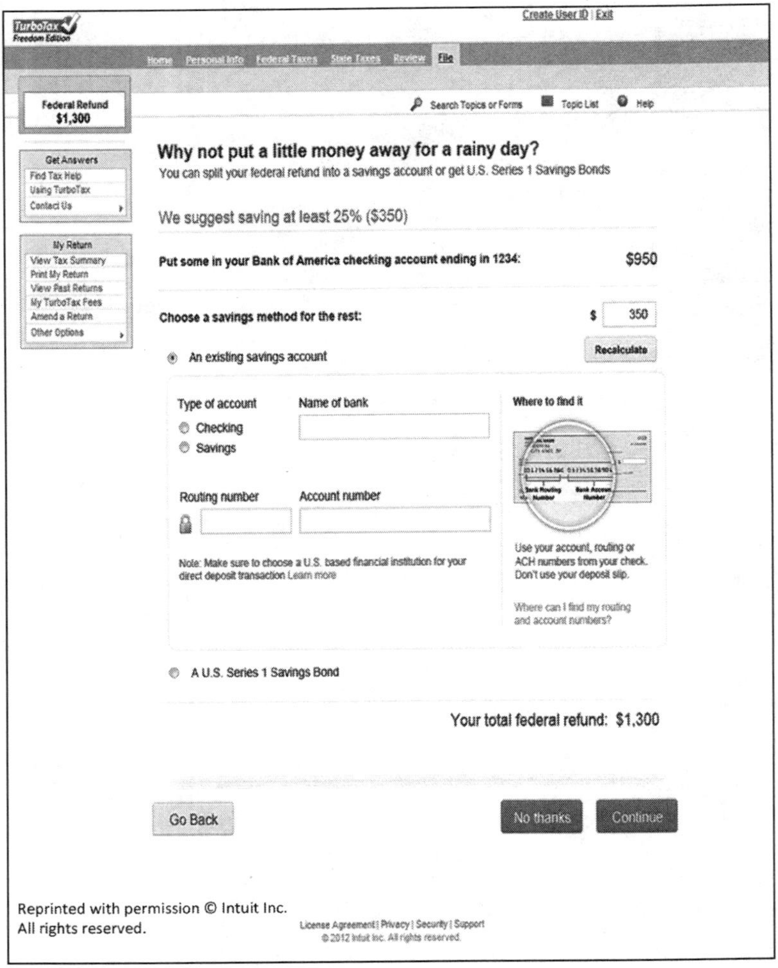

Figure 6.2 Direct Deposit Intervention Experience.

Source: TurboTax Freedom Edition, 2013.

(control) message encouraged them to do so without providing an explicit motivation. Any effects of the treatment messages are reported relative to the effect of the generic (control) message.

The third behavioral mechanism in the 2013 R2S intervention tested the effect of anchoring. That is, the intervention recommended a saving

Table 6.1 2013 R2S Prompts

Prompt category	Prompt description
Emergency prompt	Do you have enough money for an emergency? A Harvard study found that most Americans could not come up with $2,000 for something unexpected. We can help you stay prepared.
Family prompt	Have a family or thinking of starting one? Start building a bright future for them.
Future prompt	Save for your future, and get peace of mind. Feel more secure about your future with a little extra money in the bank.
Generic prompt	Why not save a little money? You can split your federal refund into a savings account or get a US Series I Savings Bond.

Source: TurboTax Freedom Edition, 2013.

level to treatment participants and prepopulated the web form's field with that amount. The experiment tested five anchors, presenting three as percentages (25, 50, or 75 percent of the refund) and two as dollar amounts ($100 or $200). The anchor shown to a filer varied according to his or her assigned treatment condition. Table 6.2 shows the combinations of prompts and anchors tested. For additional information on the intervention design and implementation, see Grinstein-Weiss, Perantie, and colleagues (2014).

Evaluation

The R2S team planned and conducted a rigorous evaluation to assess the impacts of the interventions. Data for this evaluation come from TurboTax Freedom Edition and two waves of the Household Financial Survey (HFS). Results show that the mechanisms used in the interventions can affect tax-refund saving behavior.

Data Collection

Administrative data collected through TurboTax Freedom Edition include the treatment assignment, tax return information, and individual

Table 6.2 Combinations of Prompts and Anchors Tested in the R2S Experiment over Three Test Periods

Period 1 (January 31–February 13)	**Period 2 (February 14–March 13)**	**Period 3 (March 14–April 17)**
Generic, no anchor (control)	Generic, no anchor (control)	Generic, no anchor (control)
Generic, 25%	Generic, 50%	Emergency, $100
Generic, 50%	Generic, 75%	Emergency, $250
Emergency, 25%	Emergency, 50%	Future, $100
Emergency, 50%	Emergency, 75%	Future, $250
Future, 25%	Future, 75%	Emergency, 25%
Family, 25%	Family, 75%	Future, 25%

Note: The tax filing season was divided into three sub periods to test more combinations of interventions.
Source: Center for Social Development.

choices concerning refunds. To identify constraints that may affect savings choices and to capture the impact of tax-time choices in the economic lives of participating households, the R2S team conducted the HFS with a subsample of the intervention population. The HFS is a longitudinal, Internet-based instrument fielded immediately after tax filing (n = 20,000) and again six months later (n = 8,500). The first wave of the survey captured a thorough assessment of participants' assets, liabilities, intended uses of tax refunds, product preferences, behavioral characteristics, and demographic traits. The second wave queried respondents about their actual use of the refunds. By combining the administrative data from the R2S experiment with the data from the longitudinal surveys, we can assess whether the R2S interventions affected savings outcomes six months after filing.

Results

Results from the R2S experiment show that minor design changes informed by behavioral economics principles can increase both the number of tax filers who deposit tax refunds into savings vehicles and the dollar amounts saved. We estimate that an additional 4,800 tax filers deposited some portion of their refunds into savings vehicles because of the R2S interventions, and participants directly deposited approximately $6 million more into savings accounts or savings bonds than they would have in the absence of the interventions.

Examination of savings outcomes among R2S participants shows that exposure to R2S interventions is associated with a 12 percent increase in the number of individuals who deposit refunds into savings (7.6 percent of participants exposed to one of the R2S interventions deposited a portion of their refund). On average and across treatment groups, R2S participants deposited $200–$300, and that range is significantly higher than the average savings of control-group members. We also examined a subgroup of participants who completed the HFS and reported having savings accounts (n = 7,115). In that subsample, the likelihood of saving was 28 percent higher among participants exposed to an R2S intervention than among counterparts in the control condition. Although the program effects are relatively modest, the interventions—limited to content presented on a few screens in the TurboTax Freedom Edition—were also modest.

It is noteworthy that small behavioral cues led to increases in refund deposits and continued to show positive impacts six months after participants filed their taxes. Those who saved at tax time reported improvement in financial security, reduction in levels of material hardship, and increases in ability to meet regular expenses. Not surprisingly, the HFS shows that accumulating emergency savings is a high priority among savers in the LMI population. At the six-month follow-up, when asked about reasons for saving, an overwhelming majority (75 percent) reported saving "for emergencies and other unexpected needs."

Limitations

The evaluation has identified several limitations and design features that impede implementation. First, some filers lack a bank account and so cannot directly deposit their refund. Others choose not to use their account at tax time. In the 2013 experiment, 18 percent of filers chose to receive their refunds as paper checks. However, the intervention offers these filers the option to save a portion of the refund by purchasing a Series-I US Savings Bond.

Second, many LMI filers have only one bank account. Data from the HFS show that 23 percent of respondents have a checking account but no savings account. Moreover, among HFS respondents who reported saving tax refunds for at least six months, a third reported holding the savings in a checking account. The mechanism to generate savings in the experiment requires the use of more than one product and encourages people to separate savings from money used for ordinary expenses. If a household has only one account, it can split a refund only by purchasing a savings bond.

The illiquidity of savings bonds and uncertainty about their terms or use may limit their attractiveness to households in the sample. Additional research is needed to elucidate the financial service needs and preferences of underbanked and unbanked customers at tax time. Future research might also usefully consider the regulatory framework needed to facilitate the opening of new accounts at tax time.

Third, filer fatigue can pose significant challenges to implementation of an intervention among people completing their tax returns. Intuit's usability tests on the 2012 intervention reveal that some filers skip over the motivational prompt. These tests use sophisticated eye-tracking software, and results show that some test participants quickly scan each page, ignoring the text of the offer and looking for the Continue button (Holub et al. 2013).

Finally, a true opt-out design is not feasible in the context of tax preparation. Those who have and choose to use a savings account must enter their account information. That may impede some who want to save but do not have the information at hand. If they do not want to split their refund, filers must click a button labeled "No thanks," or, "I don't need to save," in order to continue to the next screen.

New Testing and Future Directions

The R2S partnership affords the opportunity to test additional ideas for contingency-savings interventions within the TurboTax platform. In 2014, the R2S team is testing interventions that use some techniques from the 2013 effort, as well as a variety of new features. For example, R2S is exploring whether it is possible to influence saving behavior by communicating with people before they file their taxes. The 2014 effort is also testing new opportunities to open financial products at the time of filing.

Future iterations of the intervention could test whether saving behavior is influenced by the use of precommitment devices in conjunction with tax filing software. Precommitment mechanisms can help filers plan ahead by suggesting, for example, that they allocate refunds toward contingency savings. Filers who used tax software in the prior tax season could receive an e-mail or message in October or November. The communication would ask them to make a nonbinding commitment to create a rainy day fund with their refund. To make the commitment psychologically binding, the message could encourage participants to publicly announce the pledge via social media. Reminders of the commitment could be sent periodically via e-mail or text messages. During the tax-filing process, the precommitted portion of the participant's refund could be automatically allocated to a savings vehicle.

In the future, we hope to test innovations that will address barriers other than the psychological and behavioral ones that are the focus of this initial effort. Among these are numerous institutional barriers faced by low-income households. These barriers include lack of access to institutional savings mechanisms such as the ability to open an account easily, automatic features (for instance, direct deposit) that facilitate saving, and institutional incentives (such as matched retirement contributions from employers). Future innovations might make it easy to open an account at tax time and increase the number of automatic ways to save. Both ideas are promising strategies to mitigate these institutional barriers.

Conclusion

Tax filing is a nearly universal, permanent, and recurring event in the lives of US households. It is also a major financial event for most: 75 percent of households receive a sizable refund. From a behavioral economics viewpoint, tax time offers the ability to intervene at a key financial decision point and, therefore, a golden opportunity to help households overcome barriers that limit the accumulation of contingency savings.

The 2013 R2S initiative demonstrates the potential of an intervention that incorporates minor design changes, informed by behavioral economics principles, into the process of tax filing; such an intervention can help LMI filers convert the tax refund into savings. Contingency funds—that are outside the normal transactional flows—can help households weather financial shocks and allow them to invest in transformative opportunities. An innovative product of collaboration between academia and business, R2S is a unique, promising, and scalable intervention informed by a substantial body of theory and research.

Acknowledgments

The Center for Social Development at Washington University in St. Louis gratefully acknowledges the funders who made the Refund to Savings (R2S) initiative possible: the Ford Foundation, the Annie E. Casey Foundation, Intuit, Inc., the Intuit Financial Freedom Foundation, the University of North Carolina at Chapel Hill, and an anonymous donor. The research team would like to give special thanks to Amy Brown and Frank DeGiovanni with the Ford Foundation, and Beadsie Woo with the

Annie E. Casey Foundation. We appreciate their invaluable feedback, direction, and support at every stage of this process.

Refund to Savings would not exist without the commitment of Intuit, Inc., and particularly its Tax and Financial Center. We appreciate the executive sponsorship of David Williams. We also appreciate the efforts of key contributors from the TurboTax development, marketing, and analytics teams that have worked diligently on the planning and implementation of the experiment: Joe Lillie, Sacha Adams, Piritta Luoto, Julia Zhuang, Topher Stevenson, Annette Hoffard, and Kathy Kirkendall. We thank the Intuit Freedom Foundation for providing the TurboTax Freedom Edition platform and Susan Mason for her contributions. A big thanks goes to Phillip Poirier, who has championed the initiative since its inception and continues to contribute direction and insight on the team.

Our advisory committee, which includes Ray Boshara, Amy Brown, Keith Ernst, Tim Flacke, Julian Jamison, David Rothstein, Michael Sherraden, Jennifer Tescher, and Beadsie Woo, has provided outstanding advice throughout the initiative. Many people with the Center for Social Development have contributed in significant ways to the effort. Among them are Bonnie Dee, Anna DeRuyter, Lissa Johnson, Chris Leiker, and Lingzi Luo. Thanks also to Diane Wyant with the University of North Carolina at Chapel Hill.

Finally, we thank the thousands of taxpayers who participated in the research surveys and shared their personal financial information with us. We hope this research will generate evidence useful for developing policies to help LMI households increase their financial security and mobility.

Disclaimer

Statistical compilations disclosed in this document relate directly to the bona fide research of and public policy discussions concerning the promotion of increased savings in connection with the tax compliance process. All compilations are anonymous and do not disclose cells containing data from fewer than ten tax returns. IRS Reg. 301.7216.

REFERENCES

Angeletos, George-Marios, David Laibson, Andrea Repetto, Jeremy Tobacman, and Stephen Weinberg. 2001. "The Hyperbolic Consumption Model:

Calibration, Simulation, and Empirical Evaluation." *Journal of Economic Perspectives* 15 (3): 47–68.

Ariely, Dan. 2010. *Predictably Irrational: The Hidden Forces That Shape Our Decisions*. New York: Harper Perennial.

———. 2011. *The Upside of Irrationality: The Unexpected Benefits of Defying Logic*. New York: Harper Perennial.

Ariely, Dan, and Michael I. Norton. 2008. "How Actions Create—Not Just Reveal—Preferences." *Trends in Cognitive Sciences* 12 (1): 13–16.

Ariely, Dan, Uri Gneezy, George Loewenstein, and Nina Mazar. 2009. "Large Stakes and Big Mistakes." *Review of Economic Studies* 76 (2): 451–469.

Ashraf, Nava, Dean Karlan, and Wesley Yin. 2006. "Tying Odysseus to the Mast: Evidence from a Commitment Savings Product in the Philippines." *Quarterly Journal of Economics* 121 (2): 635–672.

Barr, Michael S. 2007. "Banking the Poor: Policies to Bring Low- and Moderate-Income Households in the United States into the Financial Mainstream." In *New Frontiers in Banking Services: Emerging Needs and Tailored Products for Untapped Markets*, ed. Luisa Anderloni, Maria Debora Braga, and Emanuele Maria Carluccio, 323–351. New York: Springer.

———. 2012. *No Slack: The Financial Lives of Low-Income Americans*. Washington, DC: Brookings Institution Press.

Benartzi, Shlomo, and Richard H. Thaler. 2007. "Heuristics and Biases in Retirement Savings Behavior." *Journal of Economic Perspectives* 21 (3): 81–104.

Beshears, John, James J. Choi, David Laibson, and Brigitte C. Madrian. 2009. "The Importance of Default Options for Retirement Saving Outcomes: Evidence from the United States." In *Social Security Policy in a Changing Environment*, ed. Jeffrey R. Brown, Jeffrey B. Liebman, and David A. Wise, 167–198. Chicago: University of Chicago Press.

Beverly, Sondra G., Jennifer Tescher, and Jennifer L. Romich. 2004. "Linking Tax Refunds and Low-Cost Bank Accounts: Early Lessons for Program Design and Evaluation." *Journal of Consumer Affairs* 38 (2): 332–341.

Brobeck, Stephen. 2008. "Understanding the Emergency Savings Needs of Low- and Moderate-Income Households: A Survey-Based Analysis of Impacts, Causes, and Remedies." Working Paper, November. Consumer Federation of America, Washington, DC.

Bronchetti, Erin Todd, Thomas S. Dee, David B. Huffman, and Ellen Magenheim. 2011. "When a Nudge Isn't Enough: Defaults and Saving among Low-Income Tax Filers." National Bureau of Economic Research Working Paper Series, No. 16887.

Choi, James J., David Laibson, Brigitte C. Madrian, and Andrew Metrick. 2006. "Saving for Retirement on the Path of Least Resistance." In *Behavioral Public Finance*, edited by Edward J. MacCaffey and Joel B. Slemrod, 304–351. New York: Russell Sage.

Choi, James J., Emily Haisley, Jennifer Kurkoski, and Cade Massey. 2012. "Small Cues Change Savings Choices." National Bureau of Economic Research Working Paper Series, No. 17843.

Desmond, Tyler, and Charles Sprenger. 2007. "Estimating the Cost of Being Unbanked." *Communities and Banking*, Spring, 24–26.

Duflo, Esther, William Gale, Jeffrey B. Liebman, Peter Orszag, and Emmanuel Saez. 2006. "Saving Incentives for Low- and Middle-Income Families: Evidence from a Field Experiment with H&R Block." *Quarterly Journal of Economics* 121 (4): 1311–1346.

Frederick, Shane, George Loewenstein, and Ted O'Donoghue. 2002. "Time Discounting and Time Preference: A Critical Review." *Journal of Economic Literature* 40 (2): 351–401.

Grinstein-Weiss, Michal, Dan Ariely, Clinton C. Key, and Krista Holub. 2012. "Refund to Savings." Paper presented at the FDIC Consumer Research Symposium, September 27, Arlington, VA. Grinstein-Weiss, Michal, Dana Perantie, Blair Russell, Krista Comer, and Dan Ariely. 2014. "Refund to Savings: 2013 Comprehensive Report on a Large-Scale Tax-Time Saving Program." CSD Research Report 14–16. Washington University at St. Louis, Center for Social Development, St. Louis, MO.

Grinstein-Weiss, Michal, Jenna Tucker, Clinton Key, Krista Holub, and Dan Ariely. 2013. "Account Use and Demand for Tax-Refund Saving Vehicles: Evidence from the Refund to Savings Experiment." CSD Research Brief 13–13, May. Washington University at St. Louis, Center for Social Development, St. Louis, MO.

Grinstein-Weiss, Michal, William Gale, Clinton Key, Blair Russell, and Krista Comer. 2014. "Behavioral Interventions to Increase Tax-Time Saving: Evidence from a National Randomized Control Trial." Unpublished manuscript.

Harris, Christopher, and David Laibson. 2001. "Dynamic Choices of Hyperbolic Consumers." *Econometrica* 69 (4): 935–957.

Holub, Krista, Michal Grinstein-Weiss, Clinton Key, and Dan Ariely. 2013. "Refund to Savings: Insight from the Field, 2012." CSD Research Report 13–11. Washington University at St. Louis, Center for Social Development, St. Louis, MO.

IRS, Internal Revenue Service. 2012. *Internal Revenue Service Data Book, 2011.* Publication 55B, March. Washington, DC: IRS.

Jones, Damon, and Aprajit Mahajan. 2011. "Time-Inconsistency and Savings: Experimental Evidence from Low-Income Tax Filers." Working Paper 2011-CFS.6, October. Center for Financial Security, University of Wisconsin–Madison, Madison.

———. 2012. "Present-Biased Preferences and Savings: Field Experimental Evidence from the SaveUP Study." Paper presented at the Corporation for Enterprise Development 2012 Asset Learning Conference, September 20, Washington, DC. Key, Clinton, Michal Grinstein-Weiss, Jenna Tucker, and Krista Holub. 2012. "Building Savings at Tax Time: Evidence from SaveNYC." Working Paper, Center for Community Capital, University of North Carolina at Chapel Hill, Chapel Hill.

Key, Clinton, Michal Grinstein-Weiss, Jenna Tucker, Krista Holub, and Dan Ariely. 2013. "Saving Behavior in Response to Motivational Prompts: Evidence from the Refund to Savings Experiment." CSD Research Brief 13–12, May. Washington University at St. Louis, Center for Social Development, St. Louis, MO.

Laibson, David. 1997. "Golden Eggs and Hyperbolic Discounting." *Quarterly Journal of Economics* 112 (2): 443–477.

Madrian, Brigitte C., and Dennis F. Shea. 2001. "The Power of Suggestion: Inertia in 401(k) Participation and Savings Behavior." *Quarterly Journal of Economics* 116 (4): 1149–1187.

Mammen, Sheila, and Frances C. Lawrence. 2006. "How Rural Working Families Use the Earned Income Tax Credit: A Mixed Methods Analysis." *Financial Counseling and Planning* 17 (1): 51–63.

Meier, Stephan, and Charles Sprenger. 2010. "Present-Biased Preferences and Credit Card Borrowing." *American Economic Journal: Applied Economics* 2 (1): 193–210.

Mendenhall, Ruby, Kathryn Edin, Susan Crowley, Jennifer Sykes, Laura Tach, Katrin Kriz, and Jeffrey R. Kling. 2012. "The Role of Earned Income Tax Credit in the Budgets of Low-Income Households." *Social Service Review* 86 (3): 367–400.

Mullainathan, Sendhil, and Eldar Shafir. 2009. "Savings Policy and Decisionmaking in Low-Income Households." In *Insufficient Funds: Savings, Assets, Credit, and Banking among Low-Income Households*, ed. Rebecca M. Blank and Michael S. Barr, 121–145. New York: Russell Sage.

O'Donoghue, Ted, and Matthew Rabin. 1999. "Doing It Now or Later." *American Economic Review* 89 (1): 103–124.

Romich, Jennifer L., and Thomas Weisner. 2000. "How Families View and Use the EITC: Advance Payment versus Lump Sum Delivery." *National Tax Journal* 53 (4, part 2): 1245–1265.

Schreiner, Mark, Michael Sherraden, Margaret Clancy, Lissa Johnson, Jami Curley, Michal Grinstein-Weiss, Min Zhan, and Sondra G. Beverly. 2001. "Savings and Asset Accumulation in Individual Development Accounts: Downpayments on the American Dream Policy Demonstration; a National Demonstration of Individual Development Accounts." Research Report, February. Washington University at St. Louis, Center for Social Development, St. Louis, MO.

Stango, Victor, and Jonathan Zinman. 2007. "Fuzzy Math and Household Finance: Theory and Evidence." Working Paper, September, Tuck School of Business, Dartmouth College, Hanover, NH.

Stegman, Michael A., and Robert Faris. 2003. "Payday Lending: A Business Model That Encourages Chronic Borrowing." *Economic Development Quarterly* 17 (1): 8–32.

Thaler, Richard H. 1985. "Mental Accounting and Consumer Choice." *Marketing Science* 4 (3): 199–214.

Thaler, Richard H., and Cass R. Sunstein. 2008. *Nudge: Improving Decisions about Health, Wealth, and Happiness*. New Haven, CT: Yale University Press.

Thaler, Richard H., and H. M. Shefrin. 1981. "An Economic Theory of Self-Control." *Journal of Political Economy* 89 (2): 392–406.

Thaler, Richard H., and Shlomo Benartzi. 2004. "Save More Tomorrow: Using Behavioral Economics to Increase Employee Saving." *Journal of Political Economy* 112 (Suppl.): S164–S187.

Treasury Inspector General for Tax Administration. 2012. "Processes for the Direct Deposit of Tax Refunds Need Improvement to Increase Accuracy and Minimize Fraud." Report 2012–40–118, September. US Department of the Treasury, Treasury Inspector General for Tax Administration, Washington, DC.

Tufano, Peter. 2010. "Just Keep My Money! Supporting Tax-Time Savings with US Savings Bonds." *American Economic Journal: Economic Policy* 3 (4): 172–200.

Zinman, Jonathan. 2009. "Debit or Credit?" *Journal of Banking and Finance* 33 (2): 358–366.

Chapter 7

Enhancing Financial Capability: TANF Bank Accounts

Karan Gill, Dana Mills, and Margaret McKenna

Introduction

This chapter proposes interventions to assist Temporary Assistance for Needy Families (TANF) recipients in developing financial capabilities and long-term saving behaviors. The proposed mechanism connects TANF participants, during the intake process and by default, to a low-fee or no-fee TANF bank account. Low- and moderate-income (LMI) families, especially those receiving public assistance benefits, face significant barriers to accessing and sustaining bank accounts at conventional financial institutions. Nationally, 28 percent of households with incomes less than $15,000 are unbanked, as are 12 percent of households with incomes between $15,000 and $30,000. In addition, the percentages of households that are underbanked are 22 and 26 percent in these two income groups, respectively (Burhouse and Osaki 2012). Underbanked households have bank accounts but also use nonbanking financial services such as payday loans. Families need both better access to financial services and concrete opportunities to build their financial knowledge and skills.

The premise of the proposed TANF bank account is that when individuals who receive public assistance have access to mainstream financial products, such as a bank account, financial education in individual and group formats, and behavioral supports (coaching and nudges to save, such as default mechanisms instituted by TANF and service agency staff), they are more likely to make informed financial choices and develop behaviors that lead to long-term saving and financial stability. In the proposed intervention, the TANF bank account is paired with financial education and coaching, skill building, and savings directives. This critical combination of financial knowledge (financial education) and financial inclusion (a bank account) creates what many asset-building researchers and behavioral economists call "financial capability."

To build financial knowledge, individuals need basic financial education; to build financial inclusion, they need access to affordable, financially attractive products that offer the opportunity to act (Sherraden 2010). In the TANF bank account scenario, the bank accounts are created via a contractual arrangement between the financial institution and the state social service agency that administers the electronic benefits transfer (EBT) program. The EBT contract would include a provision requiring the contracting financial institution to provide a no-fee or low-fee bank account to every TANF participant at the time of the participant's connection to public benefits. Participants could choose to opt out of the TANF bank account and elect to receive benefits via an EBT card or through their own existing bank account.

The TANF bank account is fully liquid, and thus available to cover short-term emergency needs as it serves to increase inclusion in mainstream financial services and provide a foundation for longer-term asset accumulation. To avoid penalizing TANF recipients (and discouraging savings behavior), TANF bank accounts would have no overdraft fees or minimum monthly balances. The account is also portable and owned by the participant, therefore enabling him or her to maintain a banking connection following departure from the TANF system. The pairing of a TANF bank account with financial education provides families the infrastructure to develop financial literacy, build protective savings, and eventually leave the system with the tools to maintain the habits that lead to long-term financial stability.

Temporary Assistance for Needy Families and Electronic Benefits Transfer

In most states, public benefits such as TANF are delivered largely through EBT cards, typically administered by the state's TANF program agency in partnership with a mainstream financial institution. Washington state's TANF program, WorkFirst, offers an illustration of how TANF programs typically administer such benefits. In Washington state, the Department of Social and Health Services (DSHS) partners with JPMorgan Electronic

Financial Services to issue EBT cards to those who elect to receive cash benefits in this way. As of April 2014, JPMorgan contracts with a total of 23 states to disburse benefits electronically (USDA 2014). Other financial institutions that contract with TANF administrators throughout the nation include Xerox State and Local Solutions, FIS eFunds Corporation (USDA 2014).

WorkFirst provides assistance to eligible low-income families through cash grants, work services and supports, medical assistance, and child care. As of March 2013, the maximum level of cash assistance provided to participants was $478 per month for a family of three. This assistance, divided by the 32 hours of weekly work activity required for participants to remain eligible for the program, equates to an hourly wage of about $3.73. Parents who are eligible for cash assistance can choose to be issued an EBT card that may be used as a debit card, or they can have the benefits deposited into a checking or savings account via electronic funds transfer (EFT).

The EFT option provides substantial benefits to participants by allowing those who use it to avoid transaction fees and other costs associated with both the EBT-issuing bank and with marginal financial services, such as check cashers, thus allowing them to retain more of their benefits to pay for essential needs such as housing and food. For instance, before recent action to eliminate institutional fees for WorkFirst families, Washington state families using EBTs issued by JPMorgan, WorkFirst's institutional partner, paid a $0.85 fee each time they accessed a Chase ATM. In 2011, ATM fees from welfare recipients in Washington generated more than $100,000 a month in revenue for JPMorgan (Jenkins 2011). This fee has been eliminated, but some ATM-related fees remain. Having benefits direct deposited in a bank account at an institution convenient for them would allow participants to avoid many of these fees. This suggests a need to improve participants' access to mainstream banking.

Electronic distribution of TANF benefits is now common practice in 40 states because it decreases the potential for fraud by eliminating paper coupons that can be more easily bought and sold and eliminates the administrative costs associated with printing and mailing checks. Families on TANF have also benefited from the use of EBT cards. Participants can access their money more efficiently and at multiple access points, and the EBT card has helped alleviate the social stigma associated with accessing public benefits using paper coupons. EBT cards vary by state in the set of benefits provided to the recipient; each state has its own cost per case month (CPCM) structure and each state provides different services in transferring benefits (see USDA 2014 for state-by-state information on EBT cards). Families also benefit when administration costs are lower, allowing more TANF funds to be directed to services and benefits.

However, there are also disadvantages to EBT for both families and states. For the family, since the EBT cards are owned by the state, not the recipient, participants may not deposit other sources of income to the cards and they are not portable. No formal banking or savings services are tied to EBT cards. Thus, the EBT card in its current form does not encourage the development of self-sufficiency and financially healthy behaviors that would help families remain off public benefits permanently.

The Need for Banking in the TANF Population

Public assistance recipients in the TANF program are primarily single mothers with children. In Washington state, eligibility for TANF benefits means the family must not hold more than $1,000 in liquid assets and vehicle equity cannot exceed $5,000. For a family of three, the maximum earned monthly income is $955. Such eligibility requirements and asset limits mean that TANF recipients are among the most economically vulnerable populations in the community.

Families on public assistance usually leave the system without savings to sustain them in future financial emergencies. The majority of families leaving welfare enter low-wage jobs with no benefits, and only 13 percent of them reach earnings above 200 percent of the federal poverty level within 36 months after leaving WorkFirst (OFM WorkFirst Performance Team 2008). Without emergency savings, these families are just one health emergency or vehicle repair away from falling back into the public safety net and a cycle of poverty. WorkFirst data reveal that approximately 41 percent of adults receiving TANF benefits in fiscal year 2007 cycled off and back on TANF one or more times over a three-year follow-up period (WorkFirst Subcabinet 2011). From 1997 to the present, many families have experienced multiple cycles in the program; an adult averages a total of four reentry cycles, with the average length of each cycle about 12 months. The average and median length of TANF spells have changed very little over time, while the average number of lifetime months (28.8) on TANF has steadily increased over time (OFM WorkFirst Performance Team 2008).

The high return rate of families on welfare is one of the most compelling arguments for the need to help families access mainstream banking services, build a personal safety net, and develop saving behavior that can lead to the accumulation of financial assets. A pool of savings is a critical tool on the pathway out of poverty, increasing resilience to financial emergencies. As consumer finance expert Matt Fellowes explained to a *San*

Francisco Chronicle reporter, "Bank accounts are essentially an on-ramp to economic mobility and wealth in this country. Without access to that on-ramp, people are basically living in a cash economy where there's no opportunity to convert that into wealth" (Buchanan 2007). Research supports Fellowes's argument, demonstrating a positive association between bank accounts and financial security. Stegman, Rocha, and Davis (2004) report that after controlling for income and other variables, "lower-income individuals with bank accounts are 43 percent more likely than those who are unbanked to have positive net financial assets of any kind" (384). Furthermore, 77 percent of banked households have savings, compared to one-third of unbanked households (Stegman, Rocha, and Davis 2004).

Regardless of income, many families need to improve their financial skills in order to save and build assets for the future. In a national survey to assess the financial capability of adults, only 49 percent of respondents had set aside funds sufficient to cover expenses for three months in case of sickness, job loss, or other emergency (FINRA 2009). Furthermore, research shows that individuals who grow up in low-income families that are banked are six times more likely to be banked as adult householders than children who grew up in unbanked families (Stegman and Faris 2005).

A comprehensive approach to asset building that combines opportunities to save with financial education shows strong potential for generating upward economic mobility toward financial security. Although some financial training may increase saving behaviors in the short-term, research has found that it does not affect people's long-term financial behavior unless training is combined with the opportunity to act. As one researcher noted, "if low-income families are to have the opportunity to act in their own best financial interests (be financially capable), they need access to quality financial products, including, at a minimum, a transaction account, a savings account, affordable and small dollar credit, simple insurance products, and if possible, low-cost investment and emergency savings products" (Sherraden 2010, 7).

Unfortunately, bank accounts are difficult for many low-income families to obtain, especially those accessing public benefits. Of the US households, 28 percent earning less than $15,000 a year and 26 percent of households without a high school diploma are unbanked (Burhouse and Osaki 2012). Consequently, the TANF program serves a large unbanked population.

Barriers to opening a bank account include high opening deposit minimums, mimimum balance requirements, and direct deposit or author automatic contribution requirements (Chan 2011). One-third of unbanked households report that the primary reason they are unbanked is because they do not have enough money; another 5 percent report that minimum balance requirements are too high (Burhouse and Osaki 2012). The most common account products typically require $25–$100 for an opening deposit and either a minimum balance of $300 or direct deposits of $25 each month to avoid paying a monthly fee for the account. These fees are significant barriers for LMI families, considering that only 8 percent of people making less than $25,000 a year have enough money in their bank accounts to meet these minimum balance requirements (Chan 2011). A report using data from the 2011 FDIC Survey of Banks' Efforts to Serve the Unbanked and Underbanked recommends that financial institutions broaden their offerings of low-cost savings and checking accounts and better market their small-dollar loans (Rhine and Robbins 2012).

Behavioral economists also reveal multiple behavioral barriers for low-income families in accessing products in mainstream institutions. They describe a vivid scenario for many families: "to the extent that the poor find themselves in situations (e.g., filling out an application at a bank) that are somewhat unfamiliar, threatening, or stigmatizing (all of which can consume cognitive resources), fewer resources will remain available to process the information that is relevant to the decision at hand" (Bertrand, Mullainathan, and Shafir 2006, 12). To alleviate these cognitive barriers, behavioral economists recommend making the task of meeting with the bank more appealing, through programs like the First Accounts Program, which offers automatic enrollments.

Behavioral economists have also identified a host of other barriers to participation in the financial mainstream (Bertrand, Mullainathan, and Shafir 2006):

- Low-income employers often do not require or offer direct deposit of wages. As a result, many low-wage workers cash their paychecks (often after hours) at alternative financial institutions, at relatively high interest and cost.
- The mainstream alternatives that do exist are provided without appropriate financial education, further dissuading the unbanked, as the number of options available to consumers may prove confusing or challenging to navigate.
- Mainstream banking institutions are not typically situated in high-poverty neighborhoods, making them difficult to access physically if regular transportation is unavailable.
- Low-income people believe that banking is for those with wealth and may not identify with the persona of being banked.

Such factors emphasize the importance of connecting every public assistance participant to a bank account and financial education to build financial capability.

Proposed Intervention: TANF Bank Accounts

Providing low- or no-fee bank accounts to public benefit recipients would help participants access the banking system, encourage them to build financial capability, and give them the tools to develop long-term saving behavior. To accomplish this, state contracts with EBT-administering financial institutions should require that the institution provide low- or no-fee bank accounts to public assistance participants at the time they first connect to public benefits. Benefits would then be directly deposited into these accounts. Participants who opt out of this option would access their benefits via an EBT card or their own preexisting bank account. The TANF accounts should ideally be combined with best-practice financial education and coaching, including savings directives and behavioral nudges at key transition points in the program.

In this proposed intervention, the provision of bank accounts would serve as the default option for new TANF participants; participants would have to opt out in order to receive benefits on an EBT card. The opt-out structure would support broad participation. As Thaler and Sunstein (2009) explain, people often choose options that require the least amount of effort. If, for any given choice, there is "an option that will [be selected] if the chooser does nothing," a default option, it may be expected that "a large number of people [will] end up with that option" (85). Given the challenges the low-income population faces in connecting to mainstream banking services and engaging in saving behavior, this supportive infrastructure is crucial to encouraging the development of assets and long-term financial stability in this population.

The option to become connected to a low- or no-fee bank account upon entering public assistance eliminates many common barriers that low-income families experience at mainstream financial institutions. This intervention provides a foundational product for households to begin building a personal financial safety net for emergencies and developing asset-building opportunities, preserves personal choice in the receipt of public benefits and access to mainstream banking services, and offers opportunities for recipients to gain financial education. In this way, the intervention addresses both elements of financial capability: financial inclusion and financial education.

Financial Inclusion: A Bank Account

Studies show that liquid assets, such as emergency savings funds, can play a greater role than income in protecting families against hardship and preventing them from falling back on the government safety net (Gill, Kinne, and Watts 2011). Lusardi, Schneider, and Tufano (2011) find that 28 percent of households report they "certainly" could not come up with $2,000 in 30 days to cover an unexpected expense, with 22 percent reporting they "probably" could not do so. The frequency of hardships provides insight into the high return rates for government assistance; it also demonstrates the need for tools such as bank accounts that can help families build a personal safety net to sustain them during financial emergencies.

Financial Knowledge: Education and Coaching

Providing access to a bank account as a first-step financial product could have more lasting benefits if the recipient has the opportunity to participate in financial education and coaching, which promote successful money management and the development of persistent saving behavior. Financial coaching is a practice model that focuses on both the nature of the client-worker relationship and the practical development of financial knowledge and skills. This approach to asset-building affirms that all people, regardless of their financial situation, have the capabilities to engage in purposeful action to build financial assets. In the coaching model, the client is in the driver's seat while setting personal goals, making informed choices, and working to develop concrete knowledge, skills, and abilities to achieve financial stability. In the proposed intervention, TANF recipients who choose not to opt out of a bank account at program intake receive targeted financial education and coaching by a state-level agency case manager at three specific transition points within the TANF lifecycle: at intake, TANF-associated transitional employment, and TANF exit.

Transition Point 1—Intake: On-Ramp to Savings

The first financial decision point occurs at TANF intake. At intake, for participants who do not opt out of the bank account option, a DSHS case manager provides an overview of the mechanics of bank accounts, explaining such key elements as the differences between checking and savings accounts, where a participant's benefits will be held, and how benefits can be accessed.

Transition Point 2—Transitional Employment: Building Savings

Following intake, TANF recipients typically embark on one of several parallel job-readiness pathways. In Washington state's WorkFirst,

Community Jobs offers one such pathway. Community Jobs is a full-time activity that provides participants with paid, temporary employment for up to six months. During this time, the participant's employer, a community-based organization (CBO), pays the employee wages in place of the TANF cash grant. This transitional employment experience offers an opportunity for increased financial capability, as earned income is paired with further coaching regarding available financial products and the financial skills needed to manage a bank account effectively. An additional opt-out feature is activated at this juncture, under which a percentage of the participant's wages is deposited into his or her new savings account each pay period. The participant may choose the amount to be diverted, opt out altogether, in which case the full paycheck will be deposited into the TANF checking account. The inclusion of an automatic savings mechanism will further empower families to build assets and develop the habit of saving.

Transition Point 3—TANF Exit: Maintaining Savings

TANF recipients who obtain permanent employment following participation in Community Jobs transition out of the TANF system. Financial education and coaching at this point consists of developing skills and methods to support the continuation of newly established saving behaviors, including the continued redirection of a portion of every paycheck to savings. Participants are provided the tools to access their bank account and links to other community financial literacy resources.

TANF recipients who do not obtain employment following participation in Community Jobs continue to receive TANF benefits through their bank account. The continuation of savings behavior is encouraged by a state-level agency case manager with the expectation that clients will determine the amount of savings set aside as they receive TANF benefits each month. The recipient may reduce the amount of money directed into savings due to a reduction in income.

Scale of Impact

Forty states (including Washington) disburse TANF benefits electronically. Achieving maximum scale (national adoption) of a TANF bank accounts program will require each state to renegotiate their existing contracts with EBT providers to include the provision of bank accounts, or include the provision in requirements for future contracts. The change could also be enforced by a federal policy change in the TANF program. (The reach of the program could be further expanded by connecting it to other federal public benefit programs, such as the Supplemental Nutrition Assistance Program (SNAP).) Separate collaborations between financial institutions and state agencies, structured as extensions of existing relationships, offer an opportunity to reach scale more quickly than policy changes or contract renegotiations might.

Policy Discussion

States can act to implement the proposed intervention by adopting a provision for bank accounts within the state's EBT contract without legislative action, enforced either through contract renegotiations or via separate agreements or collaborative arrangements with EBT providers. However, the option that provides the greatest protection against having the provision negotiated away later is a statutory change—at either the state or federal level—to require the inclusion of bank account access in future contracts.

Though the savings directives outlined in this chapter may not result in TANF recipients exceeding the current $1,000 liquid-asset limit, states may also need to consider statutory changes that allow for the accumulation of adequate savings to support a permanent transition off public benefits. Although asset limits are seen as a critical qualifier for these programs, states without asset limits demonstrate reduced administrative costs and have not experienced significant caseload increases due to the elimination of asset limits (Rand 2007). Still, many states have strict limits for the amount of countable assets public assistance recipients are permitted to hold. Washington state continues to enforce one of the most restrictive asset-limit policies in the nation.

However, Washington state stakeholders and advocates of asset-building strategies have already opened some policy windows to make the statutory changes needed to implement the program. Senate Bill 5921, which revises social services within the WorkFirst program, was signed into law during the 2011 state legislative session The law includes a directive for the Department of Social and Health Services to "develop strategies to increase opportunities for public assistance recipients to maintain bank accounts, increase financial education and management skills that will help minimize recipients' costs associated with banking fees and automated teller machine (ATM) transaction fees" (Department of Social and Health Services 2011, 3).

At the federal level, issues regarding banking, financial education, and savings for low-income households should play a more significant role in congressional deliberations around reauthorization of the next generation of welfare reform.

Evidence of Effectiveness

According to research and piloted programs, four essential elements are needed in the design of low-cost, high-quality bank account option for low-income consumers: minimal fees, direct deposit ability, convenient features, and appropriate incentives (Chan 2011). Three promising programs have integrated these components into their design on a smaller scale than the proposed TANF account program: First Accounts, FDIC Model Safe Accounts, and AutoSave.

First Accounts

The First Accounts program was a 2002 initiative of the US Department of the Treasury intended to expand access to traditional financial institutions for the unbanked. The program, which piloted in Chicago, partnered community organizations and financial institutions to provide low- or no-fee checking accounts with no balance requirements.

During the pilot period, 1,428 accounts were opened. Over 89 percent of savings accounts carried a balance, with an average savings account balance of $134.92. Other savings came as program participants used fewer alternative financial service providers: about 72 percent of participants used check-cashing services an average of 3.8 times a month prior to entering the program, but only 18 percent of participants surveyed who opened an account were still using check-cashing services after accessing the program. The accounts also had a significant impact on financial behavior, with 89 percent of participants stating that the checking account changed the way they managed their finances (Marzahl et al. 2006).

FDIC Model Safe

The FDIC Model Safe Accounts program, launched as a national pilot in January 2011, reduces opening deposit and minimum balance requirements to $5 and monthly fees to $1 for savings accounts. Under the program, nine financial institutions have volunteered to offer unbanked and low-income consumers deposit accounts with core features to provide safe, low-cost transactions and basic savings account products. As with the EBT system, the accounts are predominately electronic and card-based, allowing withdrawal through ATMs. Additionally, there are no overdraft or insufficient funds fees associated with the transactional accounts.

During the one-year pilot, more than 3,500 Safe Accounts were opened, and retention rates were higher than expected, with more than 80 percent of transaction accounts and 95 percent of savings accounts still active upon conclusion of the pilot (FDIC 2012).

AutoSave

AutoSave is an initiative of the New America Foundation and MDRC that tests the implementation of automatic savings program for employees administered through partnerships between financial institutions and employers. AutoSave streamlines account opening and minimizes the need for consumer decision making and paperwork by automating savings through direct deposit. Once a participant joins the program, savings deposits are made automatically each pay period, until the employee either decides to stop the deposits or separates from the employer (Lopez-Fernandini and Schultz 2010). AutoSave is relatively new, but it is worth monitoring for its effects on job performance, retention, pursuit of education, and the effectiveness of the working relationship between low-income consumers, mainstream financial institutions, and employers. It is also worth learning what account balance participants can accumulate in lower-wage employment.

The evidence from these programs not only dismisses the perception that low-income families cannot save, it also shows the potential to help these families build financial safety nets by providing a simple foundational product. The three programs mentioned and other research have consistently shown that low-income families can save and still pay for essential needs if they are given access to banking services. A TANF-associated bank account that includes the key elements shown to be effective in these programs and in other research could help families on public assistance attain financial capability on a large scale.

Barriers and Cautions

A number of potential limitations may surface with the implementation of the proposed mechanism. The first lies in the EBT contracts that states have with financial institutions. For the program to scale, social service agencies and financial institutions must be willing to enter into renegotiations of existing contracts. The agencies must believe that providing bank accounts to TANF participants is as important for participants' financial well-being as connecting TANF participants with work.

The second limitation arises from the knowledge and skill base of service providers. Staff may not have the competencies needed to support effective transfer of financial knowledge, making it necessary to provide ongoing, high-quality service provider training. This training should provide staff with the right level of knowledge and skills to implement a new benefits vehicle and engage recipients in a financial education framework that encourages saving behavior. Service providers should also have sufficient knowledge of the mainstream banking system, the mechanics of traditional bank accounts, and the theoretical importance of a behaviorally informed education plan. This will require time and resources on the part of the state as well as engagement by service providers, who may be strained by their current client responsibilities or apprehensive about learning a new approach. Training and support for staff should be offered on a continuous basis, given the high level of turnover of frontline staff in the social and human services industry.

A third limitation concerns the economic incentive for EBT contractors to provide bank accounts for TANF participants. Under some state EBT contracts, financial institutions are paid a lower fee CPCM for clients who receive cash benefits via direct deposit than for those who receive benefits via EBT (Stegman, Lobenhofer, and Quinterno 2003). But evidence shows that direct deposit to a bank account may have differing costs than a deposit onto an EBT card. For example, about a decade ago Missouri reported that a direct deposit account costs about $0.10 per month to maintain, compared to $0.58 per month for an EBT cash account (Stegman, Lobenhofer, and Quinterno 2003).

Measuring Impact

To measure the impact of the TANF bank account intervention, the effectiveness of the mechanism as a driver to move TANF families toward financial capability must be compared to existing bank accounts and the EBT. The evaluation will describe the extent to which the program contributes to three results: participant demonstration of financial capability, as evidenced by financial self-efficacy and knowledge of financial habits; the number of TANF participants who have savings and checking accounts and who save money regularly; and the amount of money families have in emergency and opportunity savings as they transition off assistance. The evaluation will also analyze how the combination of features contribute to participants' development of financial capability and saving behavior. The long-term goal is to assess the effectiveness of the full mechanism by analyzing the change in the number of clients who exit and remain off TANF or who have an extended delay before returning to TANF.

The evaluation will include a randomized multigroup design implemented in matched sites to compare the outcomes of different groups of TANF participants. Assignment to either the program or the comparison group will be done at the site level, so that all eligible clients in one office are in the same group. At selected sites, no enhanced financial education will be offered by DSHS case managers or CBO staff. This approach will reduce a potential contamination effect that would be more likely to occur with individual-level assignment to groups within the same office. While random individual assignment to groups would be a preferred design, there are many logistical challenges to implementing and maintaining accurate individual random assignment when the evaluation is carried out by different staff members in multiple sites. The designation of offices as program

Table 7.1 TANF Bank Accounts Program and Comparison Groups

Group	Financial option	Financial education	Optional service
Program group	New bank account	Yes, at transition points 1–3	Automatic savings offered when engaged in employment program
Comparison 1	Existing bank account	Yes, at transition points 1–3	None
Comparison 2	Existing bank account	Intake financial overview on direct deposit	None
Comparison 3	EBT card	Yes, at decision points 1–3	None
Comparison 4	EBT card	Intake financial overview on EBT card	None

Source: Authors' own.

or comparison sites is also more acceptable to the cooperating regional administrators at the DSHS.

The program group will open a TANF bank account, receive financial education and financial directives, and be offered automated savings. The four comparison groups will be given some combination of the typical services, either direct deposit into the participant's own bank account or an EBT card, along with the addition of enhanced financial education components provided at the defined transition points. See Table 7.1 for full descriptions of the program and comparison groups.

The design allows assessment of the results of the full program in relation to its components in order to identify the most effective approach to build saving behavior that will lead to increased financial stability and decreased TANF return rates. The analysis will include logistic regression techniques for each of the outcome variables, using the intervention assignment (bank account, financial education, automated savings, or existing accounts with financial education) as the predictors. The evaluation will initially be conducted in one state, with the cooperation of selected DSHS offices.

Conclusion

Giving families who receive public benefits the opportunity to establish a bank account supported by a savings directive can serve as a tool to build a personal safety net. Establishing a default bank account, supported by financial education and savings directives, can be a critical method for promoting long-term asset development. The TANF bank account product and model outlined in this chapter is one such instrument. To promote successful saving outcomes, it is recommended that the appropriate state agency emphasize outcome-based accountability that measures two key objectives: (1) families with TANF bank accounts create and grow their personal savings, and (2) TANF families with bank accounts return to public assistance at a reduced rate. In measuring the first objective, the state is assured that participants leaving TANF have acquired the financial literacy to develop and maintain personal savings accounts, which can increase their potential for financial self-sufficiency. Measurement of this objective also indicates the level of quality education and support provided by state-level agency case managers. The second objective measures change that occurs at the systems level, revealing a possible connection between providing TANF families bank accounts and decreased rate of return to the system.

This single systemic change to the EBT structure could create an asset-building opportunity for the most economically vulnerable families. The creation, maintenance, and protection of TANF bank accounts require involvement and effort from all parties—public assistance systems, financial institutions, and most importantly, the families. Public assistance systems that promote asset-building opportunities with this model will not only improve access to bank accounts, but also create greater opportunities for financial education. The financial institution that offers a low-cost product as part of its return for profitable contracts with the state can show value in a financial institution's stake and effort in the community. Finally, families who are committed to building assets in pursuit of financial security improve their chances of leaving the TANF system with an infrastructure that supports their movement toward financial self-sufficiency and well-being.

REFERENCES

Bertrand, Marianne, Sendhil Mullainathan, and Eldar Shafir. 2006. "Behavioral Economics and Marketing in Aid of Decision Making among the Poor." *Journal of Public Policy & Marketing* 25 (1): 8–23.

Buchanan, Wyatt. 2007. "Program Helps Low-Income S. F. Residents Start Bank Accounts." *San Francisco Chronicle*, December 4.

Burhouse, Susan, and Yazmin Osaki. 2012. "2011 FDIC National Survey of Unbanked and Underbanked Households." September. FDIC, Washington, DC.

Chan, Pamela. 2011. "Beyond Barriers." Working Paper, November 14. New America Foundation, Washington, DC.

Department of Social and Health Services, Washington State. 2011. "Strategies to Increase Access to Bank Accounts, Financial Education and Money Management Skills for Public Assistance Recipients: ESSB 5921, Section 13 (1)." Report to the Governor and Legislature, December. Department of Social and Health Services, Olympia, WA.

FDIC, Federal Deposit Insurance Corporation. 2012. "FDIC Model Safe Accounts Pilot: Final Report." April 2012. FDIC, Washington, DC.

FINRA, Financial Industry Regulatory Authority. 2009. "Financial Capability in the United States: National Survey–Executive Summary." December 2009. FINRA, Washington, DC.

Gill, Karan, Alicia Kinne, and Julie Watts. 2011. "Prosperity Blueprint: Building, Leveraging, and Protecting Washington State's Future." The Prosperity Agenda, January. Washington Asset Building Coalition.

Jenkins, Austin. 2011. "Chase Bank Collecting Hundreds of Thousands in ATM Fees from Welfare Clients." KUOW (Published online May 8, 2011). http://www2.kuow.org/northwestnews.php?storyID=136072292

Lopez-Fernandini, Alejandra, and Caroline Schultz. 2010. "Automating Savings in the Workplace: Insights from the AutoSave Pilot." Asset-Building Program Policy Paper, January. New America Foundation.

Lusardi, Annamaria, Daniel Schneider, and Peter Tufano. 2011. "Financially Fragile Households: Evidence and Implications." National Bureau of Economic Research Working Paper Series, No. 17072.

Marzahl, David, O. S. Owen, Steve Neumann, and Joshua Harriman. 2006. "First Accounts: A U.S. Treasury Department Program to Expand Access to Financial Institutions—Program Study by the Center for Impact Research." *Profitwise News and Views*, February. University of Chicago Graduate School of Business, the Center for Economic Progress and ShoreBank, Chicago, IL.

OFM WorkFirst Performance Team. 2008. "Length of Stay and Re-entry Rates of Adult Clients on TANF." Fact Sheet. September.

Rand, Dory. 2007. "Reforming State Rules on Asset Limits: How to Remove Barriers to Saving and Asset Accumulation in Public Benefit Programs." *Clearinghouse Review, Journal of Poverty Law and Policy* 40 (11–12): 625–636.

Rhine, Sherrie, and Eric Robbins. 2012. "2011 FDIC Survey of Banks' Efforts to Serve the Unbanked and Underbanked." December. Federal Deposit Insurance Corporation, Washington, DC.

Sherraden, Margaret. 2010. "Financial Capability: What Is It, and How Can It Be Created?" CSD Working Papers No. 10–17. Center for Social Development. University of Missouri, Columbia, MO.

Stegman, Michael, and Robert Faris. 2005. "Welfare, Work and Banking: The Use of Consumer Credit by Current and Former TANF Recipients in Charlotte, North Carolina." *Journal of Urban Affairs* 27 (4): 379–402.

Stegman, Michael, Jennifer Lobenhofer, and John Quinterno. 2003. "The State of EBT." Working Paper, December. Center for Community Capitalism, The University of North Carolina at Chapel Hill, Chapel Hill, NC.

Stegman, Michael, Marta Rocha, and Walter Davis. 2004. "The Role of Technology in Serving the Unbanked." December. Center for Community Capitalism, The Frank Hawkins Kenan Institute of Private Enterprise, The University of North Carolina at Chapel Hill.

Thaler, Richard, and Cass Sunstein. 2009. *Nudge: Improving Decisions about Health, Wealth, and Happiness*. New York: Penguin Books.

USDA. 2014. "Electronic Transfer Benefits Status Report by State." http://www.fns.usda.gov/snap/ebt/ebt_status_report.htm.

WorkFirst Subcabinet. 2011. "Resetting Washington's WorkFirst for the 21st Century." January. Washington WorkFirst.

Chapter 8

Building Emergency Savings through "Impulse Saving"

Kim Manturuk, Jessica Dorrance, and Jayson Halladay

Introduction

Into all good saving plans a little impulse spending often falls. A meal out and some new shoes, and the intended savings are gone. But what if impulsivity could be leveraged to help people save money, rather than spend it? This is the idea behind MAGIC Mojo, a recently piloted product that allows people to transfer money to savings instantly via text message. The MAGIC Mojo approach aims to help underbanked consumers build emergency savings and reach their financial goals. The approach is highly scalable, has the potential to reach a broad base of consumers, and incorporates ideas from behavioral economics to increase the likelihood that people save successfully.

Generally speaking, the act of consuming is an enjoyable experience; people buy things on impulse because it feels good to get something new unexpectedly. Saving money is also enjoyable, but the "feeling good" aspect is delayed, sometimes very far into the future, until the savings can be applied toward a goal. The MAGIC Mojo pilot sought to provide an immediate reward for the act of saving by leveraging the enjoyment inherent in impulsive action. Through MAGIC Mojo, consumers could experience both the short-term enjoyment of doing something impulsively and the longer-term benefit of saving for future consumption.

While the MAGIC Mojo concept is based on sophisticated principles from behavioral economics, it is a very simple tool to use. Designed to help underbanked consumers build savings, it is attached to a prepaid card rather than to a traditional bank account. When the MAGIC Mojo feature is activated, the consumer can send a simple text message at any time or use the MAGIC Mojo website to move money from the prepaid card balance to a designated savings fund also attached to the card. Participants set a savings goal when they sign up; each "impulsive save" moves them one step closer to achieving it. This mechanism can help card users get immediate gratification for forgoing impulse expenditures by instantly transferring the money not spent to a savings account, which gradually builds up a balance on the strength of these impulse savings. For example, a participant who refrains from buying a latte could send a text to MAGIC Mojo to move the money she did not spend on the latte to the savings side of her card.

This approach to building savings is distinctly different from the now-famous "latte factor" approach. The idea behind the latte factor is that people can build savings rapidly if they eliminate small, regular luxury spending—such as a daily latte—and invest the money saved in high-yield stocks (Bach 2004). Bach claims that this one change—investing the latte money—will generate nearly $2 million in savings over the course of a lifetime. Critics have pointed out the flaws in this approach to building savings. For example, in *Pound Foolish* (2012), Helaine Olen counters Bach's claims by pointing out that people are not depleting their emergency funds by buying $5 lattes. For Olen, the lack of living-wage employment opportunities for many workers and the soaring cost of higher education are far greater problems than the amount of money spent on coffee. Furthermore, a primary reason lower-income families need emergency savings is so they have access to liquid funds to cover unexpected expenses or income loss; working towards a $2 million retirement fund is not their most immediate need. That being said, while skipping lattes probably will not turn very many people into millionaires, skipping small impulse purchases can be an effective way to add savings. The act of saving a few dollars here and there and leveraging the impulsivity of that act can transform small, unexpected saves into a crucial financial cushion.

This chapter first presents some background information on the importance of access to an emergency fund for lower-income families. The chapter then highlights some of the challenges lower-income families face when it comes to starting or maintaining an emergency fund, as well as promising techniques for helping these households increase savings. The chapter will then discuss in detail how impulse savings programs can fill the unmet need for an easy-to-use tool to build savings. In this context, the discussion focuses on MAGIC Mojo, describing how and why it may offer one answer to the emergency savings challenge. Although the MAGIC

Mojo product is no longer being offered, lessons from the pilot experience can inform future development of the impulse savings concept. The chapter concludes by looking at potential limitations and opportunities for scaling this model.

Background

Unforeseen events, such as unemployment, prolonged illness, or a necessary car repair, can be difficult or impossible to manage financially without some type of emergency savings fund. Many families struggle to build emergency savings, or to manage through crises without such a cushion. As a result of the Great Recession that began in 2007, fewer families now have the resources needed to handle an emergency and buffer the effects of short-term financial difficulties (Taylor et al. 2010). While public assistance is available, it is not possible to rely entirely on such assistance to handle financial emergencies.

These events are difficult in themselves, but the addition of associated financial difficulties can create a domino effect for individuals and their families; financial hardship has been shown to have a negative impact on marital stability (McLoyd 1990), health (Kahn and Pearlin 2006), child development (Jackson et al. 2000), and emotional well-being (Price, Van Ryn, and Vinokur 1992). McKernan, Ratcliffe, and Vinopal (2009) found that having liquid assets or emergency funds above the level of asset poverty—the ability to pay one's expenses without income for three months—significantly reduced the financial hardship families experienced following divorce, job loss, and disability. According to a survey by the Consumer Federation of America (Brobeck 2008), lower-income families report they need an average of $1,500 in emergency savings while moderate-income families report needing an average of $3,000. However, less than 30 percent of low-income families and less than 50 percent of moderate-income families have even $500 in savings (Brobeck 2008). The same study found that people who identified a specific savings goal and created a saving plan were more likely to be successful in building savings. However, it is often difficult to stick with these types of plans, and the approach does not work for everyone.

Emergency Savings Approaches for the Unbanked

Christen and Mas (2009), exploring how unbanked households maintain emergency savings, find that lower-income families use a wide range of strategies, none of which fully meet their needs. These strategies include storing cash at home, asking a trusted family member to hold cash, participating in a savings circle, and investing in physical assets that can be sold to generate funds. However, these informal methods of saving do not offer as much security, liquidity, or reliability as more formal financial products such as those offered by banking institutions. Christen and Mas conclude that low-income households are thus vulnerable to "more risk of loss or theft, and their availability and liquidity are highly correlated with the saver's own circumstances" (2009, 277). Automatic savings deposits are a promising alternative, but they are not available to low-wage workers who may not have direct deposit or bank accounts. Thus we have a seemingly intractable situation: the people who most need to build emergency savings are not well served by products outside the financial mainstream, yet they struggle to build savings through the traditional approach of planning and making regular deposits in a mainstream bank account.

General Barriers to Building Emergency Savings

A recent report released by Corporation for Enterprise Development (CFED) shows that nearly half (44 percent) of American households are liquid-asset poor (Brooks and Wiedrich 2013). This means they do not have enough easily accessible funds, such as money in a savings account, to live at the poverty level for three months in the absence of regular income. Embedded in this number, however, are households that do not have enough savings to sustain themselves for even one month or to cover a single unexpected expense. Data from the 2010 Survey of Consumer Finances indicates that about 20 percent of people spend as much as they make; 6 percent report that they spend more than they make (Bricker et al. 2012). These numbers are rising also; the asset poverty rate has been rising steadily since the 1980s (Caner and Wolff 2004; Haveman and Wolff 2005). Additionally, the personal savings rate, which stands at 2.6 percent as of March 2013 according to data from the US Department of Commerce, has been mostly on the decline since the mid-1980s. Furthermore, even this dismally low savings rate does not capture differences in savings by income; low-income households are saving significantly less and people earning less than $9,000 a year are saving practically nothing (Davis and Schumm 1987). All of this paints a picture of families extremely vulnerable to even the smallest unexpected expense. Households that are unable to tap into savings to cover an emergency often find themselves relying on high-cost, short-term financial fixes, which often lead to a greater financial crisis.

Leading up the financial crisis and continuing into the present, several factors have created barriers to saving, particularly for low- and moderate-income (LMI) households. The most obvious and difficult to overcome is the lack of livable wages, which keeps many families living paycheck-to-paycheck. For families experiencing material hardship as a result of insufficient income, building savings is difficult or impossible. There simply isn't enough money left over to put anything aside, even for the rainy day you know is coming.

Another barrier to building savings is a lack of savings tools that meet lower-income families where they are. Approximately 8 percent of the population—nearly 10 million US households—are unbanked, meaning they do not have any type of deposit account at an insured financial institution (Gross, Hogarth, and Schmeiser 2012). The majority of those are households earning less than $15,000 a year. The unbanked population is diverse and the demand for banking products within this population is not entirely clear because people have a variety of reason for not interacting with mainstream financial institutions (Caskey 2005). What is clear, however, is the need for financial products and services that provide opportunities to safely manage money and save to people who do not have, do not want, or prefer not to use a traditional bank account.

In addition to structural barriers to saving, there are significant psychological and behavioral barriers. Research has documented that people tend to have difficulty accurately predicting their future financial needs and learning from past experiences (Bertrand, Mullainathan, and Shafir 2004). Thus lower-income families may not grasp how much they should aim to hold in savings, even when they have previously encountered emergency expenses or income loss. Another psychological barrier to saving is present bias, the tendency to favor consuming money today over saving it and consuming a greater amount later (Benhabib, Bisin, and Schotter 2010). When asked to decide between having $10 today or $15 in one month, a person with present bias will take the $10 today. For the same reason, people tend to find it more gratifying to consume money when it is available than to save it for the future.

On the behavioral side, research has documented that small hassles can become large hurdles when it comes to saving money. These small situational barriers, collectively termed "hassle costs," are often-cited reasons for people's failure to open bank accounts or save money regularly. In their discussion of the hassle costs associated with opening a bank account, Bertrand, Mullainthan, and Shafir (2004) write:

> These barriers might be a testy bus ride, challenging hours, or the reluctance to face a contemptuous bank teller. Such barriers are not unlike the

> embarrassment and anxiety that impede many people, including medical doctors, from administering medical self-exams which they know to be highly valuable. (420)

However, there are ways to overcome these psychological and behavioral hurdles. First, present bias can be countered through goal setting and goal visualization. People who identify a savings goal and see indicators of their progress toward the goal are more successful saving than those who do not have a specific goal (Beverly, McBride, and Schreiner 2003). Similarly, money that is unlabeled is more likely to be spent. By identifying a savings goal, people essentially label that money as already allocated, making it easier to save (Thaler 1999). When money is labeled as "emergency fund" or "rainy day savings," it is psychologically easier to save that money for true emergencies.

Second, programs can open channels to overcome the hassle costs associated with saving money. Instead of requiring people to travel to a bank to open a savings account, for example, potential savers could be given a prepaid card with a savings feature that links to an account. If potential savers use direct deposit, setting up an automatic transfer to savings can also reduce the hassle costs (Bertrand, Mullainathan, and Shafir 2004). Finally, barriers arising from a lack of trust in financial institutions can be overcome by delivering information about saving and providing access to savings tools through a trusted community organization or reputable partner.

MAGIC Mojo and Impulse Savings

MAGIC Mojo sought to overcome some of the psychological and behavioral hurdles that often prevent lower-income individuals from building emergency savings. MAGIC Mojo required little planning, promoted goal-setting, did not require a bank account, and allowed people to access their emergency savings when they needed it.

The MAGIC Mojo pilot was launched in January 2013 and ended in June 2014. The program was offered as an optional added feature to the MAGIC Card, a celebrity-endorsed prepaid MasterCard. Users who purchased MAGIC Cards could activate the MAGIC Mojo feature online. Each time an enrolled cardholder impulsively saved money—by buying something on sale, for example, or foregoing an impulse purchase—the user texted the amount saved to MAGIC Mojo. That amount was then securely moved and safely stored on the savings side of the card. Users were also able to move money to the savings side of the card using the MAGIC Mojo website. To access their savings, cardholders went online and moved the money back to the spending side of the card.

Users signing up for MAGIC Mojo were asked to identify a savings goal. In the sign-up process, users named their savings accounts, chose an image to represent their goal, and identified an amount of time to achieve the goal. MAGIC Mojo broke the goal into weekly target amounts and sent regular text message reminders to help savers stay on track and achieve their savings goals. While some people elected to save for a large purchase or an upcoming special event, the initial data show that the most common savings goal identified was to build an emergency fund.

Without a designated savings account, it can be extremely challenging to maintain safe access to liquid savings, which is a crucial component of effective emergency savings. Because MAGIC Mojo was attached to a prepaid card, it provided a way for participants to build emergency savings without relying on access to a bank account to keep those savings secured. Thus, it offered a crucial opportunity to save for people who did not have checking or savings accounts, including those who may be unable to open an account. MAGIC Mojo is also highly accessible to a wide range of traditionally underserved groups. Additionally, the web-based technology can be adapted for people with auditory or visual impairments, and speakers of any language can use the service.

Capitalizing on Impulsivity

A key strength of MAGIC Mojo is that it capitalized on the fact that impulsive actions are fun. Research has found that, when faced with an opportunity to purchase something on impulse, people who buy the item experience an emotional response (Weinberg and Gottwald 1982). After an impulsive purchase, people report feeling joyful, excited, and enthusiastic about the purchase. Interestingly, some research suggests that positive feelings are directed at the act of unplanned spending, not necessarily at the actual item purchased (Gardner and Rook 1988; Rook and Hoch 1985). These studies suggest that even if the buyer has no real attachment to the item purchased, simply the act of spontaneously spending money may make people happy.

Research has found that the external act of impulse buying is significantly connected to internal emotions and psychological states, and particularly to feelings of anxiety, stress, and guilt (Youn and Faber 2000). People who feel anxious or stressed are more likely to spend money impulsively as a way to reduce their negative emotional states. In fact, impulsive spending is driven more by the person's psychological state than by factors such as advertising, product placement, or even price. Taken together, these findings suggest that consumers may experience the same emotional rush and positive feelings from impulsively saving money as they do from impulsively spending it, since the good feelings come from acting impulsively, not necessarily from acquiring an item.

Addressing the Lack of Willpower and Planning

A second strength of MAGIC Mojo is that it not only requires no willpower, it actually takes advantage of the fact that most people do not have the willpower to stick with an unpleasant task for a long period of time. As economist Richard Thaler (1994) wrote:

> Even if an individual were capable of calculating the optimal amount to save this year in order to maximize lifetime utility, he might well find it difficult to resist the temptation of current consumption. Saving requires willpower, which humans (or at least men) have sometimes had trouble summoning since the time of Adam and Eve. Many households undoubtedly think they should be saving more but find that saving is a luxury they cannot afford. (187)

MAGIC Mojo did not require participants to stick with a savings plan, or even to save with any regularity. Rather, the opportunity to directly transfer money to savings was always available, whenever a user skipped an impulse purchase. And there was no feeling of failure associated with choosing not to skip a purchase. Thus, MAGIC Mojo offered a win-win experience on the emotional front; participants could feel good when they made an impulse save and they did not have to feel bad when they made an impulse buy and skipped saving.

Other Impulse Savings Tools

MAGIC Mojo is not the first financial tool to try to capitalize on impulsivity to improve consumers' bottom line. While none of the existing tools fill exactly the same niche as MAGIC Mojo, they do offer evidence that people can be nudged to save money on impulse. For example, RiteCheck Cashing, Inc., partnered with Innovations for Poverty Action and Bethex Federal Credit Union to give people the opportunity to open a savings account or add to an existing account when they cash checks. Under this program, when a customer comes in to cash a check, the teller asks if the customer would like to open a savings account. By targeting customers when they have cash in hand, the program reaches people at the best possible moment to prompt them to save. A similar product, called 5 for Me, is offered at Community Trust Prospera, a division of Self-Help Federal Credit Union. The 5 for Me club account is aimed specifically at check-cashing customers who commit to saving $5 from each check they cash.

Another approach linking impulsivity to savings is PriceCheck&Save, a mobile application that attempts to make impulse spending smarter and increase contributions to retirement accounts. The application, created by Putnam Investments, LLC, allows consumers to compare prices on items they want to buy. Consumers scan the bar codes of items they want to buy, and the application scans the prices of area stores to identify ones where the item can be found at a lower price. The amount saved by buying the item at the lower price can then be transferred directly to a Putnam-administered 401(k) account.

Savings and Prepaid Card Lifespan

Prepaid cards are becoming an increasingly common financial tool, particularly among the unbanked. Between 2009 and 2012, the number of prepaid card payments increased at a faster rate than debit and credit card, Automated Clearing House (ACH), and check payments (Federal Reserve System 2013). A recent focus group study by the Pew Health Group (2012) found that, for some lower-income consumers, using a prepaid card is less expensive than using a checking account. Respondents in this study reported that they were attracted to the transparent fee structure and anonymity offered by prepaid cards, as well as the inability to overdraft or spend on credit. Contributing to the increase in prepaid card use is the fact that some government benefits are now disbursed via prepaid cards. According to the Federal Reserve Board, 67 percent of government-provided assistance was distributed on prepaid cards in 2011, including nearly $73 billion in SNAP (Supplemental Nutrition Assistance Program, formerly known as the Food Stamp program) benefits (Board of Governors 2012).

However, prepaid cards are still fairly new and there are limited data on how consumers use them. The data that is available show a good deal of variation in frequency of usage, transaction amounts, and the length of time consumers maintain active cards (Wilshusen et al. 2012). Prepaid cards generally have a short lifespan—consumers stick with the same card for six months or less, on average—which could pose a barrier to the use of such cards as a tool to help build savings. General-purpose reloadable (GPR) cards sold through retail outlets have the shortest lifespan, at an average of only 63 days, while cards sold through websites, like the MAGIC Card, typically remain active nearly twice as long, at an average of 184 days (Wilshusen et al. 2012). Additionally, cards purchased online are typically reloaded more often and with larger amounts. More than 70 percent of GPR cards sold via retail outlets are loaded three or fewer times, while 43 percent of cards sold via the Internet are loaded four or more times. It seems reasonable to think that a built-in savings feature may increase the lifespan of the card. Recent research on the Rainy Day Reserve (RDR), a savings feature on the UPside Visa Prepaid Card, showed that cardholders who did not utilize the savings feature were 21 percentage points more likely to close their accounts during the study period compared to RDR users (Abbi, Hasan, and Straghalis 2013). Research currently being conducted by the UNC Center for Community Capital (CCC) is exploring whether consumers who activated the MAGIC Mojo feature during the pilot used the prepaid card longer than those who did not use the savings feature.

As prepaid cards become more common, it is important for policymakers to remain aware that financially vulnerable consumers often use these cards. Prepaid card users may also have less experience with financial products and disclosures. Therefore, regulatory policies should be established to ensure that prepaid cards with savings features, such as MAGIC Mojo, function as intended. Disclosures need to clearly state all fees so consumers can make the right decisions about how to use their cards. Ideally, card providers should also offer education so consumers learn how to manage their savings and achieve their goals.

Limitations and Scalability of the MAGIC Mojo Program

While MAGIC Mojo and similar impulse saving tools hold great promise as ways to help lower-income families build emergency funds, there are some limitations worth noting. Looking specifically at MAGIC Mojo, the primary limitation is that, as previously noted, prepaid cards tend to have short lifespans. Often, the short duration of these cards is due to customer decisions, but the card provider may also terminate cards. As a case in point, the MAGIC Prepaid MasterCard program ended in June 2014 due to the card's inability to compete profitably with other, more generic prepaid cards.

A second limitation of impulse savings programs in general is that the money saved tends to be accessible. While it is important for emergency funds to be liquid, when money is too accessible it becomes easy to spend savings on routine expenses or other items. However, this limitation can potentially be countered by many of the mechanisms incorporated into MAGIC Mojo. Specifically, individuals must go online to transfer money from the savings to the spending side of the card. This helps balance the need for liquidity with the ability to protect and separate savings by creating a minor hurdle to accessing the funds. Other mechanisms such as goal setting and reminders about progress toward savings goals may help create mental barriers that keep users from accessing funds for purposes other than their stated savings goals.

A final significant limitation to consider is that MAGIC Mojo does not necessarily reach people at certain key moments when they have access to money that can be moved to savings. Tax time has emerged as a critical opportunity to help LMI households save because it capitalizes on the tax refund windfall (Schreiner and Sherraden 2007; Duflo et al. 2006; Barr 2004). This relatively large sum of money comes outside of the usual flow of funds and provides a unique opportunity for households to put a portion of the influx into savings. Similarly, impulse savings projects that reach people when they are in the process of cashing a check leverages a critical decision moment. In that case, the customer is literally holding a sum of cash in his hand at the moment he is asked to put a small amount in savings.

One of the most promising aspects of the MAGIC Mojo concept, however, is that it is easily and affordably scalable. Once the technological infrastructure is developed, the saving feature can be added to any prepaid card. Given the growing popularity of prepaid cards, especially among underbanked consumers, impulse savings tools tied to prepaid cards, should they become nationally available, have the potential to help hundreds of thousands of people start saving for emergencies. The affordability and security-related issues of prepaid cards continue to raise concerns, but additional research on card usage, best practices for card providers, and necessary regulation can help address these concerns.

The largest program expense associated with MAGIC Mojo is the cost to develop the technology that automates the saving process. The initial costs associated with creating the technical infrastructure and functionality have already been met. The relatively minimal costs to sustain the program and bring it to scale will be covered by the fees prepaid card issuers will pay to add MAGIC Mojo to their cards. We anticipate that card issuers will accept these costs, especially if research in progress shows that MAGIC Mojo increases card "stickiness," extending the use life of the cards.

Evaluation

A large body of research documents the positive emotional rewards people reap from impulse purchases. MAGIC Mojo offered this same sense of gratification for impulsively saving money. CCC is currently conducting research on the effectiveness of MAGIC Mojo using data collected during the pilot period. CCC will analyze data on how people used MAGIC Mojo, including adoption rates, frequency and amount of saving, achievement of identified savings goals, withdrawal patterns, and what participants reported using withdrawn savings for. The research will also seek to better understand the impact of the savings feature on the usage patterns and lifespan of prepaid cards.

Although data analysis is just beginning, there is some very initial information on program participation and measures. In the first three months of the pilot, nearly 500 people signed up for MAGIC Mojo. More than one-third reported saving for an emergency fund, and there is evidence that people personalized their goals in ways that were meaningful to them, assigning a variety of names, such as Save Me, What Happened!, I Will Never Be Broke, and Don't Touch.

Table 8.1 Impulse Savings Texts over Three Weeks for Representative Client

Savings text message	Date
$3 get started	January 16
$6 didn't have to buy smokes	January 18
$7 no eating out	January 19
$5 no dinner out	January 22
$6 no cigarettes needed	January 25
$2 no mountain dew tonight	January 27
$2 coupon for smokes	January 28
$2 free redbox rental	January 28
$8 no cigarettes or mountain dew	January 29
$6 no drive thru	January 29
$6 no smokes last night	February 1
$10 coupon for oil change	February 3
$6 no smokes needed	February 5

Source: Data provided by PiggyMojo, parent company of MAGIC Mojo.

The case of John (not his real name) illustrates how users interacted with MAGIC Mojo. John bought his card shortly after the product launched; he was saving for a vacation and set a goal of $500, with an automatic transfer to savings of $10 per week and a weekly savings target of just over $21. Over the next three weeks, John saved a total of $69 by skipping a handful of small expenses and using coupons. Table 8.1 shows the amounts he saved and the accompanying texts sent by John. Some of John's savings were the result of skipping fairly small purchases; for instance, he saved $2 by not having a soft drink. Other savings were more substantial, such as skipping meals out or not buying cigarettes. Finally, John saved some money by using coupons and moving the amount he saved from the coupon to his savings account.

John's story provides a glimpse into the types of impulse savings opportunities that exist. It also shows the potential to use very small savings moments and turn them into significant progress toward a larger savings goal. Alternatively, in the event of an unexpected expense, the savings could be utilized instead of having to rely on a higher cost option such as a payday loan. For example, if John gets a flat tire or his child needs a new inhaler, the money he has put aside can cover that expense.

Conclusion

MAGIC Mojo is an innovative new approach to helping underserved consumers build emergency savings by overcoming two key barriers to saving—economic constraints and behavioral biases. Lower-income families often find it difficult to build an emergency fund because their incomes fluctuate from month to month. This makes it hard to save a specific amount regularly. MAGIC Mojo, which operates from the premise that lower-income people can still save money even if they can't budget savings, works by allowing people to save small amounts of money when they have it, and not feel guilty when they do not. It accomplishes this by replacing one source of immediate gratification—impulsive spending—with another—impulsive saving. People who save using MAGIC Mojo experience immediate gratification from each impulse save, both in the actual act of moving money and in seeing progress toward a goal. While MAGIC Mojo may not work for all consumers—there is no one-size-fits-all approach to saving—it can fill an important unmet need by allowing people to quickly and easily transform small money-saving opportunities into longer-term savings habits while providing a little satisfaction along the way. In this way, the MAGIC Mojo concept can help lower-income and financially underserved families build emergency savings, leaving them better equipped to manage shortfalls, handle unexpected expenses, and build financially security.

While MAGIC Mojo was specifically intended to help people save money and build emergency funds in a new and exciting way, the concept of impulse saving is potentially more broadly applicable across a wide range of savings tools and key decision points. Any point at which a person is considering spending money—whether funds from their usual cash flow or "extra" money—is a point at which he or she could decide to save it instead. The key challenge going forward will be to find ways to bring those opportunities to consumers when and where they spend. MAGIC Mojo does this via text messaging and the web, but there are many other possibilities that have yet to be explored. From check cashing to tax refunds, loan interest-rate reductions to cash rewards for retail loyalty, consumers receive unexpected payments and face impulsive spending opportunities frequently. Each of these decision points represents an opportunity to transform fleeting instant gratification into a safety net for the future, an opportunity ripe for innovative thought and experimentation.

Acknowledgments

The authors wish to gratefully acknowledge the helpful feedback and research support provided by Lorlita Spann, Janneke Ratcliffe, and the staff at the University of Wisconsin's Center for Financial Security. Research on MAGIC Mojo is generously supported by a grant from the Center for Financial Services Innovation.

REFERENCES

Abbi, Sarika, Shaheen Hasan, and Elizabeth Straghalis. 2013. *Paving the Way Forward: Savings on Prepaid Cards* (July). D2D Fund, Allston, MA.

Bach, David. 2004. *The Automatic Millionaire: A Powerful One-Step Plan to Live and Finish Rich*. New York: Broadway Books.

Barr, Michael S. 2004. "Banking the Poor: Policies to Bring Low-Income Americans into the Financial Mainstream." Report, October. Brookings, Washington, DC.

Benhabib, Jess, Alberto Bisin, and Andrew Schotter. 2010. "Present-Bias, Quasi-Hyperbolic Discounting, and Fixed Costs." *Games and Economic Behavior* 69 (2): 205–223.

Bertrand, Marianne, Sendhil Mullainathan, and Eldar Shafir. 2004. "A Behavioral-Economics View of Poverty." *The American Economic Review* 94 (2): 419–423.

Beverly, Sondra G., Amanda Moore McBride, and Mark Schreiner. 2003. "A Framework of Asset-Accumulation Stages and Strategies." *Journal of Family and Economic Issues* 24 (2): 143–156.

Board of Governors of the Federal Reserve System. 2012. "Report to the Congress on Government-Administered, General-Use Prepaid Cards." Federal Reserve Board, July. Washington, DC.

Bricker, Jesse, Arthur B. Kennickell, Kevin B. Moore, and John Sabelhaus. 2012. "Changes in U.S. Family Finances from 2007 to 2010: Evidence from the Survey of Consumer Finances." *Federal Reserve Bulletin* 98 (2), July.

Brobeck, Stephen. 2008. "Understanding the Emergency Savings Needs of Low- and Moderate-Income Households: A Survey-Based Analysis of Impacts, Causes, and Remedies." Working Paper, November. Consumer Federation of America.

Brooks, Jennifer, and Kasey Wiedrich. 2013. "Living on the Edge: Financial Insecurity and Policies to Rebuild Prosperity in America. Findings from the 2013 Assets and Opportunity Scorecard." CFED, Washington, DC, January.

Caner, Asena, and Edward N. Wolff. 2004. "Asset Poverty in the United States, 1984–99: Evidence from the Panel Study of Income Dynamics." *Review of Income and Wealth* 50 (4): 493–518.

Caskey, John P. 2005. "Reaching Out to the Unbanked." In *Inclusion in the American Dream: Assets, Poverty, and Public Policy,* ed. Michael Sherraden, 149–166. New York: Oxford University Press.

Christen, Robert, and Ignacio Mas. 2009. "It's Time to Address the Microsavings Challenge, Scalably." *Enterprise Development and Microfinance* 20 (4): 274–285.

Davis, Elizabeth P., and Walter R. Schumm. 1987. "Savings Behavior and Satisfaction with Savings: A Comparison of Low- and High-Income Groups." *Home Economics Research Journal* 15 (4): 247–256.

Duflo, Esther, William Gale, Jeffrey Liebman, Peter Orszag, and Emmanuel Saez. 2006. "Saving Incentives for Low- and Middle-Income Families: Evidence from a Field Experiment with H&R Block." *The Quarterly Journal of Economics* 121 (4): 1311–1346.

Federal Reserve System. 2013. "The 2013 Federal Reserve Payments Study: Recent and Long-Term Payment Trends in the United States: 2003–2012, Summary Report and Initial Data Release." Federal Reserve System, December, Washington, DC.

Gardner, Meryl Paula, and Dennis W. Rook. 1988. "Effects of Impulse Purchases on Consumers' Affective States." *Advances in Consumer Research* 15 (1): 127–130.

Gross, Matthew B., Jeanne M. Hogarth, and Maximilian D. Schmeiser. 2012. "Use of Financial Services by the Unbanked and Underbanked and the Potential for Mobile Financial Services Adoption." *Federal Reserve Bulletin* 98 (4) (September): 1–20.

Haveman, Robert, and Edward N. Wolff. 2005. "The Concept and Measurement of Asset Poverty: Levels, Trends and Composition for the U.S., 1983–2001." *The Journal of Economic Inequality* 2 (2): 145–169.

Jackson, Aurora P., Jeanne Brooks-Gunn, Chien Huang, and Marc Glassman. 2000. "Single Mothers in Low-Wage Jobs: Financial Strain, Parenting, and Preschoolers' Outcomes." *Child Development* 71 (5): 1409–1423.

Kahn, Joan R., and Leonard I. Pearlin. 2006. "Financial Strain over the Life Course and Health Among Older Adults." *Journal of Health and Social Behavior* 47 (1): 17–31.

McKernan, Signe-Mary, Caroline Ratcliffe, and Katie Vinopal. 2009. "Do Assets Help Families Cope with Adverse Events?" Perspectives on Low-Income Working Families, Brief 10. The Urban Institute, Washington, DC.

McLoyd, Vonnie C. 1990. "The Impact of Economic Hardship on Black Families and Children: Psychological Distress, Parenting, and Socioemotional Development." *Child Development* 61 (2): 311–346.

Olen, Helaine. 2012. *Pound Foolish: Exposing the Dark Side of the Personal Finance Industry*. New York: Penguin Books.

Pew Health Group. 2012. "Key Focus Group Findings on Prepaid Debit Cards." Issue Brief, April 11. The Pew Charitable Trusts, Washington, DC.

Price, Richard H., Michelle Van Ryn, and Amiram D. Vinokur. 1992. "Impact of a Preventive Job Search Intervention on the Likelihood of Depression Among the Unemployed." *Journal of Health and Social Behavior* 33 (2): 158–167.

Rook, Dennis W., and Stephen J. Hoch. 1985. "Consuming Impulses." *Advances in Consumer Research* 12 (1): 23–27.

Schreiner, Mark, and Michael Sherraden. 2007. *Can the Poor Save? Saving & Asset Building in Individual Development Accounts*. New Brunswick, NJ: Transaction Publishers.

Taylor, Paul, Rich Morin, Rakesh Kochhar, Kim Parker, D'Vera Cohn, Mark Hugo Lopez, Richard Fry, Wendy Wang, Gabrial Velasco, Daniel Dockterman, Rebecca Hinze, and Soledad Espinoz. 2010. "A Balance Sheet at 30 Months: How the Great Recession Has Changed Life in America." Social and Demographic Trends Report, June 30. Pew Research Center, Social Demographic Trends Project, Washington, DC.

Thaler, Richard H. 1999. "Mental Accounting Matters." *Journal of Behavioral Decision Making* 12 (3): 183–206.

———. 1994. "Psychology and Savings Policies." *American Economic Review* 84 (2): 186–192.

Weinberg, Peter, and Wolfgang Gottwald. 1982. "Impulsive Consumer Buying as a Result of Emotions." *Journal of Business Research* 10 (1): 43–57.

Wilshusen, Stephanie M., Robert M. Hunt, James van Opstal, and Rachel Schneider. 2012. "Consumers' Use of Prepaid Cards: A Transaction-Based Analysis." Payment Cards Center Discussion Paper, August. Federal Reserve Bank of Philadelphia.

Youn, Seounmi, and Ronald J. Faber. 2000. "Impulse Buying: Its Relation to Personality Traits and Cues." *Advances in Consumer Research* 27 (1): 179–185.

Chapter 9

Prosperity SmartSave Card: An Incentivized Emergency Savings Strategy

Sharon Henderson

Introduction

The Great Recession affirmed the need for families across all income strata in the United States to build contingency funds, yet saving for future emergencies is most difficult in households that most need help in weathering unexpected expenditures—those with little to no disposable income. Building emergency savings alone will not bring significant improvements in families' economic security; promoting savings is only one element of a broader effort to move families toward financial security. Building strong credit histories is another pivotal component of improving financial security within the US financial systems. The Prosperity SmartSave card, developed by Prosperity Works, is designed to address both of these critical components of financial security, providing access to emergency savings funds and helping consumers build credit histories, especially for those who are un- or underbanked.

The Prosperity SmartSave card is a secured credit card offered in conjunction with financial education. The product allows consumers to build credit histories and accumulate contingency funds for use in emergencies. The card incentivizes savings and promotes future-oriented planning by depositing savings matches into children's savings account. Holding emergency funds on a secured credit card is aimed at ensuring ease of transactions and enhancing clients' credit histories, thereby opening the door to more competitive rates on goods and services and supporting financial mobility. For the un- and underbanked, the card can serve as a gateway to greater engagement with mainstream financial institutions.

The Prosperity SmartSave card is based on Prosperity Works's understanding of both consumer behavior and the financial management practices of families with very limited resources. This understanding is based on 15 years' experience working with low-income families to design financial strategies that support saving money and building credit. The Prosperity SmartSave card takes advantage of the popularity of prepaid credit cards and consumers' familiarity with preloaded cash cards from employment or benefit payments. Neither prepaid credit cards nor preloaded cash cards build credit worthiness. In order for payment behavior to be reported to the credit bureaus, a consumer must borrow funds and make payments on that loan. A secured credit card is a product that allows consumers to use their own funds as collateral against their line of credit; they borrow from and repay themselves. In contrast, prepaid credit cards allow consumers to deposit an amount onto a card and then spend those funds, rather than borrow against them. Preloaded cards are simply a transfer of funds from a company or government agency to a card that may be used as cash.

In 2012, Prosperity Works tested the idea that "parents will do for their children what they will not do for themselves" though an intense 12-month mother/child savings and financial education program. When mothers knew that the only way their children would gain access to a matched savings account was for them to also open a savings account, each mother was willing to save for herself. Testimonials at the end of the program indicate that if there had not been a direct benefit for their children, mothers would not have put away funds in their own accounts. The Prosperity SmartSave card is structured in a manner that offers financial incentives for saving. These incentives may tie to children's savings accounts, if appropriate in the context of the specific program offering the card. Using a dual-generation approach to savings may increase future orientation of the entire family unit.

Although the Prosperity SmartSave concept may prove useful for a wide array of audiences, the card is best targeted to the 28 percent of the US population that is un- or underbanked, meaning they either lack a bank account altogether or combine the use of a bank account with nonbanking services such as payday loans or pawnshops (Burhouse and Osaki 2012). More specifically, the Prosperity SmartSave card is targeted to lower-income, unemployed, young, and single-parent households, groups that are disproportionately more likely to be un- or underbanked (Burhouse and Osaki 2012). Access to common financial services and transactions is a challenge for financially underserved households, and these households tend to pay more for the financial services they need. Whether the issue is lack of reasonable access to financial institutions or lack of trust in financial institutions, those who are not participating in the banking system pay higher costs for daily financial transactions (Lusardi, Schneider, and Tufano 2011). Un- and underbanked households may have limited access to credit and zero funds available to develop an emergency savings account. Nonetheless, the benefits of mainstream financial systems are not always obvious to these families, as they compare the cost of alternative financial systems to the high cost of overdraft fees and other banking penalties.

The goal of the SmartSave card strategy is not to build savings patterns as much as it is to open an opportunity for individuals to participate in a full suite of financial services. By securing saved funds, the opportunity becomes a tool to build economic security and bring families into the mainstream banking system. The card brings consumers who may be suspicious of banks into the mainstream financial system through a side door. By engaging with the secured credit card and its accompanying financial education, participating consumers will develop banking behaviors and learn of products and services that may create a stronger financial foundation for the household. Participants will build emergency savings and positive credit. Each of these actions is a step toward reducing the financial fragility experienced by over 50 million families in the United States.

Background

The face of banking in America is changing rapidly, yet large pockets of low-income and rural consumers remain unable to access financial institutions and services. However, it is not only poor and low-income households that lack emergency savings cushions. Of the 2,667 individuals responding to a July 2011 online poll conducted by the National Foundation for Credit Counseling, 64 percent stated they would need to tap a source other than their savings account to satisfy a $1,000 unplanned expense. Although 17 percent indicated they would borrow funds from friends and family, another 17 percent reported they would need to neglect existing obligations in order to meet the emergency need. Similar percentages of respondents, about 10 percent each, said they would sell or pawn something they owned, take out a loan, or use a cash advance on a credit card to meet an unexpected $1,000 expense. (National Foundation for Credit Counseling 2011). Likewise, data from BankRate.com show that

26 percent of Americans have no emergency savings in a checking, savings, or money market account, and another 24 percent have insufficient savings to cover three months' expenses (Ross 2014).

Left to depend on service providers outside the financial mainstream, un- and underbanked families must pay high fees for services such as check cashing and higher interest rates for credit. Un- and underbanked families form the population that will most benefit from the Prosperity SmartSave card, as they are most likely to use alternative financial services. The SmartSave card provides another way to access the mainstream financial system in a form that provides the convenience of nonbank financial services without the high fees.

Problem to Be Addressed

Data show that over half of Americans currently manage their lives in a critically fragile financial state, without the resources to accommodate even a minor unexpected expense (Lusardi, Schneider, and Tufano 2011). For the most financially fragile, this situation is further complicated by disincentives to save that come from liquid asset tests families must pass to receive public assistance. Without access to either financial savings or credit, these families are devastated when an emergency arises. Something as minor as a $200 car repair can lead to loss of employment, and ultimately leave a family hopeless as well as homeless.

Many of these families are also un- or underbanked, cut off from the mainstream financial system by a lack of funds or a lack of understanding of how the system works. Without access to the mainstream financial system, these families rely on alternative service providers to access the financial services they need. The "small-dollar credit options" available to underbanked consumers include payday lenders, pawnshops, auto-title lenders, refund anticipation lenders, depositories, and installment lenders (Financial Education Division 2010). A substantial portion of these alternative services come with high fees.

Those who rely on these alternative services are also off from credit by a lack of credit history, as these nonbank financial services typically do not feed into the credit-building system. Access to credit and credit-building products builds financial independence. A positive credit report has become essential in every area of consumer behavior including employment, rental deposits, utility deposits, and cost of insurance and basic consumer purchases (Fellowes 2006). Establishing strong credit and learning how to use that credit wisely contribute to child, household, and community economic security. Chenven (2014) notes that "Without a strong credit history it is difficult, if not impossible, for households to get and stay ahead," (3) adding that "Most people require some minimum level of stability—a place to live and an income—before they can begin to sustainably build assets. Credit building is critical in successfully laying that groundwork" (7). However, even as access to banking becomes more widespread, it remains difficult for many low-income households to access credit, and hence to build a strong credit history.

Helping consumers develop and maintain strong credit histories and high credit scores may be one step toward reducing the wealth gap between white and African American families in the United States, a gap that has tripled in the past 25 years. Although African American family income has increased over time, white families have accumulated much more wealth. In 1984, the median wealth of white families was $85,070 more than that of African American median family wealth. By 2009, the difference in median wealth between white and African American families grew to $236,500 (Shapiro, Meschede, and Osoro 2013)

Furthermore, African Americans and other minorities are discriminated against when they apply for credit, either through the mainstream financial system or through alternative financial services. People of color continue to experience redlining and unnecessary subprime lending and are denied access to small dollar credit (Been, Ellen, and Madar 2009). A 2008 study by the Federal Reserve Bank of Boston compared credit card applications from people with identical risk profiles and payment histories across zip codes. The author found significant differences in the likelihood of credit application approvals based on the racial makeup of the study neighborhoods (Cohen-Cole 2008). These data provide conclusive evidence that redlining is still a factor in whether consumers can access credit, regardless of the amount of credit being requested. Thus, increasing access to safe credit-building products presents an opportunity to accelerate the financial growth of families that may be experiencing discrimination in the financial system.

Addressing these gaps in the financial system and helping low-income and minority families establish economic security requires an accessible, affordable, mobile financial product that facilitates accumulation of emergency savings while it helps families build credit and provides financial education. The proposed solution is a credit product that links key principles of behavioral economics with an opportunity to build knowledge that aids in credit building and lifelong financial management. Because it relies on a secured credit card, which is an established mainstream financial product, the intervention requires little new development; rather, the program can leverage existing products and resources, making it relatively simple to implement and scale. Used as a companion to existing programs, the product can be tailored by community-based organizations to fit the context of use and the goals of the organization.

This project has two primary goals: (1) to connect low-income consumers with the products and services available through mainstream financial institutions, even if they do not actually hold an account in a financial institution, and (2) to develop a low-touch system that rewards emergency savings behavior and builds credit capacity across geography, race, culture, economic class, age, and language boundaries. For individual consumers, the proposed product should (1) simplify, demystify, and mobilize the US financial transaction system, (2) establish an accessible conduit that provides incentives for emergency fund savings deposits and helps establish savings for children, and (3) offer a viable method to build or repair credit.

Target Market

Key elements of the proposed intervention include ease of use, ease of access, affordability, and mobility. Each of these elements feeds into the ability of people who are un- or underbanked to build financial security, supporting the development of healthy financial behaviors by providing a safe and affordable financial product. While this product is available to individuals of all income ranges, the specifics related to incentives, marketing, and versatility of use, as well as the focus on building emergency savings, are targeted to the needs of households earning less than 300 percent of the federal poverty level.

The SmartSave card will initially be available through organizations that serve the target population; eventually, as the project scales, the card will be available through convenience stores where competitive products, such as prepaid debit cards, are sold. Building on the hypothesis that parents will do for their children what they will not do for themselves, the product design includes rewards that establish secondary savings accounts for children, depositing a small amount in the child's account for each deposit made into the adult's account. The parent would make this choice when opening the account and could alter it any time later.

A small SmartSave pilot was launched in New Mexico in April 2014. In this pilot, the parent savings accounts and SmartSave cards are tied to the savings accounts of their children. There are future plans to test the SmartSave card independent of children's' savings. New Mexico was chosen as a pilot ground for its diverse population, including a large Hispanic community as well as Native American tribal territories and deep rural pockets. These will allow for testing of the product in diverse cultures and settings.

How the Product Works

Under the SmartSave program, incentives to save are tied to both savings and repayment behaviors. The incentives are designed utilizing insights from behavioral economics. Behavioral economics is the study of how individuals make decisions, what is happening in their heads as they do so, and how people might become better decision makers. It is not uncommon for humans to disregard facts or logic and behave in irrational ways. Incentives help the brain focus beyond the immediate decision and look to connections of additional behavior.

The major saving incentive is a 5 percent match, deposited into a child's savings account or back into the adult's account, for deposits into the adults account up to $1,000 for the first two years after the account is opened. Distributions of the incentives will be made monthly during the first year and quarterly the second year. For example, if the parent deposits $20 into his or her emergency savings account during month one, a credit of $1 will appear on the next account statement. The credits, which are not available to the parent's credit line or account balance, will continue to build until the parent transfers them to a child's savings account.

On the repayment side, on-time payments to the secured credit card account during the first three months after borrowing against the account will be rewarded with a $5 bonus, deposited either into the children's savings account or back into the emergency savings account, as directed by the account holder. An additional $10 bonus will be deposited at the next quarter if months four through six are paid on time. There are no bonus dollars after the first six months.

The SmartSave card engages low-income families by tying parents' motivation to provide long-term financial security for their children with the need for emergency savings to create immediate financial security for the family. The card includes a range of features designed to increase convenience of use, motivate savings, and help families build a secure financial future, including emergency savings accounts accessed through secured lines of credit; bonus deposits into children's savings accounts and incentives to parents; credit reporting to at least one of the three main credit bureaus; and financial education in the form of credit-building tips included in each monthly statement, automated savings hints and reminders, financial coaching messages delivered via text messaging, and a mobile household budgeting tool.

Engaging consumers in new financial products and systems creates a space for financial education and coaching and the development of increased ability to navigate financial systems. Previous success with gaming tools tied to financial incentives indicates that people enjoy games and will engage with them regardless of the value of the prize. One such success is known as "prize-linked savings" where participants' names are entered into a raffle drawing for a prize every time they make a deposit into a specified account.[1] Savings challenges provided through automated systems bring the saver the satisfaction of earning a reward at little administrative cost. These challenges, which will be delivered via text message, can be used to educate consumers while helping them build savings with small rewards deposited into savings accounts.

For example, a message for the month of February, which is Black History Month, could be pushed out to the account holder that launches a treasure hunt, executed through a social networking platform, to locate the biography of Chicago investment banker Michelle L. Collins. Once the consumer locates the biography and responds to the challenge, a reward of $1 will be deposited to his or her savings account. The abbreviated biography would include links to terms related to investment banking, such as stocks and bonds, and introduce the concept of purchasing US Savings Bonds during tax time, an option that is now available on the US tax return. To manage the expense of this effort, prizes will be limited to the first 2,000 winners. These short-term challenges would be supplemented by an ongoing game, developed on a social network platform, focused on building credit. Points would be awarded for achieving credit-building defined behaviors such as making on-time payments, diversifying loan types, and maintaining low balances.

Scaling the SmartSave card will require heavy dependence on existing automated systems. The Prosperity Network will establish a cross-financial institution system with the SmartSave card, initially by piggybacking on the shared branching system used by credit unions (http://sharedbranching.org/).[2] Over 6,000 credit union branches throughout the United States participate in shared branching; credit union members may walk into any of these and access the full services of their home credit union. Hosting the SmartSave card through the credit union branching system will allow card users to access their account features at any of these branches and eliminate many regulatory barriers.

The costs associated with launching SmartSave will depend on the ability to tie together existing products to create this new structure. Costs for the two-year pilot are estimated at $195,000 per year. This includes evaluation costs, staffing (the pilot is operating with two full-time staff members), and initial technical assistance to organizations that will assist with product distribution. Following years will average $145,000 per year for product expansion. Marketing materials will cost $75,000 and the initial technology costs are budgeted at $43,000. The primary additional costs, not already managed within existing systems, are associated with the incentives and administering the financial education games. The cost of incentives includes:

- A 5 percent gift to a child's savings account for every dollar saved in the first two years up to $1,000, for a maximum of $20 per card holder
- A maximum of $25 per card holder for on-time payment incentives

Some of these costs will be recouped in the form of fees and interest charged to cardholders; these include 11 percent interest on charges to the secured card, an application fee of $15, and an annual renewal fee of $10.

Evidence of Effectiveness

Research on the tie between saving incentives and savings behavior has increased significantly over the past two decades. The Research Plan for The American Dream Demonstration project, conducted in the 1990s, demonstrated that savings is an institutional phenomenon, meaning that when access and incentives are right, people—including poor people—are more likely to save. This assumption runs contrary to mainstream economic thinking about savings behavior, which focuses more on an individual's propensity to save. In their report on the American Dream Demonstration, Schreiner, Clancy, and Sherraden (2002) conclude that higher match rates, higher match caps, use of direct deposit, and financial education are associated with an increased likelihood of being a saver.

In a large, randomized field experiment carried out in cooperation with H&R Block, about 14,000 H&R Block clients across 60 offices in low- and middle-income neighborhoods in St. Louis were invited to deposit a portion of their tax refunds in Individual Retirement Accounts (IRAs) and randomly offered either a 20 percent match on their contribution, a 50 percent match, or no match (the control group). Higher match rates significantly increased IRA participation and contributions: participation rates were 3 percent for the control group, 8 percent for the 20 percent match group, and 14 percent for the 50 percent match group, and average contributions were 4 and 7 times higher for the 20 percent and 50 percent groups, respectively, than for the control group (Duflo et al. 2006).

Limitations

Practical limitations of the Prosperity SmartSave card are associated with the functionality of making deposits to the account associated with the card. Assuming that the card will rely on the shared branching system of the credit unions, prospective participants will need to join a local credit union in order to open the associated accounts. Membership into credit unions is often restricted by geography, employment, or participation in a membership-based organization, so some potential card users may not be eligible. The approach to overcoming this limitation is fairly simple: SmartSave card holders will be qualified as Prosperity Works' participants, making them eligible for several credit unions where Prosperity Works is a qualifying member.. Once participants have joined a credit union, they can access their funds through any shared branching participant.

Helping consumers understand credit and build strong credit requires accessing and sharing their credit scores with them. This effort may also encounter limitations, in the regulations and procedures around credit scores. Each credit bureau restricts how credit score information may be shared with consumers. The credit report, also referred to as the consumer report, is available to the consumer for free once each year; however, the credit score must be purchased. There are strict limitations on the use of the credit score by third parties, including on sharing the score with the consumer. The FICO company is examining ways to allow credit scores to be shared with consumers for credit-building purposes. This product will fall within that area.

Evaluation

During a pilot period where up to 1,000 cards will be issued, measurements will be taken on a defined schedule. Participant uptake, including numbers of applicants, numbers of participants enrolled, and numbers of cards issued, will be reviewed quarterly, as will savings amounts and the relationship between the child savings incentive and increases in savings. Surveys will be conducted every six months to request input from savers regarding the impact the child savings incentive has had on their savings behavior. On-time payment rates among users will be reviewed every six months and credit-building indicators, including credit scores, will be surveyed annually. Following the pilot period, a six-month development period will allow for refinements before making the card available to the public at large.

Conclusion

Incorporating a credit-building mechanism into an emergency savings product allows people to build sustainable systems to meet ongoing financial needs and reduce the costs of purchasing goods and services. Providing automated financial education at the same time allows users to understand the high costs of alternative financial products and the benefits of building good credit and adequate emergency savings.

A key strategy for this product is its mobility and lack of dependence on any one financial institution. The Prosperity SmartSave card is as flexible and mobile as the consumers it serves. By incorporating the parent's motivation to care for their children, this strategy helps overcome the tendency of parents to go without savings. It also brings attention to the need to pass on financial knowledge from parent to child, thus building a more secure financial future for the next generation.

Notes

1. In-depth discussion around prize-linked savings can be found at the D2D Fund's website (www.d2dfund.org).
2. See http://sharedbranching.org for more information.

References

Been, Vicki, Ingrid Ellen, and Josiah Madar. 2009. "The High Cost of Segregation: Exploring Racial Disparities in High-Cost Lending." *Fordham Urban Law Journal* 36 (3): 361–393.

Burhouse, Susan, and Yazmin Osaki. 2012. "2011 FDIC National Survey of Unbanked and Underbanked Households." FDIC. September, Washington, DC.

Chenven, Sarah. 2014. "The Power of Credit Building: Credit-Building Strategies for Funders." Asset Funders Network, April. Credit Builder's Alliance.

Cohen-Cole, Ethan. 2008. "Credit Card Redlining." Working Paper QAU08–1, February. Federal Reserve Bank of Boston.

Duflo, Esther, William Gale, Jeffrey Liebman, Peter Orszag, and Emmanuel Saez. 2006. "Saving Incentives for Low- and Middle-Income Families: Evidence from a Field Experiment with H&R Block." *The Quarterly Journal of Economics* 121 (4): 1311–1346.

Fellowes, Matt. 2006. "Credit Scores, Reports, and Getting Ahead in America." Research Report, May. Brookings, Washington, DC.

Financial Education Division, US Department of Treasury. 2010. "Developing a Research Agenda on Small-Dollar Credit and Financial Empowerment, March 4, 2010." Convening Overview. Washington, DC.

Lusardi, Annamaria, Daniel J. Schneider, and Peter Tufano. 2011. "Financially Fragile Households: Evidence and Implications." National Bureau of Economic Research Working Paper Series, No. 17072.

National Foundation for Credit Counseling. 2011. "Majority of Americans Do Not Have Money Available to Meet an Unplanned Expense." News Release, July, http://www.nfcc.org/newsroom/newsreleases/floi_july2011results_final.cfm

Ross, Allison. 2014. "Financial Security Index: Saving for a Rainy Day." Bankrate, June 23. http://www.bankrate.com/finance/consumer-index/saving-for-a-rainy-day.aspx.

Schreiner, Mark, Margaret Clancy, and Michael Sherraden. 2002. "Saving Performance in the American Dream Demonstration—A National Demonstration of Individual Development Accounts." Final Report, October. Center for Social Development, George Warren Brown School of Social Work, Washington University in St. Louis.

Shapiro, Thomas, Tatjana Meschede, Sam Osoro. 2013. "The Roots of the Widening Racial Wealth Gap: Explaining the Black-White Economic Divide." Research and Policy Brief, February. Institute on Assets and Social Policy, Brandis University.

Chapter 10

Accelerating Savings among Low-Income Households

Ed Khashadourian

Introduction

The conversation around low-income savings habits is historically inspired by the developments in the field of asset building, where existence of long-term assets is believed to lead to changed behavior. In this context, saving, while it is generally viewed as an important vehicle that makes accumulation of financial wealth possible, is treated mostly as a transitory component in a household's asset-building process. In other words, in the asset-building discourse, savings is a repository of financial resources. When savings reach a critical level, they are used to leverage other forms of assets, because such assets usually offer higher long-term returns and contribute to overall financial well-being more effectively than does cash in a bank account. This view characterizes the resource-oriented approach to saving.

Our understanding of emergency savings is different from the more traditional resource-oriented approach, however, in that the purpose of having money saved for emergencies is for it to never be spent (or converted into other forms of assets). This is because the primary function of emergency savings is to provide protection against financial uncertainties. Similar to an automobile insurance policy, which drivers obtain not to get into accidents, but to attain the peace of mind that having the coverage offers, the idea of having emergency savings is to build cash and near-cash reserves in order to improve the ability to cope with uncertainty. Under this analogy, when individuals save, their deposits function like premium payments on an insurance policy, expanding the coverage and thus expanding their ability to manage even larger financial emergencies.

This view of saving is different from a resource-oriented approach as it does not directly relate to rates of return or valuation of assets. In addition, unlike investments, which require planning in terms of both timing and the amount of savings needed to leverage investments, individuals cannot plan how and when emergencies will occur and are often unable to make a realistic assessment of the expenses they'll incur in the event of an emergency. Moreover, as a fact of life, uncertainty and the degree of exposure to it change through the life cycle and may be influenced by individual circumstances. For this reason, emergency savings models are usually designed under a different set of structural and behavioral parameters than are other traditional models of savings, such as Individual Development Accounts (IDAs), that are inspired by a resource-oriented approach.

Savings and the Financial Vulnerability of Low-Income Households

Five years after the Great Recession, there are reasons to believe that personal savings rates may very well remain higher than their prerecession lows, at least for the foreseeable future (Dynan 2012). Uncertainties in the US economic outlook have presented an opportunity to revisit the notion of personal savings and built momentum to promote policies that support healthier savings rates among American households. Emergency savings is one critical component of savings rates and savings habits that needs to be addressed in the policy discussion.

The importance of focusing on emergency savings is often brought up in policy papers and by researchers in the field. For example, a 2010 policy paper by the Center for Economic Progress suggests that, "For some workers, particularly LMI [low- to moderate-income] ones as well as people in their 20s and 30s, making savings for retirement the default over other valuable forms of savings may 'put the cart before the horse'" (Center for Economic Progress 2010, 11). Others, including Cramer (2010) and Boshara (2010) to name a couple, have also discussed the urgency of considering the short-term savings needs of low-income households.

The pronounced emphasis on low- to moderate-income (LMI) households in this conversation is logical from a practical standpoint, as these households are generally believed to be more vulnerable to financial emergencies than higher-income families. But a focus on low-income families is also important from a macroeconomic perspective: evidence suggests that increasing savings among low-income households can have the largest marginal effect on total national savings in the United States. In fact, the US national savings could increase by as much as 53 percent if households in the bottom two quintiles of income increased their savings by just $1,000 a year (Johnson, Mensah, and Steuerle 2006).

In spite of this significant potential contribution, available data and research on the actual savings levels of low-income households are not encouraging; an increasing number of American households report that they face financial emergencies every day. In a nationwide survey of 2,000 households conducted by the Pew Research Center in late 2006, 34 percent of respondents reported that they had faced an unexpected financial expense that set them back financially within the past year (Taylor, Funk, and Clark 2010). Taken at face value, this finding implies that there is almost a 100 percent chance that a typical household will experience a major unexpected expense within a three-year period.

Literature on behavioral economics suggests that unrealistic expectations, behavioral biases, and blind spots may explain why many people remain vulnerable to even relatively small financial emergencies. Fortunately, the literature also demonstrates that relatively small changes, such as default options, mental accounting, or channel factors and behavioral nudges, could produce large impacts in savings outcomes (Thaler, Sunstein, and Balz 2010; Mullainathan and Shafir 2008; Pronin and Kugler 2007; Bertrand, Mullainathan, and Shafir 2006). Motivated by these developments, a host of new programs and initiatives have been introduced in conferences and publications. The Savings Accelerator Account (SAA) platform, one such example, is described in the following sections.

Savings Accelerator Accounts

In discussing the conceptual underpinnings of different low-income savings models, reference is frequently made to the institutional theory of saving (ITS). Developed by Beverly and Sherraden (1999), and later expanded by Beverly et al. (2008), ITS assumes that low-income earners save less than higher-income individuals primarily because of differences in their level of access to financial institutions and not because of individual preferences and values. According to Beverly et al. (2008, 90), "The term *institutions*... refers to purposefully-created policies, programs, products, and services that shape opportunities, constraints and consequences." The authors include in the extended list of institutions seven constructs: access, information, incentives, facilitation, expectations, restrictions, and security. Of these seven institutional constructs, this chapter will focus primarily on the role of incentives and restrictions in accelerating savings.[1]

Key Mechanisms: Deposit Structure and Incentives

The central hypothesis of the SAA model is that behavioral biases that impede the long-term accumulation of savings can be mitigated by essentially disguising the long-term focus in a platform that structures saving as a sequence of short-term decisions, motivated by a series of independent actions and rewards. In SAA programs, participants earn rewards that are instantaneous and partially independent of past and future deposit activities. A similar approach is taken in prize-linked or lottery-based savings programs; however, whereas in prize-based models the incentives are contingent on the saver winning a raffle prize, they are not subject to probability in the SAA model.

SAA models are designed by manipulating three main program elements: deposit structure, incentive components, and incentive duration.

Deposit Structure

Participants can make deposits in any amount and at any time and earn corresponding rewards. They can, however, maximize their benefits by depositing at least once a month and at levels recommended by the program. In other words, incentives increase with the amount of deposit but reach a maximum at a set monthly level. So, if the deposit cap is set at $40 per month, then incentives apply to the first $40 deposited in that month; deposit caps are typically $25 to $50 per month. Incentives are applied to each deposit independently and there is no time restriction. This means that participants can choose to withdraw their funds at any time and still earn proportional benefits for the length of time they participated in the program.

Typically, SAA programs feature a higher opening-month deposit compared to subsequent monthly deposits. While higher introductory deposits may be seen as a barrier limiting the ability of at least some participants to join the program, a range of different savings plans are often available, each featuring different contribution levels. Thus, programs can address this barrier by offering an alternative plan to individuals who find the introductory deposit in one plan too high. At the same time, several behavioral and economic factors rationalize the use of higher introductory deposits. For example, if a program is offered during the tax season, a higher introductory deposit might actually be more attractive to an individual who receives a significant tax refund and is interested in saving a part of it. In fact, Ramp-UP accounts, a category of SAA featuring an introductory deposit of $500, have been very popular at participating VITA (Volunteer Income Tax Assistance) sites in the Los Angeles area in the past few years.

While the separation between the first and subsequent monthly deposits may sound trivial, they may have a significant behavioral effect. The higher introductory deposit can actually set in motion the strong behavioral heuristic of anchoring, which may affect retention rates in the program. For example, in a savings plan featuring a $200 introductory and a $25 monthly deposit, the monthly deposits can appear more affordable in the context of the high initial deposit. Brooks (2011) uses the example of a liquor store to explain the effect of anchoring: "A $30 bottle of wine may seem expensive when surrounded by $9 bottles of wine, but it seems cheap when surrounded by $149 bottles of wine" (181). In this way, the choice of a higher introductory deposit, which is often rewarded by a sign-up bonus, can play an important role in helping participants to continue saving.

Incentives

ITS recommends financial incentives as an important stimulant for savings and program adoption, but the theory refers to incentives, by and large, as dollar figures and does not elaborate on the mechanisms through which incentives incite behavior. Yet, the literature on behavioral economics demonstrates that situational and channel factors, as well as cognitive principles resulting from the bounded rationality of economic agents, can generate different responses to a given financial incentive based on how it is structured. Working from this insight, SAA programs incorporate a multicomponent incentive structure in which rewards are offered not only in relation to amounts saved, but also based on the consistency of deposits. This is one of the more salient features of SAA that separates it from alternative incentivized savings models.

To understand how incentives are incorporated in an SAA, a partial list of incentive subcomponents is provided in table 10.1. In table 10.1, a sign-up bonus is a reward that applies to the initial deposit; it is typically offered in plans where the initial deposit is substantially higher than subsequent monthly deposits. In many cases, the sign-up bonus could be a strong mechanism to address the status quo bias, which can impede individuals from taking action.

Another subcomponent of the SAA incentive structure is the straight deposit match. This mechanism, which targets the frequency of deposits, is important from a behavioral perspective. The reward is applied when

Table 10.1 Examples of Incentive Components in Savings Accelerator Account

Incentive component	Description
Signup bonus	A benefit applied to the first deposit in the program. The signup bonus does not depend on the amount deposited. For example, if the first deposit is $100 and participants are promised a $50 signup bonus, a deposit of less than $100 would still earn the signup bonus.
Straight deposit match	A direct match offered on deposits. The straight deposit match does not depend on the amount deposited. As long as a deposit in any amount is registered at any time during the month, a straight deposit match is applied.
Interest	Annualized rate of interest applied to monthly deposits. The rate is compounded monthly.

Source: Savings Plan Agreement document, Opportunity to Assets.

a monthly deposit is made. The incentive amount is fixed and does not depend on the amount saved. As long as a deposit in any amount is registered within the calendar month, the straight deposit match will apply to that deposit. Therefore, participants making contributions at least once each month earn higher rewards regardless of how much they save, compared to others who may save the same total amount at a more sporadic rate. This may help savers avoid the cognitive load required to make long-term decisions, as it signals the importance of not missing the deposit in a given month regardless of the saver's ability to make a full contribution in any given month. In other words, the straight deposit match helps participants to focus on the immediate future. Thus, this mechanism may improve consistency of deposits, increase deposit rates, and support habit-forming behavior among participants. Although conclusive evidence does not exist to support this hypothesis, in a survey of a small group of SAA holders, North (2012) notes that 67 percent of participants who indicated that they would continue to save after the end of the program had reduced their monthly expenses to allow for more savings, indicating a long-term change in consumption habits.

The third common SAA incentive component, often referred to as a fractional match, is similar to interest payments on expected monthly deposits. Following Khashadourian (2009), the interest amount is calculated on a monthly basis and applied to the deposit cap, typically at a rate of 15–23 percent. This high rate reflects the common belief that low-income households face a high rate of time preference, which is a measure of readiness to sacrifice present pleasures for future ones (Carvalho 2010; Pennings and Garcia 2005; Lawrance 1991). To offset this time preference, Khashadourian (2009) recommends that the interest rate should be set sufficiently high to motivate savers to more easily make the sacrifice of saving, rather than spending, their hard-earned dollars. Since interest is paid for both current and past deposits, the amount of incentive awarded each month increases with every monthly deposit, and participants see a higher benefit amount with successive deposits. This process characterizes the "acceleration" in the SAA.

It should be pointed out that the choice of interest as an incentive mechanism is important not only because of its role in accelerating savings, but also because of the role it plays in allowing the model to take advantage of the reinforcing effect of construal. Bertrand, Mullainathan, and Shafir (2006) provide examples demonstrating that people's responses to different stimuli depend on how they understand and interpret those stimuli. Since monthly deposit amounts in SAA are limited, the high rates of interest do not translate into significant amounts in terms of dollars, but they can be very effective in attracting deposits. This is because although many low-income households understand the mechanics of interest quite well, their circumstances are such that they most often find themselves on the paying end of it. In that context, in the mental processing of incentives, an interest rate of 19 percent may appear even more appealing than a higher-valued match rate.

Incentive Duration

To make the cost of incentive payments manageable, the plan duration in SAA is limited. That is, incentive payments are limited to a set period, typically ranging from 12 to 18 months. In effect, the plan duration is framed as the number of monthly opportunities a participant has to make deposits and earn rewards. If a deposit is missed in one month, the participant has lost one opportunity to draw the full benefit from saving. And since incentives are treated independently, a lost reward in one month cannot be regained with a deposit in a subsequent month, even if that subsequent deposit is larger. Each month, a participant faces decision points and has to decide whether to close the account and withdraw the funds, leave the funds in the account for another month without making additional contributions, or make another deposit and defer the decision regarding the fate of the account to the following month. Therefore, another hypothesis suggests that offering incentives through

Table 10.2 Examples of Two SAA Savings Models

Plan features	Model 1	Model 2
Plan period (months)	12	18
Initial deposit	$200	$50
Other deposits	$25	$30
Signup bonus	$50	-
Straight deposit match	$5	$3
Interest (fractional match)	19%	23%
Total deposits	$475	$560
Total incentive reward	$190 (0.4 to 1)	$183 (0.33 to 1)
Final account value	$665	$743

Source: Plan Selection Guide, Opportunity to Assets.

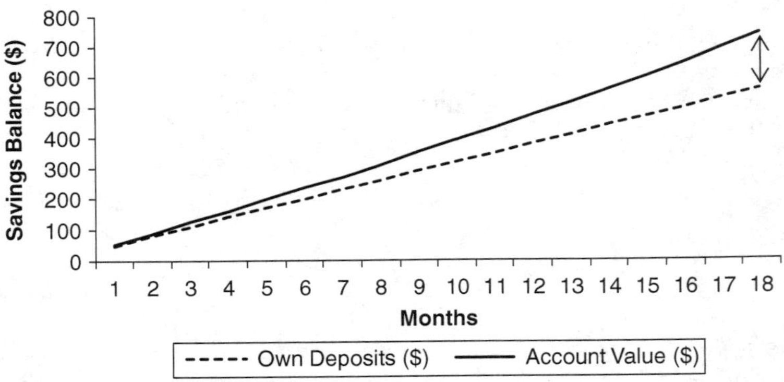

Figure 10.1 Deposits and Total Account Value in SAA plan T16 over 18-Month Savings Period.

Source: Author's calculations using Savings Path, a database operated by OPTA used to calculate incentives in savings accelerator accounts.

acceleration will help depositors stay on track and make a decision in favor of continuing saving rather than withdrawing funds in the absence of any restrictions. Table 10.2 presents the primary features of two sample SSA models. Figure 10.1 shows the deposits and total account value (deposits plus rewards) in a savings plan that features the components listed in model 2 from table 10.2.

The Significance of Time Restrictions

Restrictions are a common aspect of different types of savings programs. From retirement savings accounts to college savings plans and matched savings programs for low-income households, access to the dollars saved remains restricted until participants reach a defined milestone. The most common restriction is a time restriction, which requires that participants wait a specified period of time before accessing funds. Other examples involving use restrictions (funds are available only for specific types of expenses), minimum or maximum contribution levels, and sources of deposited funds are also common in various types of matched savings programs.

By far, the most prevalent type of restriction is the time restriction. In most cases, participants are still able to access the amounts they have contributed to their accounts at any time and for any purpose, but they run the risk of forfeiting program incentives if they violate the time restriction—that is, if they withdraw funds too early. It is often argued that time restrictions are needed in incentivized savings programs to offset the temptation to spend money rather than saving for the future. Mullainathan and Shafir (2008) suggest that because of such self-control problems, saving is a weak vehicle for transforming small deposits into large sums of cash. Therefore, when incentives are offered to encourage saving, automatic time restrictions may be needed to guarantee accumulation. On the other hand, restrictions may make it difficult to assess the effect of incentives in stimulating savings, as the presence of restrictions may obscure the real effect of incentives.

Furthermore, in an emergency savings model, imposing time restrictions may not make sense, as such restrictions may not only reduce participants' ability to cope with financial emergencies, but also lead to welfare losses in consumption. Programs that impose time restrictions on incentive payments in effect adopt an all-or-nothing approach, offering no middle ground for participants who make a good-faith attempt to save, yet are unable to continue with the program. Given the generally short decision horizons of low-income households, a program that requires participants to lock their cash in a 12-month restricted account introduces an element of uncertainty that increases the mental pressure of the decision to participate. Saving is already a complicated decision for the poor; programs need to make participation as appealing as possible by reducing such mental barriers.

SAA does not adopt the all-or-nothing approach common in other savings programs. Rather than creating hard restrictions, which may negatively influence a potential saver's experience, it imposes a soft barrier: incentives are offered regardless of when a participant leaves the program, but the incentives are distributed exponentially (through acceleration) to increase the opportunity cost of an early withdrawal. Opportunity cost, like time restrictions, could nudge behavior in the desired direction, prompting participants to remain in the program until maturity while minimizing the risk of a welfare loss due to early withdrawal from the program.

This aspect of the model, coupled with the mostly independent treatment of deposit rewards, constitutes a clear example of what Camerer and colleagues (2003) call "asymmetric paternalism." The SAA incentive structure offers significant benefits to those who may withdraw, yet imposes no harm on those who make the rational choice of completing the program. The higher opportunity cost of withdrawing will support the decision to save for another month, but a participant who decides to terminate retains the benefits he or she has already accrued. Each month, participants must choose between continuing with the program for another month or giving up on the higher reward in the following month by withdrawing funds. Acceleration, or the increased opportunity cost of early termination, makes the sequence of these short-term decisions compatible with the long-term goal of increased savings.

Acceleration versus Savings Match

As a model for emergency savings, SAA focuses on habit-forming behavior rather than on targeting a predefined level of savings as the primary financial goal for participants. Accordingly, it utilizes acceleration instead of matching as the underlying incentive mechanism. In its technical definition, a match is a reward offered on a set amount of savings. In other words, it applies to a stock measure of assets. Acceleration, on the other hand, is applied to a flow measure: the amount an individual can set aside each period (for instance, each month) to accumulate savings over the long term.

Why is acceleration different from a match payment? Part of the reason traces back to the overarching philosophy of a resource-oriented savings program. When the focus is on savings as a resource, it implies that the program will try to offer a significant match amount on a per-account basis. Since the approach is resource oriented, it is natural for a program to offer as high a reward as possible under existing program budget and cost constraints in order to help savers build a larger nest egg. Acceleration, on the other hand, is concerned only with finding the minimum dollar amount required to entice an individual to make a spot decision—that of spending a relatively small amount of money in a given month or saving it until the next period in order to earn an instant reward. Because of this difference in approach, incentive amounts required to accelerate savings are typically much smaller than match payments.

A second and related difference between a match and an acceleration relates to the time value of incentives. If, in the presence of time restrictions on match payments, the incentives are back-ended—that is, offered only to people who complete the program at a certain time—then the present value of the offered incentive will be smaller compared to a scenario, such as in SAA, where incentives are earned with every monthly deposit.

This is because long-term results in SAA are products of a sequence of short-term actions. The goal is to nudge the individual to save a nominal amount in a given month, and the incentives are structured to make each monthly deposit *appear* as a separate decision, independent from deposits made in the past or those that will be made in the future. This is because lost incentives resulting from a missed deposit in one month cannot be made up in the future. By focusing attention in this way on an instant reward or a short time interval, this mechanism enables participants to avoid complications that result from biases such as hyperbolic discounting. Hyperbolic discounting is defined as the declining rate of time preference when the delay for receiving a reward is prolonged (Frederick, Loewenstein, and O'Donoghue 2002). To the extent that hyperbolic discounting is the governing mental process in the decision to save, it doesn't make a material difference whether receiving a match on savings requires a wait period of six months or two years (for example), since most of the discounting happens in the near term anyway. This means that it is difficult to entice an individual to make a deposit in a savings account if his mental timeframe with respect to saving needs to expand beyond the very short term.

Still, other developments in this area, such as subadditive discounting, suggest that the perception of a delay depends on whether or not the participant considers the time between the present and the delayed future reward as one unit or subdivides it into smaller intervals. To the extent that such subdivisions occur, individuals will assign a higher discount rate to processes that involve shorter intervals. According to Read (2001), subadditive discounting may result in more discounting than that predicted by hyperbolic discounting, therefore making the decision to save for the long term even more difficult for a low-income saver.

To put things into perspective, given that a month is the shortest time interval a low-income household may consider (primarily because a majority of household payments, such as rent or utility bills, occur on a monthly basis), it is likely that the decision to save in one month with the option to revisit the decision the next month will be discounted at a lower rate compared to a situation in which a decision to save in one month must be made in the context of a long-term vision involving several intervals of delay. Yet, if the sequence of such recurring short-term decisions—that is, those involving smaller discount rates—is often resolved in favor of saving, then the individual has automatically moved closer to the long-term goal of accumulating liquid assets.

Implementation of SAA

SAA programs have been in existence in small numbers in Southern California since 2011. A simpler version of the SAA model, known as the Ramp-UP account, was debuted in 2009 across four nonprofit organizations in Los Angeles as a tax-time savings initiative. The technology to implement SAAs is currently offered by Opportunity to Assets (OPTA),

Table 10.3 Basic Demographic Information of SAA Participants

Demographic indicators	**Figures from 2011–2012 Enrollments**
Gender	
Female	68%
Marital Status	
Married	**28%**
Single	56%
Other	16%
Education	
High school diploma or below	65%
Postsecondary education	35%
Income-area median income (AMI)	
Below 30% of AMI	48%
31–50% of AMI	36%
51–80% of AMI	13%
Household characteristics	
Average household size	3.1
Average minors per household	0.86

Source: Data compiled by Opportunity to Assets using information obtained from standard program enrollment forms used by partner organizations.

a social enterprise based in Los Angeles, California. In 2011, OPTA launched the Savings Path database system, which is designed to support large volumes of transactions and allows customization of savings plans based on different program parameters.

Since 2009, more than 1,000 individuals have opened accounts through one of several nonprofit organizations partnering with OPTA across Los Angeles and Orange County, California. OPTA supports participating organizations by setting up the program and designing savings plans based on the specific needs of the target population (North 2012). OPTA also provides back-office data management and centralizes data collection and reporting. The organizations enroll participants by referring them to their partnering financial institutions. A selection of demographic and financial information regarding the program is provided in tables 10.3 and 10.4.

The numbers reported in the first section of table 10.4 are based on information available on December 31, 2012. Customization of the programs resulted in the creation of 33 different SAA plans. These programs differ in terms of deposit amounts, duration, and total incentives. Therefore, the average amounts reported should be interpreted with caution. For example, the average incentive amount per dollar saved is $0.21 across all programs. However, this amount is lower for tax-time savings programs that feature high introductory deposits (for which the average

Table 10.4 Selected Program Financial Information

Participation and savings by time period	Program metrics
Program years 2009–2012	
Total number of accounts (2009–2012)	1,028 (399 during 2009–2010)
Total amount deposited (own deposits)	$729,568
Average account balance	$709
Total incentive payments	$156,217
Average incentive per dollar saved	$0.21
Program YEARS 2009–2010	
Average deposit activity rate (per month)	79%
Average deposit amount (per month)	$34
Completion rate (graduating accounts)	73%
Percentage of accounts never funded	15%
Premature termination (funded accounts)	12%

Source: Data compiled by Opportunity to Assets using information from its Savings Path database, which tracks deposit amounts and incentive payments by partner organizations.

incentive per dollar saved is around $0.19) and higher for youth savings models.

One significant result of the program is the high rate of deposit activity across these accounts. As is seen in table 10.4, during 2009–2010, on average, 79 percent of all open accounts posted a deposit each month throughout the entire program.[2] This number is significantly higher than that reported for IDA programs; for example, Boshara (2005) reports a 50 percent deposit rate for the IDA program he studied. While these results have not been subjected to independent statistical evaluation in an experimental setting, they seem to corroborate the idea that the incentive mechanisms provided by SAAs can potentially influence the savings behavior of accountholders.

Financial Incentives and Savings Accelerator Accounts

Are SAAs scalable? The answer to this question depends partly on our understanding of the concept of scale as well as the costs related to offering incentives in savings programs. The reasons for having a robust dialogue around incentives are manifold. Most importantly, on an operational level, the inclusion of incentives in savings programs has major implications for the cost and scalability of low-income savings programs. The direct cost of offering incentives as well as the indirect costs associated with administering programs, including determining participant eligibility, tracking participation, keeping records, and meeting other program management requirements, makes savings programs that offer incentives very resource intensive.

Some of the most prominent examples of savings initiatives that do not involve direct payments of incentives to savers include local Bank On campaigns and the FDIC's Model Safe Accounts pilot project.[3] These initiatives have been launched in various parts of the country with the goal of increasing access to safe, low-cost transactional and savings products for LMI households. The programs, which are generally offered in close collaboration with local financial institutions, financial regulators, and community advocacy groups, are based on customization and marketing of bank products to appeal to LMI households. It should be noted that incentives are still present in a significant way, in the discounted pricing of the financial products offered. But while the implementation of these programs also requires financial resources, they appear to be more cost-effective compared to programs involving direct match payments, largely because the costs related to discounted pricing of financial products is absorbed, at least initially, by the participating financial institutions, who can internalize these costs by distributing them across their large consumer base and expansive product lists.

The conversation regarding incentives should distinguish between these two types of cases, which can be characterized as demand-side versus supply-side incentive models. A demand-side incentive includes any kind of payment that directly supplements amounts saved by an individual; a supply-side incentive takes the form of reduced costs or price discounts on financial products and transactions. In theory, both demand- and supply-side incentives can yield higher utilization rates for bank accounts and increases in savings; however, supply-side incentives may be more cost effective and may scale more easily. Moreover, demand-side incentives are not only costlier, but may not even be sufficient on their own; supply-side incentives may be required in addition to facilitate access to safe and affordable bank accounts. It is partly for this reason that supply-side initiatives have gained popularity among both practitioners and policymakers.

However, supply-side incentives are necessary to spur emergency savings, but not sufficient. They are necessary because they offer access to safe and affordable bank accounts, which is a prerequisite to the accumulation of savings. But if the demand for emergency savings is inelastic (i.e., unresponsive to changes in the price of financial products and services), then supply-side incentives will generally not result in any significant increase in emergency savings. Of course, without a formal analysis, it is impossible to judge with any degree of certainty whether the demand for emergency savings is in fact inelastic. However, data from surveys of those who are unbanked indicate that a significant portion (around 20 percent) of low-income individuals and households that have bank accounts still utilize alternative financial services (AFS), such as check-cashing outlets, conducting financial transactions through these establishments at a higher cost than traditional banks would incur. For example, Khashadourian and Syldy (2007) offer a synopsis of findings from two studies conducted in the Los Angeles area regarding the utilization of check-cashing outlets by people who have bank accounts; more recent results are provided in the FDIC's 2011 National Survey of Unbanked and Underbanked Households (Burhouse and Osaki 2012). This apparent insensitivity to transaction costs implies that the demand for emergency savings may be close to perfectly inelastic with respect to the cost of transactions.

Still, while supply-side incentives alone may not be effective in stimulating savings, this does not automatically imply that demand-side incentives alone will do the trick. There is however, some evidence to support the hypothesis that demand-side financial incentives are generally associated with increased savings. In a famous large-scale, randomized study, Duflo and colleagues (2005) evaluate the response rates and contribution levels of individuals in H&R Block's Express IRA program at selected H&R Block tax preparation locations. Individuals were randomly assigned to the control group (with no match on their Express IRA contributions) or to one of two experiment groups, one with a 20 percent match and one with a 50 percent match for Express IRA contributions of up to $1,000. The study concludes that matching had a significant effect on contributions. While the average contribution in the control group was reported at $765, that number increased to over $1,100 in the groups with matches.

Beverly and colleagues (2008) provide additional support, mainly from the literature on IDAs, to explain the effect of demand-side incentives on savings contributions. However, they also caution that the evidence supporting the role of such incentives is mixed. Individuals who have fixed savings goals may, in the presence of financial incentives, reduce their own savings and rely on the match to achieve their goals; this is called an income effect. Individuals may also reallocate assets from categories that have no or low incentives into ones that have higher incentives, resulting in zero net impact on savings. Finally, the introduction of incentives may create income and substitution effects that can work in opposite directions, canceling the effect of incentives on net savings. For instance, a financial incentive on savings will lower the relative price of future to present consumption, potentially prompting the consumer to substitute future consumption for current consumption (by saving more). At the same time, the income effect could lead consumers to reduce net savings.

These arguments make a logical case for questioning the effectiveness of demand-side incentives; however, they may not be applicable to emergency savings of low-income households for a number of reasons. First, it is not clear that low-income households have fixed savings goals. In fact, according to ITS, savings programs can set participant expectations regarding how much to save and since incentives are typically conditioned upon contributions, the likelihood of a financial incentive diminishing savings is rather slim. Second, assuming that current and future consumption (saving) are normal goods, the theoretical argument regarding income and substitution effects holds true only for households with net positive assets who may reshuffle their portfolios in order to contribute to a matched savings program without increasing net savings. Yet, in the case of low-income savings and asset-poor households, the likelihood of such canceling effects is questionable at best, in part because low-income households often face a higher degree of future income vulnerability, which according to Muellbauer (1996) will generally prompt individuals to shift income away from the present to the uncertain future, and in part because many low-income households have very low (if not negative) net asset values—they cannot reshuffle assets they do not have.

Of course, some type of reshuffling could happen even if net asset values are negative, for instance, through borrowing money and saving a part of it (Lusardi, Schneider, and Tufano 2011). But even in this context, financial incentives may still play a significant role in stimulating low-income savings. For example, Schreiner, Graham, and Miranda (1998) show that when the spread between borrowing rates and return on savings narrows, low-income households are more likely to both borrow and increase savings at the same time (although, they also point out, in some cases the optimal choice is neither to borrow nor to save). This finding, while not supported through additional research, is important on its own merit, as it suggests that narrowing the spread between saving and borrowing rates (e.g., by offering higher rates of return on savings through program incentives such as those incorporated in the SAA model) may prompt low-income households to start saving at lower levels of wealth and accelerate their rate of saving as their asset levels increase.

Notwithstanding this possibility, demand-side incentives are still necessary for the indirect role they play in increasing low-income savings. Beverly and colleagues (2008) explain the role of incentives in increasing participation rates in matched savings programs, suggesting that they function as a defense against the status quo bias. Increasing participation and adoption rates are also a key highlight in the study by Duflo and colleagues (2005); the authors indicate a significant difference in participation rates with incentives: 3 percent participation among the control group versus 8 percent for the group offered a 20 percent match and 14 percent for those offered a 50 percent match.

The effectiveness of demand-side incentives could be explained from a behavioral perspective as the harnessing of group dynamics to influence the behavior of individuals. The choice, timing, and payment of demand-side incentives could provide potent mechanisms to promote savings, for example, by adding an element of novelty or creating a sense of competition among participants in a matched savings program. Such design elements can influence behavior in the desired direction regardless of the amount of the incentives offered. From this perspective, the more important question is not whether incentives matter, but rather how incentives should be structured to generate the best results.

Policy Implications of SAAs

The emergency savings model offered by the SAA model is currently implemented within the same regulatory environment as other matched savings programs. SAA utilizes account structures that are almost identical to traditional matched savings programs such as the IDA. And SAA faces some of the same challenges as other savings programs in offering meaningful savings opportunities to low-income households. For example, existing asset and property limits in public benefit programs remain a big factor in limiting program participation rates. Although in most cases, the amount of savings including incentive payments remains well below $1,000 or $1,500, an amount usually well within the asset thresholds for most public benefit programs, the perception that savings may affect public benefits creates challenges in recruiting participants.

The tax consequences of SAA incentive payments also present challenges. These payments are typically small, ranging from $150 to $250 per account, and so should incur no significant income tax consequences. Any tax impact is further mitigated by the fact that most programs offer incentives periodically across the course of the program. As a result, depending on when an account is enrolled, the total incentive payments are typically split across two calendar years. Furthermore, in most cases, the payments are treated as gifts, which come with no tax consequences for the saver. Still, policy interventions to formalize any tax consequences of incentive payments in this and other programs could help address cognitive barriers for potential participants.

Financial institutions could also play a significant role in streamlining the process and supporting incentivized savings programs. Existing partnerships through projects such as the Bank On initiative are extremely valuable, but anecdotal evidence suggests that these campaigns place a high emphasis on transactional products such as checking accounts. Investment in resources to create low-fee or no-fee accounts should also include products designed for matched savings programs, offering flexibility in setting up the accounts, online access, and reporting capabilities. Several currently available account platforms, such as reloadable debit cards, offer the kind of functionalities that could help facilitate the management of incentivized savings programs, but many financial institutions are reluctant to offer these products to community-based organizations on a low- or no-fee basis, due to costs or other considerations. These platforms could present an opportunity for financial regulators to play a more active role in guiding financial institutions to more effectively support matched savings programs.

Conclusion

The main theme of this chapter is to highlight the importance of saving as a sound financial habit for LMI households. While most of the literature on building wealth for the poor has focused on the transformational power of accumulating assets, reference is typically made to long-term assets, such as human capital, or tangible assets. But changes in the economy in the aftermath of the Great Recession underline the need for closer attention to the role of asset allocation decisions through which households balance liquid and illiquid assets.

Justification for increasing savings does not necessarily stem only from the need to prepare for financial emergencies. Building and maintaining liquid assets can also offer speculative benefits to households and make it possible for them to take advantage of opportunities as they arise. America is not a nation of savers, however, so interventions such as programs to help increase savings are necessary to effect change. But identifying a model or a collection of models that can effectively address this problem is not easy. Considerations regarding cost, effectiveness, and scalability of models are important elements in the discussion around low-income savings.

This chapter introduces the concept of SAAs. In line with its overall philosophy of achieving long-term outcomes through a sequence of short-term actions, an SAA program provides small monetary rewards for behavior consistent with long-term savings outcomes. In this model, a sequence of small decisions made independently of each other results in the accumulation of liquid assets over the long term. SAA programs achieve this goal by focusing on how and when incentives are offered to savers. By applying lessons from behavioral economics instead of focusing on dollar amounts, SAA deploys incentives as a combination of independent mechanisms that are embedded in a savings program to influence behavior in both the short and long term.

Further development of the SAA platform can be informed by a comprehensive evaluation of the different components embedded in it. Statistical models can be developed to evaluate the relative importance and effectiveness of the multicomponent incentive mechanism. Multivariate techniques can be employed to determine the simultaneous impact of each incentive component, on deposit frequency and on amounts saved. These evaluations can help fine-tune the model, for example, by identifying the minimum rate of fractional match (or interest) needed to create a meaningful acceleration of savings. Such an analysis can also help determine the most effective combination of available incentive mechanisms, some of which have not been introduced in this chapter.

The SAA concept is an interesting idea to explore further, but it is only one among several alternative approaches that could increase low-income emergency savings. Therefore, a full-fledged experimental study of SAA programs should be pursued. SAA can be tested against other incentivized savings models to determine the advantages and limitations of each in stimulating low-income emergency savings. A comparative analysis could test the effect of time restrictions or the significance of backending the savings match as compared to the gradual distribution of benefits offered by the SAA platform. The results of such a study could pave the way for communities to raise funds and engage financial partners more effectively, justify future investments in program delivery options, and catalyze the development of technological tools to reduce the administrative costs of such programs.

Notes

1. In speaking of incentives, Beverly et al. (2008), make a distinction between subsidies and rates of return. However, this distinction does not make a practical difference in terms of our present analysis. Therefore, in this chapter, incentives will be defined as any kind of financial reward offered to low-income participants in a savings program.
2. Data regarding deposit activity in the program is available upon request.
3. For more information regarding Bank On and Model Safe Accounts, see http://joinbankon.org/ and http://www.fdic.gov/consumers/template/. It is important to note that these initiatives are not particularly focused on savings accounts, although most try to incorporate options to facilitate savings for low-income customers.

References

Bertrand, Marianne, Sendhil Mullainathan, and Eldar Shafir. 2006. "Behavioral Economics and Marketing in Aid of Decision Making Among the Poor." *Journal of Public Policy & Marketing* 25 (1): 8–23.

Beverly, Sondra, and Michael Sherraden. 1999. "Institutional Determinants of Saving: Implications for Low-Income Households and Public Policy." *The Journal of Socio-Economics* 28 (4): 457–473.

Beverly, Sondra, Michael Sherraden, Reid Cramer, Trina R. Williams Shanks, Yunju Nam, and Min Zhan. 2008. "Determinants of Asset Holdings." In *Asset Building and Low-Income Families*, ed. Signe-Mary McKernan and Michael Sherraden, 89–151. Washington, DC: The Urban Institute Press.

Boshara, Ray. 2005. "Individual Development Accounts: Policies to Build Savings and Assets for the Poor." Welfare Reform and Beyond Policy Brief 32, The Brookings Institution, Washington, DC.

———. 2010. "Seven Surprising Findings from the Asset Building Field." *Bridges*, Winter. Federal Reserve Bank of St. Louis, https://www.stlouisfed.org/publications/br/articles/?id=2058.

Brooks, David. 2011. *The Social Animal: The Hidden Sources of Love, Character, and Achievement*. New York: Random House.

Burhouse, Susan, and Yazmin Osaki. 2012. "2011 FDIC National Survey of Unbanked and Underbanked Households." FDIC. September, Washington, DC.

Camerer, Colin, Samuel Issacharoff, George Loewenstein, Ted O'Donoghue, and Matthew Rabin. 2003. "Regulation for Conservatives: Behavioral Economics and the Case for 'Asymmetric Paternalism.'" *University of Pennsylvania Law Review* 151 (3): 1211–1254.

Carvalho, Leandro. 2010. "Poverty and Time Preference." RAND Working Paper WR-759. Rand Corporation, Santa Monica, CA.

Center for Economic Progress. 2010. "Universal Savings for American Workers." Policy Paper. National Community Tax Coalition, Center for Economic Progress, Chicago, IL.

Cramer, Reid. 2010. "Homeownership and Individual Development Accounts: An Assessment of Recent Research." Asset-Building Program, May. New America Foundation, Washington, DC.

Duflo, Esther, William Gale, Jeffrey Liebman, Peter Orszag, and Emmanuel Saez. 2005. "Saving Incentives for Low- and Middle-Income Families: Evidence from a Field Experiment with H&R Block." National Bureau of Economic Research Working Paper Series, No. 11680.

Dynan, Karen. 2012. "Higher Savings: Who Needs It?" Opinion. *Brookings*, October 1, http://www.brookings.edu/research/opinions/2012/10/01-personal-saving-dynan.

Frederick, Shane, George Loewenstein, and Ted O'Donoghue. 2002. "Time Discounting and Time Preference: A Critical Review." *Journal of Economic Literature* 40 (2): 351–401.

Johnson, Suzanne N., Lisa Mensah, and C. Eugene Steuerle. 2006. "Savings in America: Building Opportunities for All." Spring. Global Markets Institute at Goldman Sachs and the Initiative on Financial Security.

Khashadourian, Ed. 2009. "Decision Risks and Individual Development Accounts: An Alternative View." *Journal of Income Distribution* 18 (2): 142–159.

Khashadourian, Ed, and Syldy Tom. 2007. "The Unbanked Problem in Los Angeles." Working Paper, October. United Way of Greater Los Angeles.

Lawrance, Emily C. 1991. "Poverty and the Rate of Time Preference: Evidence from Panel Data." *Journal of Political Economy* 99 (1): 54–77.

Lusardi, Annamaria, Daniel J. Schneider, and Peter Tufano. 2011. "Financially Fragile Households: Evidence and Implications." National Bureau of Economic Research Working Paper Series, No. 17072.

Muellbauer, John. 1996. "Consumer Expenditure." In *Readings in Macroeconomics*, ed. Tim Jenkinson, 92–125. Oxford, UK: Oxford University Press.

Mullainathan, Sendhil, and Eldar Shafir. 2008. "Savings Policy and Decision-Making in Low-Income Households." In *Insufficient Funds: Savings, Assets, Credit, and Banking among Low-Income Households*, ed. Rebecca M. Blank and Michael S. Barr, 121–145. New York: Russell Sage Foundation.

North, G. 2012. "Learning to Save: Tailoring Matched Savings Accounts to Meet the Savings Needs of Low Income Earners in Los Angeles." Master's thesis, Heller School for Social Policy and Management, Brandeis University.

Pennings, Joost M. E., and Philip Garcia. 2005. "The Poverty Challenge: How Individual Decision-Making Behavior Influences Poverty." *Economics Letters* 88 (1): 115–119.

Pronin, Emily, and Matthew B. Kugler. 2007. "Valuing Thoughts, Ignoring Behavior: The Introspection Illusion as a Source of the Bias Blind Spot." *Journal of Experimental Social Psychology* 43 (4): 565–578.

Read, Daniel. 2001. "Is Time-Discounting Hyperbolic or Subadditive?" *Journal of Risk and Uncertainty* 23 (1): 5–32.

Schreiner, Mark, Douglas H. Graham, and Mario Miranda. 1998. "Choices by Poor Households When the Interest Rate for Deposits Differs from the Interest Rate for Loans." Working Paper, April. Microfinance Risk Management and Center for Social Development, Washington University in St. Louis.

Taylor, Paul, Cary Funk, and April Clark. 2010. "We Try Hard. We Fall Short. Americans Assess Their Saving Habit." Social Trends Report. PEW Research Center, Washington, DC.

Thaler, Richard H., Cass R. Sunstein, and John P. Balz. 2010. "Choice Architecture." April 2. http://papers.ssrn.com/sol3/papers.cfm?abstract_id=1583509.

Chapter 11

Start2Save: Helping Working Families Meet Unexpected Expenses and Opportunities

Ingrid Holguin

Introduction

The case for asset building as an approach to poverty alleviation dates back more than 20 years, to Michael Sherraden's *Assets and the Poor* (1991). As CFED (2013) and numerous others have recognized, *Assets and the Poor* demanded a sharper focus on the causes of poverty, as well as potential strategies to alleviate it, and made the case for the importance of household assets, including savings, in the achievement of financial stability and economic progress. Emergency savings are just one component of the asset base needed to support financial stability, but they can serve as the foundation for further asset building. Start2Save, a matched emergency savings program, is designed to help families develop this important foundation.[1] The program has the potential to provide low-income families with an opportunity to gain financial preparedness skills while building and maintaining emergency savings, empowering them to create their own safety net.

Start2Save has at its core the vision to help low-income, low-asset households save for short-term emergencies and develop long-term asset-building habits. It incorporates many features that have been found in other savings programs, such as Opportunity Fund's Individual Development Accounts (IDAs), to contribute to participant success, including a defined savings goal, saving reminders, a savings match, and financial education and case management services. Start2Save also introduces some innovative elements, including a lower savings goal with a resulting lower match, a consumer savings account that clients can keep after graduation, savings reminders sent via text message, and the ability to use match funds to open a secured credit card at graduation from the program. The most important innovation is that where IDAs typically require participants to invest in a long-term asset, the Start2Save account—with the saver's deposits and the match earned at graduation—is the asset, providing participants with a source of liquid funds to ease the task of managing through financial emergencies.

Start2Save, which was developed by Opportunity Fund in collaboration with Citibank, has been piloted in collaboration with a range of community-based agencies that serve the low-income/low-asset population. As a pilot, the program is subject to ongoing monitoring and evaluation activities designed to address two key questions: How essential are emergency savings in creating financial stability, perceptions of self-efficacy, and a positive and proactive future orientation? And, can emergency savings balances remain accessible for short-term emergency needs while being managed and leveraged to build a foundation for long-term asset building? Based on lessons learned from each evaluation cycle, the program continues to evolve, with the goal to increase both its scalability and its effectiveness in helping low-income families build and maintain critical liquid assets.

Emergency Savings: The Missing Prequel to Long-Term Savings

Nearly half of US households (44 percent) are considered liquid-asset poor, meaning they do not have sufficient financial resources to manage through an emergency, and one quarter of all households are net-worth-asset poor, meaning debts outweigh household assets; 31 percent do not have a savings account (Brooks and Wiedrich 2013). For these households, short-term financial needs and uncertainties around income flows often take precedence over longer-term asset-building goals.

Short-term savings are a critical first step toward long-term asset building, but getting started on the path to saving is a challenge for this population. One of the main reasons these populations do not engage in long-term asset building is their lack of short-term savings and the difficulty they encounter in accessing liquidity in cases of emergency. Of the 65 percent of attendees at Start2Save information sessions who don't enroll in the program, many feel they simply cannot support the additional monthly cash outflow represented by the program's $20 per month minimum deposit. Initial findings from the Kansas University evaluation that followed the pilot's first 95 participants show that at enrollment, 70 percent of participants reported that almost all of their money goes to necessities. Slightly more than half felt that, on their own, they could save a little money, but not enough to make a difference (Adams and West 2013).

Saving up enough to build a relevant emergency savings balance is even more challenging, as it requires a routine, monthly commitment to put aside present income for future expenses. This commitment frequently must overcome much more than simply stretched finances. Many households and communities place a relatively low value on saving, and pressure from family or friends to help them meet financial needs, lack of encouragement from financial service providers to save (as opposed to borrow), and lack of understanding of the tools for budgeting and saving over time are all obstacles to saving (Brobeck 1999). Once a significant savings balance has been achieved, making sound financial decisions about whether to access the savings may present further difficulties, requiring the saver to consider the nature of the emergency—is it perceived or real?—the extent of the need—is it long or short term?—the possibility of other strategies to cover the expense, and the source of funds to replenish the balance once it is drawn down.

The commitment to save must be made in the context of household finances and the messy process of day-to-day financial management. Income flows in and expenses are paid out; debt is assumed and paid down; savings are deposited and withdrawn. Some degree of money management is needed to turn funds withheld from the monthly cash flow into usefully large lump sums. This can be accomplished with debt: cash received in hand today to be repaid in the future. It can also be accomplished via saving: small chunks of cash set aside from present income over time to cover future expenses or investments. Most households manage their money by balancing both debt and savings (Rutherford 2000).

Like debt, savings can be viewed as long or short term, depending on their purpose and characteristics. How savings are characterized depends on the flexibility of the timeframe within which funds should be available and the degree of liquidity and accessibility required. Emergency savings are short term because they are designed to cover immediate and unexpected gaps in household cash flows. The timing of needs is variable and difficult to predict, and balances need to be liquid and readily accessible. Long-term savings such as IDAs and retirement accounts, on the other hand, are designed for a specific purpose and come with rigid timeframes and restricted accessibility and liquidity (Davis et al. 2012).

Thus, strategies to build emergency savings must be concerned with both access and permanence. In other words, access to liquidity for contingencies is about two things: cash balances and cash flows. Savings balances ebb and flow as they are built up with deposits and then depleted to cover liquidity needs. To be effective as a long-term, sustainable source of liquidity in times of need, emergency savings must exhibit three characteristics: balances should be of sufficient size to be relevant in an emergency, the financial instrument should include mechanisms that help manage money, and emergency savings should be a key cornerstone in the foundation upon which household net worth is built.

To provide households with the opportunity to build savings and the tools to maintain them, a program must do more than simply provide financial support for saving. It must also take into account both this daily messiness and the other factors that affect the ability to save, engaging a diverse set of strategies to ensure that the message and its timing resonate with individual experiences and aspirations related to saving. One component of this effort should be financial education and coaching efforts to shape the behavioral aspects of saving and help savers build long-term savings habits. Financial education and coaching can help participants make more informed choices about their finances and lead to positive outcomes, including improved savings outcomes (Davis et al. 2012).

As a learning innovation, Start2Save seeks to address these gaps and make emergency savings an essential piece of the asset-building spectrum, by helping low-income households build an emergency savings account that can be at once an asset and a source of liquidity in times of need.

Start2Save: Short-Term Liquidity and Long-Term Asset Building

The Start2Save program builds on Opportunity Fund's IDA program, which has enrolled more than 4,000 participants over 12 years. IDAs are restricted-access matched savings accounts set up as trusts for the sole purpose of paying qualified expenses (US Congress 1998, Sec. 404 (5) (A)); the timeframes for saving, spending down balances, and closing the account are fixed. IDAs have been shown to help the poor save toward long-term goals (Schreiner, Clancy, and Sherraden 2002); they are designed in a way that likely supports the formation of savings habits (Loibl, Kraybill, and DeMay 2011). However, while the IDA program has proven successful in many respects, the experience has shown that many low-income households are not prepared to save toward the long-term goals—homeownership, small business development, or college education—that are usually the focus of an IDA.

Opportunity Fund developed Start2Save to reach these more vulnerable households, helping them both to build liquidity to fund emergency needs and to establish long-term savings habits that can lead to the accumulation of additional assets. It accomplishes these dual goals by helping participants create a liquid account that they can access anytime, but deferring match rewards until the end of the program. The Start2Save account meets the criteria for a short-term savings instrument for emergencies: access is driven by the saver, and balances are readily available and can be withdrawn as needed. However, participants only have access to their own funds until they complete the program; the match is only added to their savings and made accessible when the participant reaches the savings goal, creating an incentive to continue building savings at least over the period of the program.

The Start2Save account looks somewhat like an IDA, in that it offers a defined savings plan with a match incentive, but it is very different. Unlike IDAs, Start2Save graduates keep their savings and match in liquid form in an unrestricted, commercial interest-bearing savings account that comes with an ATM card. The program combines the account and matching funds incentive with financial education, behaviorally informed nudges, and "soft" debiasing mechanisms to help participants build savings balances and healthy financial habits.

The matching fund is itself a powerful tool to keep participants focused on their savings goals. Other mechanisms designed to keep participants on track include the option to sign up for automatic monthly deposits and a requirement that savers call the program to initiate an emergency withdrawal. Emergency withdrawal request calls build in a pause to rethink the expenditure, discuss and assess the alternatives, and consider strategies for rebuilding balances. They are also opportunities for participants to receive financial coaching and information about alternative resources.

Missed deposit follow-up reminders, now supplemented with proactive text-based deposit reminders (for those who opt in to this service), also help participants make better decisions and build successful financial habits. An unauthorized withdrawal request or two missed deposits are indicators of financial stress that activate case management and financial coaching services. Not correcting these behaviors can result in termination from the program. Program attrition from both drop outs and terminations remains low, around 20 percent, on par with Opportunity Fund's IDA saver attrition rate.

Participants can also engage with the educational elements of the program in a classroom environment (a function outsourced to community partners who offer financial education as part of their service offerings) or online (as a free service offered by the FDIC). Through the program's online portal, savers can monitor their savings and accrued match. Progress toward the savings goal and earned match is further reinforced through paper statements sent quarterly. Proactive, text-based deposit reminders were recently added to supplement emailed deposit reminders sent after a deposit is missed.

The savings goal for participants is $500 over a one- to two-year period, with monthly deposits between $20 and $40. Each deposit earns a 2:1 match, which is transferred into the saver's account once the savings goal is met, after at least 12 monthly deposits. On average, Start2Save participants reach the goal and graduate in 15 months with a savings account balance of $1,500 ($500 in monthly deposits plus the match). This amount is just over the average participant's monthly household income. When added to the average savings balances at enrollment, it puts graduates at the halfway point on the journey out of liquid poverty, defined as having sufficient savings to cover basic expenses for three months (Brooks and Wiedrich 2013). (For this population, whose incomes barely meet basic household expenses, household income and expense are essentially synonymous.) In addition, this amount is sufficiently low so as not to interfere with eligibility for public programs that maintain asset or savings limits as part of their eligibility requirements.

In its final development stage, launched recently, Start2Save graduates have been offered the option to deposit a portion of their savings ($200–$600) as collateral for a secured credit card. In the first group of participants offered the credit card option, 15 percent opted in; of these, 80 percent have activated their cards and 100 percent of those are paying on time. Graduates also have access to continued automatic deposits to the savings account and email and text deposit reminders.

Opportunity Fund administers the Start2Save program in collaboration with a range of partners. Citibank provides the savings accounts, which are designed to channel savers into Citi's microfinance savings platform. As the program administrator, Opportunity Fund has online access to clients' account data to monitor activity and provide data for management and evaluation functions. The Kansas University School of Social Welfare evaluates program effectiveness and impact to supplement Opportunity Fund's an annual internal assessment; these activities serve as the basis for continued learning and innovation as the program scales up.

Most importantly, Opportunity Fund partners with community-based agencies serving the target populations to offer the accounts. Partners are typically one of three types: social services agencies, transitional or low-income housing organizations, and community-based financial education and tax preparation providers. The program is intended to enable these organizations to provide a low-cost, high-impact savings and asset-building program alongside other services. At the client level, Start2Save's goal is to empower participants with an increased sense of self-efficacy and provide the tools to build, access, and maintain a rainy-day fund.

Reaching Potential Savers Where They Are

The goal of Start2Save is to reach populations that are more economically vulnerable than those served by the IDA program. The data collected thus far show that the program has been successful in reaching this population, as figure 11.1 demonstrates. Figure 11.1 compares average net household assets, household monthly income, and combined checking and savings balances at enrollment for Start2Save and traditional IDA participants who started their respective programs at Opportunity Fund in March 2012. Figure 11.1 also displays average ending account balances for these two groups, again over the same time period (March 2012 through February 2013). Not shown in the figure, monthly deposits over the one-year timeframe averaged $37 for Start2Save and $101 for IDA participants.

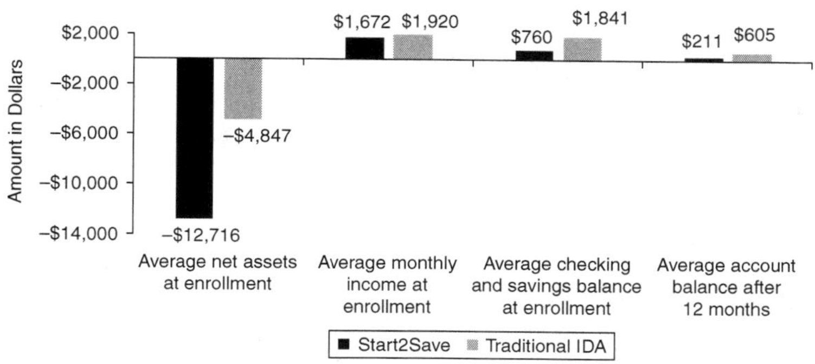

Figure 11.1 Financial Indicators for Start2Save and Traditional IDA Participants at Opportunity Fund: March 2012–February 2013 Cohort.

Source: Opportunity Fund data on Start2Save and Traditional IDA participants collected from their applications.

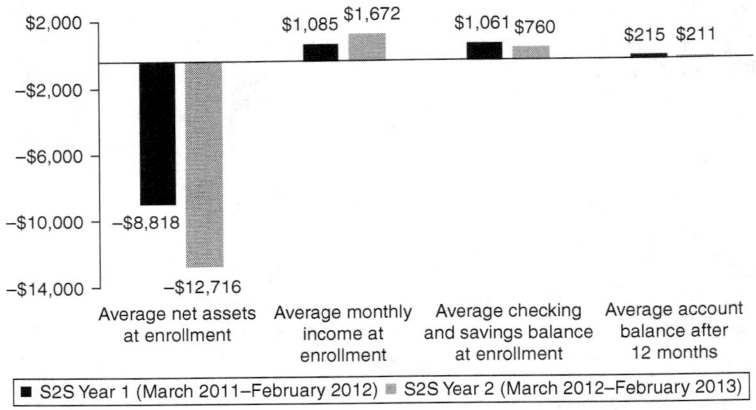

Figure 11.2 Financial Indicators for Start2Save Year 1 and Year 2 Cohorts.

Source: Opportunity Fund data on Start2Save participants collected from their applications.

All of these averages are significantly lower across the board for Start2Save participants, reflecting this population's increased financial vulnerability.

Figure 11.2 compares the same figures for Start2Save's Year 1 and Year 2 cohorts. What is striking about the two cohorts taken together is that while household income was higher in Year 2, household net worth was not. Not shown in the figure, monthly deposits were essentially the same for the two cohorts, averaging $35 in the first year and $37 in the second. These data again demonstrate that Start2Save is effectively reaching low-income, low-net-asset households. The average Start2Save household consists of 1.5 members; 60 percent of median monthly household income for families of 1.5 members in Santa Clara County, California, where Start2Save has most of its participants, averages just under $4,000.

While attrition is low, about 20 percent, savers can, and do, miss deposits: savers who successfully complete the program miss, on average, 3 out of 10 deposits; those who drop out or are terminated miss 6 out of 11. Of active savers, 25 percent call to request an authorized emergency withdrawal at least once. Less than 20 percent of participants have signed up for automatic deposits, far short of the goal of 60 percent. This low rate reflects the realities faced by this more vulnerable population, which must cope with more uncertainty in household income flows, lack of access to bank accounts, low bank balances that can approach zero when household expenses are paid, and discomfort with electronic banking technologies.

Only 35 percent of those who attend a Start2Save information session enroll in the program. Some of the others are not eligible, but a host of issues, financial, behavioral, and emotional, affect the decision to enroll. Becoming a saver from not saving at all takes a leap of faith. What is Opportunity Fund? Why is it doing Start2Save? Where does the money for the match come from? Can savings be accessed while I'm in the program? What if I can't save? How can I sustain an additional drain on monthly income when I'm barely covering expenses? Facing these very valid questions, Start2Save outreach and messaging has had to evolve to reach potential savers where they are.

For example, one of the program's most successful outreach efforts has been a campaign that positions emergency savings as a way to avoid predatory lending products, such as payday loans. The idea of becoming one's own lender in times of economic distress resonates with individuals who have experienced the economic impacts of high-cost predatory loans.

Reaching the target population at tax time has also proved very effective. Over a five-week period, in collaboration with SaveUSA (a national replication of New York City's $aveNYC tax-time matched-savings program), Start2Save was promoted at a Volunteer Income Tax Assistance (VITA) site; those seeking tax assistance were offered onsite account opening and direct deposit for up to $200 in tax refunds. The VITA site strategy gave Start2Save its most successful outreach effort: 14 percent of VITA participants served during the promotion became Start2Save clients. The strategy has since been replicated at five partner sites, where it has generated an uptake rate of 16 percent.

Melissa's Story: Navigating the Transition from Short-Term Savings to Long-Term Asset Building

Melissa's story illustrates both the strengths of Start2Save, and its remaining gaps. Melissa was among the first Start2Save program participants and one of four subjects who participated in the Start2Save Video Diaries project, for which she was interviewed periodically over the course of her participation in the program. Her journey, documented in excerpts from the interview footage, demonstrate the evolving but constant mental financial management triggered by the development of a saving habit. At the beginning of her enrollment in the program, Melissa was anxious about the demands of saving but aware of the role that developing emergency savings could play in her long-term goals. She says,

> I am trying to go forward in my life and become a cosmetologist, work in a salon and take care of my daughter. I'm nervous about saving over that [two-year] period of time. I need to save money if my car breaks down, or I can't get to school or rent gets raised that 8 percent, [like] it can do every year. I wouldn't know where that money would come from.

Midway through the program, she found herself developing new confidence in her ability to manage her finances and accommodate emergencies.

> I'm making that deposit every month. I know I'm in control because I have it written down: what's coming in, what's going out, what I have to pay every month, and how much I have to spend and play with. I've never had money left over for emergencies. So it's kind of exciting and good. I like that feeling of stability in my life.

As she neared graduation, Melissa reported feeling empowered by her savings account and excited to have a sense of flexibility in her finances.

> I definitely can't wait to get that money back. I decided not to touch it because I want that money there and I want to do something important with it. I feel really good that I'm saving and that I have something to put toward a new car. When I look back at this year, I wonder how I made it through and I'm just so happy that I have money left over. I've been responsible for that money and I know that if something does happen that my daughter and I will have some money.

Unfortunately, Melissa has not sustained the gains she made in the program. Although she reached her savings goal, she has not continued to make regular deposits and subsequent withdrawals without corresponding efforts to replenish the account have left her with a savings balance too low to provide the security she had so valued. As a result, the sense of control she had gained has unwound.

From the point of view of emergency savings intended for consumption in the short term, Melissa's Start2Save story is one of resounding success. When viewed through the asset-building lens, however, it is clear that there is more work to be done. Why? Ongoing evaluation work will be asking graduates this question. It is not necessary, however, to wait for these results to pursue ways to prevent this outcome. In order to enhance household net worth over time, emergency savings balances should, on average, demonstrate permanence without relinquishing the essential features of flexibility in the purpose, timeframe, and liquidity of the funds. The benchmark for effective graduate strategies would be that balances depleted to cover emergency expenditures would be replenished over time such that, at a minimum, average balances would hover at 1.5 times household income. A stretch goal would be to grow average balances to 3 times the household's basic monthly expenses.

A number of actions are being taken to help sustain these outcomes. One is to extend the "nudge" features of the program—automatic deposit, proactive text-message reminders, electronic missed-deposit notifications, and deposit reminders—beyond the participant's graduation. Monthly statements and online banking tools from Citibank should also help some graduates continue their savings habits.

The newly introduced secured credit card can enhance long-term asset building through three mechanisms. First, it builds a firewall between the easily accessible funds that are pledged as security for the credit card and slightly less accessible savings balances, which must be withdrawn in cash via an ATM card or bank visit. Second, the credit card builds in behaviorally informed nudges to replenish savings balances via the monthly bill and built-in incentives to pay on time in the form of interest charges and penalties on unpaid balances. Third, the secured credit card limits the savings that can be accessed to the amount of savings pledged.

This hybrid saving-and-credit approach also offers graduates the opportunity to build credit, giving them access to the other critical tool of asset building, debt. Forty percent of Start2Savers have no credit score and another 22 percent have poor credit scores. Credit is a critical component for long-term asset building; using a debt mechanism to access and replenish emergency savings securitizes a portion of the emergency savings. Diversifying the savings asset into two pots, one secured and one unsecured, creates a sound, flexible money management tool.

Cost and Sustainability: Scaling Up Start2Save

Mobilizing savings is an expensive proposition, and Start2Save, still in its pilot phase, with its iterative cycles of doing-learning-innovating, cannot yet offer a scalable program model, although it is clear there is demand for the program: enrollments increased by 50 percent from the first year of the pilot to the second and could very well increase nearly that much again in the third year.

Early evaluation results and Opportunity Fund's experience with the IDA program do suggest some ways in which the program might be made scalable. Start2Save compares favorably with IDA even in its current form. The largest expense of any matched savings program is the match. Start2Save cuts matching costs by 75 percent over IDA by limiting the size of the account. A traditional college or small business IDA has the same 2:1 match as Start2Save, but the $500 emergency savings goal limits the maximum match to $1,000, compared with $4,000 per traditional IDA saver. This lower ceiling is also more reachable for the lower-income households the Start2Save program serves.

Experience elsewhere suggests that matching costs could be reduced even further. Evidence from the SaveUSA model shows that a 50 percent incentive is sufficient to enroll large numbers of savers when the opportunity to save is presented at the right time and place (Azurdia et al. 2014). For Start2Save, these data would suggest that the matching ratio could be reversed, from 2:1 to 1:2, and the saver contribution increased to reach the same $1,500 target balance. Given the average deposit amount of $37, the average Start2Saver could be expected to reach a $1,000 savings goal, and earn a $500 match, in 27 months. The program cost model is currently built on a maximum savings period of 24 months; the cost implications of adding three to six months to the participation period would not be significant compared to the cost reduction gained by reducing the match ratio.

Start2Save's operations costs also compare favorably to IDA: direct operations costs for Start2Save run at about 90 percent of what it costs to graduate an IDA saver. One of the principal drivers of costs is back-office account management and transaction processing. With traditional IDAs, participants can make any number of withdrawal/payment requests; the average is 3.5 per participant. For Start2Save, participants are allowed only one emergency withdrawal request before they are required to participate in counseling and additional requests may lead to termination from the program. And, where IDA matches are paid at several points in the program, there is only one match transaction for Start2Save, completed as a single electronic funds transfer process at graduation.

Back-office account management currently accounts for about 50 percent of total operations costs. Start2Save's strict limit on withdrawals reduces these costs substantially. These costs could be halved with additional investment in the two technology platforms that Start2Save relies on: Citibank's microfinance platform and VistaShare's Outcome Tracker, the account management and database system used by Opportunity Fund.

A key element in this reduction would be the ability to open accounts online rather than relying on time-intensive manual processes. The paper-based account-opening process currently in use increases back-office costs, works as a deterrent to account opening, and opens the door to error as paper moves from client, to Opportunity Fund, to bank branch, and beyond. Citibank continues to work on developing a feature that would allow Opportunity Fund to open Start2Save accounts online.

Outcome Tracker is a web-based client management system offered by VistaShare specifically for nonprofit agencies; it is used by many agencies to manage their IDA programs. Although it offers important features, it is designed for traditional IDAs, which Start2Save is not. As a result, the program team has had to develop workarounds to force Outcome Tracker to work for both programs. This creates inefficiencies that increase account processing and transaction coding time and create delays in account monitoring and reporting. Whether the solution is to invest in further development of Outcome Tracker or source a new system, added investment is necessary to create a system that works for Start2Save, reducing access and processing time and ensuring efficient operation.

Over the next five years, as Start2Save matures and scales, per-account costs could be reduced by as much as 50 percent through a number of developments, including reductions in match incentives and investment in enhanced management technology. The baseline number for new account enrollments within the framework of a pilot is 150 per year. The expectation is that, at scale, one program coordinator would have the capacity to enroll 250 accounts per year, with additional support to oversee the graduate portfolio. If these assumptions prove true, Start2Save would have the capacity to more than triple enrollments while increasing direct costs by only a factor of 1.5. On an account-by-account basis, a conservative estimate would suggest that like back-office costs, front-office costs—principally outreach, enrollment, case management, and data collection—could be cut in half.

Learn first, then Scale: Scaling Front-Office Functions

Getting to the right match rate and building the technology platforms are precursors to scaling up. As work continues to address the cost elements of the model, innovation will continue to create a program that can scale in all three phases of the Start2Save process: (1) reaching and enrolling participants, (2) supporting clients as they save up through emergencies to reach the savings goal and trigger the match deposit, and (3) building in mechanisms to facilitate ongoing savings and creating money management tools that diversify savings and build credit.

Ongoing evaluation activities provide the feedback on which the next cycle of innovations is built. Complete evaluation results provide an indication of program impact at graduation, addressing key questions including the degree of changes in attitudes and behaviors regarding household finances; perceptions of self-efficacy are measured using the Self-Mastery Scale. This evaluation does not consider Start2Save graduate program features, as the final survey is administered at graduation. However, Opportunity Fund is seeking funding for a follow-up evaluation that will include post-graduation outcomes and impacts.

Evaluation results can point to opportunities for exponential leaps in learning and design. However, incremental improvements and iterative learning can emerge from anecdotal evidence and interaction with savers and agency partners. They can also be distilled from an analysis of outcomes compared to goals with respect to quantitative data on demographics and savings and withdrawal transactions.

A more significant outreach effort will yield benefits on two fronts: sharing the model and learnings with peers in the field and pushing toward a programmatic sweet spot where funding opportunities match minimized operating costs and outcomes and impacts are on par with expectations and benchmarks. On the first point, Opportunity Fund has and will continue to invest in assessment, evaluation, documentation, and dissemination. On the second, the momentum is already in place for year-on-year growth. Opportunity Fund has not yet fully engaged with the question of what scale is in the long term for Start2Save.

Policy Change as a Lever to Achieve Scale

Even with dramatic reductions in costs, savings programs remain expensive. Empowering low-income/low-asset households to save is not a task that can be accomplished at the needed scale without an intentional and progressive policy framework that specifically targets these populations. Start2Save is working on the question of how to identify and work with low-income households to increase savings and enable the maintenance of sufficient liquid balances to allow them to manage through emergencies. The first step in this work is to adopt the premise that especially for low-income families, savings are an asset that reduces financial vulnerability. The particular focus on emergency savings balances is warranted, as these liquid balances make up the first building block of the household balance sheet.

Start2Save also offers an opportunity to provide insights on the policy front, specifically with regard to identifying the policy barriers and incentives that could be adjusted to power scalable and sustainable gains in savings behaviors and wealth-building outcomes among low-income households. Four policy imperatives emerge from Opportunity Fund's work to date.

The first of these imperatives is to Support the Financial Security Credit Act (FSCA) or similar policy proposals that provide tax credits to incentivize savings among low-income tax filers. Under FSCA, savings, including emergency savings, would be rewarded with a tax credit structured as a match on savings. Administering and funding a savings match through the tax code would go a long way in addressing the high cost of matching funds as the largest impediment to sustainability, and therefore scale, for savings incentive programs.

A second priority is ensuring the continuity of the Earned Income Tax Credit (EITC) and adequate funding for the VITA program, which together work to increase income for low-income households. Lump-sum cash refunds at tax time increase the possibility for savings, and the VITA program provides support services that facilitate tax filing.

Third, all federal and state asset limit tests should be eliminated. These upper limits on savings punish savers by making households with assets above certain thresholds ineligible for social safety net programs such as Temporary Assistance for Needy Families (TANF) or Supplemental Security Income (SSI). Asset limits force the most vulnerable households to choose between savings or subsistence subsidies, rather than encouraging savings while benefiting from subsidies.

The fourth imperative is to expand the mandate of the Assets for Independence Act (AFI) to include a broader interpretation of assets beyond traditional long-term savings to include short- and medium-term assets, including those held in cash. Three revisions to the legislation are critical: include emergency savings and other cash-based assets as part of the asset-based policy to improve family stability, expand the definition of "emergency withdrawal" to make it more flexible and better aligned with the challenges of saving up for and through emergencies, and add an additional modality for the use of funds to include transfers of participant savings and matching funds into a qualified savings account.

Conclusion

In tackling the question of how to build emergency savings, the goal of asset building cannot be disregarded. Strategies to build emergency savings must be concerned with both access and permanence, with cash flows and cash balances. To be effective in the short term, emergency savings must be flexible and readily accessible. To be effective as a long-term strategy, balances should be of sufficient size to offer meaningful support in an emergency, and products must have built-in mechanisms to help savers manage funds. Program features and interventions must be driven by a focus on achieving outcomes and impacts that lead to improvements in financial stability and net worth.

Savings mobilization is difficult and expensive, and matched savings programs are often deemed particularly so because of the match. Public policy already supports savings on a massive scale. The imperative, therefore, is not to prove that tax incentives and direct spending are needed to promote savings or even that they result in more savings and investment. Rather, scarce public resources must be redirected from policies that ensure that those who have income and wealth save more, to policies that help those who have less save a little.

The importance of emergency savings as a financial safety net is now well documented in the research. Start2Save is one approach that is rising to the challenge, building on lessons learned from the evolution of the asset-building framework, Opportunity Fund's work with traditional IDAs, and new insights in behavioral economics. Through innovation, investment, and a push toward scale, Start2Save hopes to deliver a model that can have significant effect in helping low-income households build and manage savings for short-term emergencies while developing long-term asset-building habits.

NOTE

1. In this chapter, "emergency savings" denotes liquid balances held in nonrestricted savings accounts that are available to savers in case of unexpected expenses or reductions in household income.

REFERENCES

Adams, Deborah, and Stacia West. 2013. "Start2Save Research Report for Opportunity Fund: Findings from the Baseline Survey." The University of Kansas Edwards Campus, School of Social Welfare, Overland Park, KS.

Azurdia, Gilda, Stephen Freedman, Gayle Hamilton, and Caroline Schultz. 2014. "Encouraging Low- And Moderate-Income Tax Filers to Save: Implementation and Interim Impact Findings from the SaveUSA Evaluation." Report, April. MDRC, New York, NY.

Brobeck, Stephen. 1999. "Making Household Saving a Priority." *America Saves*, http://americasaves.org/in-the-newsroom/research/making-household-savings-a-priority.

Brooks, Jennifer, and Kasey Wiedrich. 2013. "Assets & Opportunity Score Card: Living on the Edge: Financial Insecurity and Policies to Rebuild Prosperity in America." January. Corporation for Enterprise Development, Washington, DC.

CFED. Corporation for Enterprise Development. 2013. "Why Assets Matter: An Overview of Research on Assets and Their Effect on Financial Stability and Economic Opportunity." Fact Sheet. CFED, Washington, DC.

Davis, Katy, Liz Greenberg, Sonia Steinway, and Ray Brescia. 2012. "Saving for a Rainy Day—or a Hurricane: Emergency Savings for Low- and Moderate-Income Consumers." Eugene and Carol Ludwig Center for Community and Economic Development at Yale Law School, New Haven, CT.

Loibl, Cäzilia, David S. Kraybill, and Sara Wackler DeMay. 2011. "Accounting for the Role of Habit in Regular Saving." *Journal of Economic Psychology* 32 (4): 581–592.

Rutherford, Stuart. 2000. "Raising the Curtain on the 'Microfinancial Services Era.'" Focus No. 15. Consultative Group to Assist the Poor, Washington, DC.

Schreiner, Mark, Margaret Clancy, and Michael Sherraden. 2002. "Saving Performance in the American Dream Demonstration: A National Demonstration of Individual Development Accounts—Final Report." October. Washington University in St. Louis, Center for Social Development, St. Louis, MO.

Sheradden, Michael. 1991. *Assets and the Poor: A New American Welfare Policy*. Armonk, NY: M. E. Sharpe.

US Congress. 1998. *Assets for Independence Act*. Washington, DC: U.S. Government Printing Office.

Chapter 12

Incorporating Savings into the Debt Management Plan

Karen Heisler and Seth Lutter

Introduction

This chapter introduces a plan to promote emergency savings among consumers who are struggling to pay off their debts, but have chosen to enroll in a debt management plan (DMP). DMPs are typically focused on the relatively short-term goal of helping clients pay off existing debt and become financially stable; adding a savings component would also promote long-term behavioral change to support enduring financial security. Encouraging consumers to save money even as they pay off their debts would underline the importance of "paying yourself first," a vital component of long-term financial security.

Background

Thousands of Americans use DMPs each year to take control of their debt with the support of certified consumer credit counseling organizations. DMPs have been found to be effective at helping consumers pay off debt, improve financial management practices, and mitigate the impact of financial emergencies later in life (Kim, Garman, and Sorhaindo 2005). However, no real research has been done to explore how DMPs affect consumer behavior with regard to savings.

Consumers typically resort to credit counseling when they are unable to meet their monthly obligations. These consumers have difficulty juggling the expenses of everyday life while making payments on their debt. Most of these consumers get into debt problems not because of bad spending habits, but as a result of bad savings habits. Financial emergencies, such as job loss or medical debt, cause financial strain and put households over the edge. According to CFED's Assets & Opportunity Scorecard (Brooks and Wiedrich 2013), 43.5 percent of households are liquid-asset poor; 30.8 percent of households do not have a savings account, and 56 percent of consumers have subprime credit. This means many consumers do not have liquid funds available to cover basic expenses for three months if they experienced a sudden job loss, a medical emergency, or another financial crisis leading to a loss of stable income or large, unexpected expenses.

When families lack sufficient emergency savings, short-term challenges become long-term problems. With no liquid resources and few short-term finance options, they may become vulnerable to high-interest predatory lending services, such as payday loans, title loans, or paycheck advances. Put deeper in debt by the fees associated with these services, families can get trapped in a vicious cycle of paying off old debt with new debt. This cycle can last only so long before it collapses and consumers find themselves over their heads in debt.

The Debt Management Plan

Under the current DMP process, counselors work with clients to determine how much income should be used to pay off debt, then negotiates with creditors to reduce interest rates and fees and create a pay-off plan. For clients working with an approved Consumer Credit Counseling Services (CCCS) agency, many creditors have a set minimum payment and interest rate they provide to consumers on a DMP. The interest rate tends to be 5–10 percent (but can vary from 0–18 percent) and the minimum payment is normally 2–3 percent of the current balance. Creditors typically also cancel many fees and bring accounts current. For these creditors, CCCS agencies do not have the ability to negotiate further; the parameters set by creditors are final. It is important to note that while many creditors, especially the large national companies, work with CCCS agencies, cooperation is not required. Creditors are motivated to cooperate because the involvement of the credit counselor increases their chances of being repaid.

Table 12.1 Potential Savings: Debt Management Plan with Savings Component versus Conventional Debt Repayment for $25,000 Debt

	Total debt ($)	**Monthly credit repayment ($)**	**Monthly savings contribution ($)**	**Total monthly payment ($)**	**Months to repayment (months)**	**Amount saved ($)**
Conventional repayment	25,000	635	0	635	240	0
Debt management plan with savings component	25,000	483	26	510	60	1,600
Difference		152	26	125	180	1,600

Source: Authors' own.

After the plan is accepted by all of the client's creditors, the counselor enrolls the consumer in the DMP. The negotiation process typically produces a DMP that results in a lower monthly payment, less interest accruing on accounts, and a significantly shorter repayment period—a typical DMP reduces the time a consumer needs to pay off debt from 20+ years to an average of 3–5 years. After signing up for the DMP, the consumer makes one monthly payment to the CCCS organization, which distributes that payment to each creditor in accordance with the DMP.

That single consolidated payment typically replaces 10–12 payments a month, each with a separate minimum balance and due date. After one creditor is paid off, the funds originally disbursed toward that creditor are then automatically put toward the balance of another creditor, usually the one with either the highest interest rate or the lowest balance, allowing remaining balances to be paid down faster. For example, as table 12.1 illustrates, an individual with $25,000 in debt could both lower his or her monthly payments, by approximately $150, and pay off the debt more quickly on a DMP, reducing the repayment time by 180 months.

While participating in a DMP can help clients repay their old debt, it does not prevent emergencies from occurring in the meantime. Consumers generally turn to a DMP when they have no other options available. A new emergency can push them even deeper in debt, often at extremely high interest rates because of their poor credit. If this new debt causes them to miss their DMP payments, they can be kicked off the program. Having emergency savings can help consumers stay on the DMP even if an emergency arises. Thus, building savings into the DMP can both provide a safety margin for the DMP itself and build savings behaviors that lead to long-term financial health.

Integrating Savings into the Debt Management Plan

Rural Dynamics Inc. (RDI) developed the concept of integrating savings into the DMP as a result of an analysis of its 46-year history of assisting consumers in financial crisis. RDI counsels over 5,000 individuals and families each year, helping them pay off over $6 million in consumer debt. While RDI is committed to helping consumers with their unmanageable debt, the organization's ultimate goal is to assist consumers in becoming financially secure. Without savings, this goal is unattainable. Approximately 1,000 clients each year work with RDI through a DMP; the DMP counseling and debt management process offers an opportunity to engage with clients about financial stability more generally, and help them build a savings habit to provide security and head off future debt problems.

This program would modify RDI's existing DMP program by adding a monthly savings component. Credit counselors enrolling clients in a DMP would discuss the importance of savings to promote both short- and long-term financial resilience in their initial meeting. The client would then have the option of adding a savings component to the DMP, under which he or she could deposit $20–$50 a month in an emergency savings account, which would be held by the credit counseling organization for the duration of the DMP. The counselor would work with the client to determine how much of monthly income should be used to cover household expenses, how much should be used to pay off debt, and how much should be put into savings. Once the consumer completes the DMP, the counseling organization will facilitate the transfer of the current savings to a new account in his or her name. Thus at the end of the DMP—typically about 40 months based on RDI's internal data—the client will have paid off his or her debt and also accumulated substantial funds in an emergency savings account.

For instance, if the client in the example in table 12.1 was able to pay $510.00 per month on the DMP rather than the minimum $483.32 required to satisfy creditors, which would allow $26.68 each month to go into a savings account. As table 12.1 shows, at the end of the DMP program, the client will have paid off all of the debt and built a savings account of $1,600.80, plus interest and match incentives offered by the counseling service.

If the client drops out of the DMP early or has to withdraw funds, no incentives or interest is paid. In the event of a withdrawal, interest may be paid on remaining balances or subsequent deposits, but no interest will be paid on the withdrawn amounts.

Structuring the Savings Account

For the duration of the DMP, the savings deposits would be held in a money market trust account in the counseling agency's name. This arrangement offers advantages for both the counseling agency and the client. First, money market accounts typically offer higher interest rates than standard savings accounts (approximately 1 percent annual interest, as opposed to 0.01 percent). Pooling all client savings funds into a single trust account will allow the organization greater accessibility to accounts that offer higher rates. For clients who complete the DMP with savings intact, this will mean higher returns on their savings. The interest on funds from clients who do not complete the DMP can be used to meet expenses associated with the program or to provide a match incentive. Second, since the savings are not held in the client's name, they cannot be levied by creditors.

The Role of Incentives

Incentives can be used to encourage clients to finish the DMP, continue saving, and resist withdrawing savings. Early dropout is a particular problem, with consequences for both clients and counseling organizations. At RDI, about 17 percent of clients drop out of the DMP before completion to pay off their debts by themselves. Many of these clients are in the final year of their DMP, after the organization has helped them decrease their debt to just one or two manageable bills. Dropping out of the program and withdrawing emergency savings before program completion eliminates the exit counseling session, which is an important component of promoting ongoing financial stability. In addition, when a client drops out early, the CCCS organization loses the income it would have collected, through fair-share payments from creditors and fees from clients, for debt that consumers pay off after they drop out of the program. This has a significant impact on the budgets of community-based CCCS organizations, many of which are struggling to survive in the current financial climate.

The simplest way to incentivize completion of the DMP is to allow clients to accrue interest only if they complete the program and only on balances that remain in the account at the end of the DMP. Because interest rates on money held in savings are fairly low, however, withholding interest may not represent a powerful enough incentive to modify behavior. Another, perhaps more powerful way to encourage consumers to complete their DMP and meet their savings goals may be to offer a small financial bonus, perhaps 10 percent of the total savings balance. Although clients could still withdraw emergency savings at any time, they would have to successfully complete the DMP, meet their savings goal, and complete an exit counseling session in order to receive the bonus. A pilot program could compare completion rates for consumers who participate in a DMP with an emergency savings component with or without a completion bonus. These data could then be used to help providers make decisions about program completion incentives based on whether the earned income from consumers who complete the program is enough to pay for the bonus. Furthermore, given the benefits credit counseling agencies offer to creditors, in the form of increased repayment rates, it is possible that creditors might adjust policies or provide funding to assist in the implementation of completion incentives.

Limitations

Because this program requires no regulatory changes, there should be few significant limitations to implementing or expanding it. The most important limitations to consider are program flexibility and cost, the cost to clients of saving money on a tight budget, and the ability of clients to spend the emergency savings fund on nonemergency consumption after program completion.

Although there are some costs associated with the research and evaluation component of this program, the costs of sustaining the program over the long run are minimal. The major costs would be the administrative costs associated with managing accounts and scheduling an additional end-of-program counseling session for each consumer. Organizations could cover these costs over the long run through a fee-for-service model in which consumers pay an additional fee for the exit counseling. Providers could also charge a small fee for withdrawals before program completion to cover administrative and banking fees associated with those transactions.

Evaluation

With the cooperation of the National Foundation for Credit Counseling and enough research capacity, there are wide possibilities for measuring the impact of an emergency savings component on DMP completion and the ongoing financial health of consumers. To study the effectiveness of the savings component at encouraging program completion and fostering financial health, researchers could engage in a randomized study in which half of new consumers at participating organizations are placed on a traditional DMP and half on a DMP with a savings component. Researchers could then evaluate the impact of the savings component on program completion by tracking the percentage of consumers who successfully completed DMPs in each group; the financial health of consumers with or without the savings DMP can be tracked by checking credit scores one to two years after program completion and comparing the results to credit scores at intake. (Although amounts held in savings are not part of the formula for determining credit scores, savings does have a strong indirect impact on credit scores by helping to mitigate the impact of financial emergencies.) This process would also provide valuable information about the impact of DMP completion on credit scores, which is something that to our knowledge has not been studied.

The impact of a completion bonus in the form of a match can by studied using a similar method. Half of consumers participating in the emergency savings component of the DMP would be offered a completion bonus in the form of a 10 percent match on their savings. Researchers could then compare completion and savings rates between clients who are offered a bonus and those who are not. Tracking this information would help determine whether or not offering a completion bonus is a necessary or even useful incentive.

Completion measures are vital because DMP completions are critical to the survival of community-based credit counseling organizations. Higher DMP completion rates mean better results for clients and increased income for organizations, through DMP fees and creditor fair share payments. Thus, increased DMP completion rates mean increased financial stability for credit counseling agencies.

A number of other important outcomes can be measured through in-person meetings, mailed surveys, and phone calls to consumers, including the percentage of clients who commit to continue saving, the percentage of clients who still have their emergency savings at three months and one year after program completion, the percentage of clients who have added to emergency savings at three months and one year after program completion, the percentage of consumers who have spent their emergency savings on emergency needs at three months and one year after program completion, and the percentage of consumers who have spent their emergency savings on nonemergency items at three months and one year after program completion.

Conclusion

Adding an emergency savings component to a DMP has the potential to promote lifelong saving among a population that would benefit from it most. The strength of this program is that it utilizes the teaching moment that occurs when consumers admit that they are overwhelmed by debt, combining financial counseling about how to avoid falling back into debt with an immediate opportunity to save. Because it can be sustained through earned income and it can be implemented through the existing infrastructure of National Foundation for Credit Counseling (NFCC) member organizations, this program has the potential to scale up to impact hundreds of thousands of financially vulnerable consumers.

Though an emergency savings fund is a vital tool to promote long-term financial stability, putting money into savings competes with many other important things consumers need to spend money on, including paying off debt that may be accruing interest more quickly than savings. However, if DMP clients complete the program with a commitment to saving, the long-term benefits of financial stability will outweigh the sacrifices made to build those savings, including any extra interest paid on debts.

References

Brooks, Jennifer, and Kasey Wiedrich. 2013. "Living on the Edge: Financial Insecurity and Policies to Rebuild Prosperity in America. Findings from the 2013 Assets and Opportunity Scorecard." CFED. January, Washington, DC.

Kim, Jinhee, E., Thomas Garman, and Benoit Sorhaindo. 2005. "Study Finds Positive Financial Behaviors Increased: Credit Counseling, Debt Management Effective." *Journal of Family and Consumer Sciences* 97 (2): 35–39.

Chapter 13

Who Said Pigs Can't Fly? A Learner-Centered Approach to Emergency Savings

Sonya Caesar

Introduction

As suggested by a number of authors in this volume, patterns of low saving, including for shorter-term contingencies, is of growing concern. This chapter introduces the concept of micro-saving for relatively small consumption emergencies. Micro-savings are small in scale—saving in terms of *coins* rather than *bills*. Micro-savings can be particularly useful for lower-income populations, who may struggle to save in larger increments, and can enhance their ability to weather unexpected financial storms. It can also begin to transform attitudes about savings and potentially enhance financial capability.

First-year students at the Community College of Baltimore County (CCBC) in Baltimore County, Maryland, participated in a savings program called Operation Silver Savings. This micro-savings field project provided each student with a piggy bank and a simple financial goal—to save all of their leftover coins over the duration of the seven-week student orientation course called "Achieving Academic Success: Transitioning to College" (course number ACDV 101). The project was piloted as part of a financial literacy curriculum offered at the college called Money Matter$ @CBCC. This curriculum is embedded in a mandatory, one-credit-hour course that targets more than 5,000 CCBC students each year. Between

February 2011 and December 2013, a remarkable 17,706 students participated in the financial literacy course. Students participating in Operation Silver Savings during the orientation course have saved over $79,000, mainly collected from loose change, since the program began. Notably, students who took part in the project reported higher financial awareness than they had prior to participating, as well as greater levels of saving.

Community college students are an especially relevant target population. Almost 50 percent of community college students live at or below the poverty level (Mullin 2012); these students are often working poor or Temporary Assistance for Needy Families-eligible (TANF-eligible). This is a well-targeted intervention because it is aimed at low-income, employment-constrained, and low-asset households. CCBC enrolls over 70,000 students annually, 50 percent of whom qualify for and receive financial aid and assistance. Approximately 5,000 students are required to take the freshman ACDV 101 orientation course each academic year. The Money Matter$ @CBCC program was piloted in spring 2011 with 350 students; over 80 faculty have been trained to teach the Money Matter$ @CBCC curriculum.

Background

Increased concern over low-income households' capability to weather a financial disaster is especially timely given the current state of the economy. The Great Recession of 2008 affected the country as a whole and especially younger people, bringing high unemployment rates, reduced hours of available employment, and significant disruptions in the housing market (Bell and Blanchflower 2011). Such economic uncertainty left household finances strained for years. A 2012 survey of Americans' financial lives provides a glimpse into the lingering effects of the recession. The survey asked more than 30,600 Americans about their financial health and financial management practices; 68 percent reported living paycheck–to-paycheck and indicated they would struggle to fulfill their financial obligations if their next paycheck was delayed by only a week (American Payroll Association 2012).

Lower-income households are less resilient to financial instability and, therefore, more likely to be affected by the ill effects of a recession, which may bring unstable or scarce employment, housing insecurity, and other financial stressors. The inability to pay for basic daily necessities can make saving for emergencies or future goals feel like a distant dream; savings feel optional while bills are immediate and mandatory, as one participant disclosed in a qualitative study of savings habits and financial education (Muske and Winter 2004, 83). Savings goals can be difficult or impossible to attain when living paycheck-to-paycheck.

What makes a financial shock an emergency? Emergencies or stressful life events are triggered when people face situations where their perceived needs exceed perceived resources (Slavin et al. 1991; Folkman et al. 1987). In the financial context, emergencies are those events that create expenses outside of the usual daily requirements and beyond the resources of the household, thereby leading to material hardships. Mills and Amick (2010) quantify material hardships using eight criteria, including whether a household is (1) unable to meet basic living expenses, (2) misses a utility payment, (3) has a utility turned off, (4) has a telephone disconnected, (5) misses a mortgage or rent payment, (6) does not go to the doctor due to a lack of money, (7) does not go to the dentist due to a lack of money, or (8) experiences food insecurity. Emergency savings might provide protection from the financial shocks that lead to material hardships (Chan 2011).

Community college students are among the most vulnerable populations. Approximately 13 million students cross the thresholds of community colleges each year; this group tends to be disproportionately female and older than their four-year university counterparts. Many community college students are the first in their families to attend college, and they are often underprepared for college, meaning that they are "not yet emotionally, socially, or academically prepared for college-level work" (Barr and Schuetz 2008, 8). These students tend to be from low-income, working-poor, and poverty-level households. Many are employed, either part or full time, while enrolled as students, and a significant number are raising families, many as single parents (Mullin 2012; Geckeler et al. 2008). As a result of the heightened economic vulnerability of community college students, a number of concerned parties, including educational institutions, nonprofit groups, governmental agencies, and educators, are interested in identifying opportunities to assist students in overcoming financial obstacles.

Barriers to Saving for Emergencies

It is important to remember that, although the focus of this discussion is lower-income households, income alone is not the cure for material hardships or financial emergencies. A shortage of funds is not the only barrier to saving. Accumulating savings is influenced by a range of behaviors, biases, perceptual blind spots, and engrained habits. People at any income level may make choices that are not optimal concerning savings and consumption. Individuals may also procrastinate, only to regret their lack of action later (Hernandez 2011). As Lusardi, Schneider, and Tufano (2011) point out, "financial fragility . . . is not just a poor person's problem" (2). Indeed, living paycheck-to-paycheck exists across income groups (American Payroll Association 2012). Furthermore, reports on the declining economic security of the middle class suggest that the problem may become even more widespread (Wheary et al. 2007).

In a study that investigated why people do not build emergency savings, even when they have funds available over time to do so, Muske and Winter (2004) followed the daily financial rituals of seven "average" families as defined by Census Bureau data—families with children in which the parents were 35–44 years old with median household incomes. In-depth interviews illustrate varying attitudes toward saving. Asked specifically about long-term planning and saving, one individual responded that "although savings [is] important, they were not important enough to cut 'their current lifestyle'"(Muske and Winter 2004, 84). Again, people tend to see savings as an optional activity while bills are considered nonnegotiable. Consumer consumption choices seem to pose a challenge for allocating income to savings.

Though people offer a number of other reasons for not saving, one reason in particular may prove especially problematic for low-income populations: the amounts suggested as minimum thresholds for emergency savings—typically three, six, or even eight months of income (Chan 2011; Brobeck 2008; Orman 2005)—may simply be too daunting, thus discouraging people from even trying. As Davis (1992) suggests, "saving may seem pointless to consumers who can at best set aside a few dollars each week" (30). People who pay out most of their income to bills may find saving to be a luxury or simply too mentally taxing (Hernandez 2011); feelings of frustration and anxiety, around savings and personal finances more generally, may lead to negative attitudes toward savings and inertia that results in inaction.

Furthermore, vulnerable student populations are also affected by what may be thought of as micro-emergencies. Small crises—the lack of money to buy a meal, replace a lost bus pass, put a few gallons of gas in the car in order to get to work or school, or buy a needed supply—may snowball into larger issues and derail students' academic progress. Community college students frequently need loans of $5 or less—suggesting that small savings is both relevant and important for student well-being and financial stability.

This insight—that micro-savings matters and may be relevant for preventing hardships—suggests that mainstream approaches to savings might be reconsidered. A better tactic may involve encouraging people to build any level savings, without regard to what financial experts consider necessary or adequate amounts. This is not a new idea, as it has been discussed in the financial education literacy field for more than three decades. For example, Davis wrote that "consumer educators, therefore, may need to demonstrate that saving small amounts on a regular basis can enable clients to achieve objectives such as building an emergency reserve fund" (Davis 1992, 30). Expert advice that neglects people's immediate financial needs and the larger behavioral context are less likely to succeed. Simple mechanisms to help people automate savings may result in better designs, following a more reflective and learner-centered approach (Thaler and Sunstein, 2008).

Micro-Savings as a Means to Accumulate Emergency Savings

The CCBC project, supported by grants from OneMain Financial and the Citi Foundation, sought to embed micro-savings into a freshman orientation course to address students' economic needs. The goal of the initiative was to build healthy financial behaviors among financially vulnerable community college students. Between February 2011 and December 2013, 5,304 students in the program completed a pre-survey and 2,515 (47 percent) students completed post-surveys. The survey was modeled after an instrument described by O'Neill and Xiao (2006) and includes information about students' financial practices and attitudes. The online survey includes both multiple-choice items and a series of open-ended questions that ask students to provide qualitative feedback about what they learned during the financial literacy portion of the orientation curriculum. Additionally, the post evaluation includes items to assess the impact of the micro-savings project on financial behavior.

The pre-survey data confirm that CBCC students are financially vulnerable. In fact, nearly half, 49 percent, reported living paycheck-to-paycheck.[1] Based on focus groups conducted with students (Miller 2011), students also face hardships including subpar living conditions, inability to pay bus fares to get to work or school, and inability to cover daycare needs or pay for needed school supplies.

Micro-saving offers a small behavioral change leading to small savings gains that, in turn, may lead to larger savings. Collecting a few pennies at a time may seem insignificant, but doing so consistently may convert a nonsaver into a habitual saver, especially among people who traditionally report being unable to save money. The CCBC post-survey supports this hypothesis: 33 percent of incoming first-year students reported being unable to save on the pre-survey; on the post-survey, 72 percent of Operation Silver Savings participants reported having started saving because they were given the piggy bank. Furthermore, 91 percent of students in the program reported saving during the class project, and 75 percent reported learning how to save money because of having the piggy bank. In total, three-quarters of students also indicated that the program changed the way they think about money. The average amount saved among students who completed the post-survey was $32, or about $4.50 per week over the duration of the course. From the time of the program's inception in February 2011 until December 2013, students reported saving nearly $80,000, an impressive number for a population that reported almost no savings at the beginning of their participation.

Student responses to open-ended questions suggest that, beyond providing small amounts to facilitate their navigation of micro-crises, the exercise increased their sense of financial competence and financial security (Williams 2013 and Miller 2013). For example, one student demonstrates applying skills in budgeting: "I am now living a paycheck ahead and I am saving money by not spending as much." Much of the work students engaged in was about thinking ahead, or as one student noted, learning "how to keep aside money for emergencies by opening a saving account at my bank and on the 25th of the month, 5 bucks gets transferred." In another quote, a student connects how even small behaviors might lead to better well-being, in this case related to housing: "In the past few weeks, since learning about saving and putting money aside, I now have enough money for a security deposit on an apartment. So changing my lifestyle with money has been a good lesson."

Because these data were not generated through a randomized field experiment, they cannot prove a causal link between the program and saving. Nonetheless, students' comments certainly support the possibility that the program had profound impacts. For example, one student wrote: "Having the pig really made me save money. Now I'm going to keep the pig and keep saving. Since I got the pig I don't waste my change anymore—where usually I would just throw it away, now I keep it and put it in my pig." Another student commented: "I learned that even a little is a lot. Saving a little at a time really does add up over time. This was a short class and just putting the change from my pocket in the piggy bank got me almost 20 dollars, mostly in pennies." The micro-savings concept appears especially relevant, for example, one student wrote learning "that saving money doesn't always have to be putting 20s or 100s in the bank; it's the little things that you save that will add up." Another noted learning to "collect all loose change that I find in my pockets. I used to just toss them aside," as well as "I've learned how to save additional money without touching it." Others commented on how they saved by "receiving change from people in my family who hate change." Students reported learning "that small savings can turn into large savings," and "that having just one cent a day adds up." The program may also lead to a greater sense of financial satisfaction and wellbeing. For example, one student wrote: "I've learned how important it was to have savings, having savings could help out with situations that may come up and relieve you from stress".

For these students, it seems that even very small savings was associated with changes in their thinking and behavior. Hopefully, these changes will help the students to remain in college and secure a stronger economic future once they graduate or transfer to a four-year institution.

It should be noted that there were considerably more pre-surveys collected than post-surveys. While community college is an important pathway to higher education, it is not uncommon for community college students to stop attending at different points throughout a term (Kalogrides and Grodsky, 2011). By some estimates, community colleges retain just half of their enrolled students over one year (Mullin, 2012; Goldrick-Rab, 2011). This reality affected response rates, and in turn may have influenced the data findings. Nonresponse bias is a strong possibility. We cannot observe the thoughts and experiences of students who did not complete the class, participate in the project, or respond to the survey. The data and observations that were collected may still prove useful for other groups interested in implementing a similar model.

Making the Case for a Micro-Savings Project

The central tool of the CCBC project is the piggy bank. Operation Silver Savings distributes light blue, see-through piggy banks with the CCBC logo on their sides. The piggy bank has long been an iconic symbol of saving; ceramic pigs and their more recent derivatives have served as visual symbols of saving for children and adults alike. Use of this symbol serves as a "choice architecture," providing the kind of "nudge" required to break the cycle of savings inertia, in line with the mechanisms popularized by Thaler and Sunstein (2008). Such behavioral nudges, or prompts to act, can play a valuable role in preparing an individual for behavioral change. The physical presence of the piggy bank itself serves as a "nudge" or reminder that people should empty their pockets and fill it with their weighty coins. Translucent piggy banks like those used by CCBC's Operation Silver Savings project provide a further prompt by allowing the saver to see the physical growth of his or her savings. Noticing these changes can contribute to feelings of financial empowerment. An added bonus is that program expenses are relatively low, as each piggy bank costs less than two dollars.

One notable dimension of the Operation Silver Savings project, also provided by the use of the piggy bank, is that students report it being fun. Although the purpose of the program is to teach a serious, potentially life-changing lesson, the piggy bank brings an enjoyable element of whimsy to the process. The lighthearted nature of gifting someone a piggy bank makes the topic of saving and financial planning less intimidating, helping people believe that anyone can do it, across age, race, or income lines. One CCBC student, a mother in her mid-fifties, described the impact the piggy bank, with its whimsical appeal, has had on her family:

> My husband is former military, accustomed to treating most of his take-home pay as disposable income. If he can get his hands on it, it is spent. He likes food and toys and things that capture his imagination. Imagine my surprise when he expressed an interest in the piggy bank. He told himself a story about how the piggy bank money would be used in the future to offset distress and regularly deposited $20 bills. He would forgo little treats to put money in that blue, translucent piggy. The pig had captured his imagination and made it possible for him to choose saving over a more immediate reward. To date, he has deposited $160 into the pig.

For some, then, the piggy bank adds an element of gamification. Gamification is the process of incorporating gaming concepts into tasks that might otherwise be less interesting, to motivate engagement. In other words, this process takes an otherwise mundane task into something more fun and engaging (Kapp 2012). While the piggy bank engages only the most basic elements of gamification, displaying progress and providing diversion, these components can engage otherwise nonsavers in building a small savings cushion. That small cushion can add up. If a group involved in a community-organized micro-savings program could commit to saving $20–$30 per month, over the course of a year, they could amass $240–$360. This amount, while still quite small, offers some degree of cushioning in the event of a micro-emergency, perhaps heading off a larger crisis, and it most certainly can serve to move the emergency preparedness and saving conversation in a positive direction.

Lessons Learned and Thoughts for the Future

Although a small cushion can be important, the saving of coins is not without challenges. Accumulated coins become heavy and can be burdensome to store, count, and cash. Some banks charge additional fees for counting coins. On the other hand, CCBC students report that the weight and bulk of coins served as a deterrent that prevented them from spending easily and thus offered less temptation to break into savings. Some students moved their savings to larger receptacles when their piggy banks were full. One possible solution for programs with longer-term savings goals would be to forge or leverage existing partnerships with financial institutions to offer deposits with no coin-counting fees, or to allow participants to open conventional savings accounts with the coins once their savings reach a particular threshold.

Conclusion

A program similar to Operation Silver Savings could be deployed as an introductory stage for a larger-scale emergency savings project, with the coins saved leading to long-term emergency savings. A longer-term savings project could move through phases with ever-expanding goals. Within that framework, the first phase could encompass micro-savings to empower individuals with the belief that they can save, beginning with small amounts of money that might ordinarily go unnoticed. Parting with $20 may seem unfathomable to a low-income parent faced with a slew of bills, but dropping leftover coins into a piggy bank may seem achievable. The program could then progress into additional phases, which may involve participation in an incentivized emergency savings club that offers bonuses and incentives for saving regularly. The overall program goals would be to move clients through the phases, helping them to develop a habit of savings along with a substantial emergency savings fund.

The CCBC Operation Silver Saving project suggests that micro-savings can, indeed, serve as a gateway to more regular saving, building a sense of the possibility of saving and the power of putting aside even very small amounts. The lesson of Operation Silver Saving is that creating the conditions to engage people in the practical act of saving creates positive awareness in a contextualized way, providing a powerful learner-centered experience.

NOTE

1. The instrument was created by Sonya Caesar, program director for Money Matter$ @CBCC, and Davis Jenkins, senior associate director for the Community College Research Center (CCRC). Natasha Miller provides more detailed survey results of pre-surveys (Miller, 2014b) and post-surveys (Miller, 2014a).

REFERENCES

American Payroll Association. 2012. "2012 'Getting Paid In America' Survey Results."

Barr, Jim, and Pam Schuetz. 2008. "Overview of Foundational Issues." *New Directions for Community Colleges* 144: 7–16.

Bell, David N. F., and David G. Blanchflower. 2011. "Young People and the Great Recession." *Oxford Review of Economic Policy* 27 (2): 241–267.

Brobeck, Stephen. 2008. "Understanding the Emergency Savings Needs Of Low-And Moderate-Income Households: A Survey-Based Analysis of Impacts, Causes, and Remedies." White Paper, November. Consumer Federation of America, Washington, DC.

Chan, Pamela. 2011. "Beyond Barriers: Designing Attractive Savings Accounts for Lower-Income Consumers." Asset Building Program Working Paper, November. New America Foundation, Washington, DC.

Davis, Elizabeth P. 1992. "Financial Management among Households with Differing Resource Constraints." *Journal of Consumer Education* 10: 27–31.

Folkman, Susan, Richard S. Lazarus, Scott Pimley, and Jill Novacek. 1987. "Age Differences in Stress and Coping Processes." *Psychology and Aging* 2 (2): 171–184.

Geckeler, Christian, Carrie Beach, Michael Pih, and Leo Yan. 2008. "Helping Community College Students Cope with Financial Emergencies: Lessons from the Dreamkeepers and Angel Fund Emergency Financial Aid Programs." Report, May. MDRC.

Goldrick-Rab, Sara. 2010. "Challenges and Opportunities for Improving Community College Student Success." *Review of Educational Research* 80 (3): 437–469.

Hernandez, Mindy. 2011. "Applying Behavioral Research to Asset-Building Initiatives: Lessons from a Year of Experimentation." Report, April. Innovation @ CFED, Washington, DC.

Kalogrides, Demetra, and Eric Grodsky. 2011. "Something to Fall Back On: Community Colleges as a Safety Net." *Social Forces* 89 (3): 853–877.

Kapp, Karl M. 2012. *The Gamification of Learning and Instruction: Game-based Methods and Strategies for Training and Education*. San Francisco, CA: Pfeiffer.

Lusardi, Annamaria, Daniel J. Schneider, and Peter Tufano. 2011. "Financially Fragile Households: Evidence and Implications." National Bureau of Economic Research Working Paper Series, No. 17072.

Miller, Natasha. 2011. "Summary of Community College of Baltimore County 'Financial Challenges' Focus Group Results: Dundalk and Essex Campuses." Report. Community College of Baltimore County, Baltimore, MD.

———. 2013. "Content Analysis of Question 10 and Question 12 of Money Matter$ @CBCC Financial Literacy Post Survey. The Community College of Baltimore County's Achieving Academic Success: Transitioning to College Freshman Orientation Course (ACDV 101)." Report. Community College of Baltimore County, Baltimore, MD.

———. 2014a. "Financial Literacy Post Survey Results (Spring 2011–Fall 2013). The Community College of Baltimore County's Achieving Academic Success: Transitioning to College Freshman Orientation Course (ACDV 101)." Report. Community College of Baltimore County, Baltimore, MD.

———. 2014b. "Financial Literacy Pre Survey Results (Spring 2011–Fall 2013). The Community College of Baltimore County's Achieving Academic Success: Transitioning to College Freshman Orientation Course (ACDV 101)." Report. Community College of Baltimore County, Baltimore, MD.

Mills, Gregory, and Joe Amick. 2010. "Can Savings Help Overcome Income Instability?" Perspectives on Low-Income Working Families, Brief 18. The Urban Institute, Washington, DC.

Mullin, Christopher M. 2012. "Why Access Matters: The Community College Student Body." Research Brief, February. American Association of Community Colleges, Washington, DC.

Muske, Glenn, and Mary Winter. 2004. "Personal Financial Management Education: An Alternative Paradigm." *Financial Counseling and Planning* 15 (2): 79–88.

O'Neill, Barbara, and Jing Jian Xiao. 2006. "Financial Fitness Quiz Findings: Strengths, Weaknesses, and Disconnects." *Journal of Extension* 44 (1). http://www.joe.org/joe/2006february/rb5.php.

Orman, Suze. 2005. *The Money Book for the Young, Fabulous & Broke*. New York: Penguin.

Slavin, Lesley, Karie Rainer, Micah McCreary, and Kalpana Gowda. 1991. "Toward a Multicultural Model of the Stress Process." *Journal of Counseling & Development* 70 (1): 156–163.

Thaler, Richard H., and Cass R. Sunstein. 2008. *Nudge: Improving Decisions about Health, Wealth, and Happiness*. New Haven, CT: Yale University Press.

Wheary, Jennifer, Thomas M. Shapiro, Tamara Draut, Tatjana Meschede, and Laura Sullivan. 2007. "From Middle to Shaky Ground: The Economic Decline of America's Middle Class, 2000–2006." By a Thread Report #3. Institute on Assets and Social Policy, Brandeis University, Waltham, MA.

Williams, Jeanine. 2013. "Content Analysis of Student Responses in the Community College of Baltimore County's Achieving Academic Success: Transitioning to College Freshman Orientation Course (ACDV 101). Money Matter$ @CBCC Financial Literacy Post Survey." Report. Community College of Baltimore County, Baltimore, MD.

Chapter 14

Epilogue: Emergency Savings as a Central Component of Family Financial Security

J. Michael Collins and Thomas Shapiro

Introduction

This volume initiates an innovation dialogue about strategies to help low-income individuals and households meet immediate, nonrecurring expenses. The chapters identify programs, products, and policies worthy of further development and testing. Collectively, this volume is meant to inspire new ideas for promoting savings.

The introductory chapters illustrate the diversity in definitions of savings, emergency funds, and liquidity. Next, the book describes potential strategies related to housing, demonstrating the breadth of opportunities in the area of emergency savings. The book also introduces a series of approaches that integrate savings into existing program infrastructures, reaching larger numbers of people and potentially operating at meaningful scale. Other chapters illustrate strategies embedded into technology, including social networks and stored value cards, as well as incentivized savings behaviors. Clearly, the clever use of technology and new financial product platforms will open new opportunities in the future. Together, these examples offer compelling models for governments and firms interested in exploring solutions that can help broaden savings among households, even those with very low incomes.

Despite the optimism that emerges from these chapters, significant hurdles remain. While a series of great ideas are presented in this text, to have impact, innovations must be both sustainable and scalable. As programs reach larger scale, it will be important to ensure that approaches are carefully targeted to the most critical populations and that the programs are in fact succeeding in helping families smooth consumption and meet unexpected needs.

Four specific issues complicate attempts to define and operationalize emergency savings. First, some households can easily borrow in some markets, so savings mechanisms need to be considered as both substitutes for and complements to credit. People can simultaneously save and borrow, using liquidity flexibly based on the timing of the particular need. Second, savings policies and programs all seem to have slightly different goals, which may include increasing the number of people who save or have savings, increasing the amount of money people have saved, and encouraging people to save more regularly. Influencing how individuals spend their savings can also be a goal, but in general it appears that promoting emergency savings involves relaxing the paternalism historically seen in savings programs. This means fewer restrictions, and therefore more opportunities for people to use their funds in ways that omniscient planners or might not judge to be appropriate.

Third, savings for unrestricted use, as might be expected, is difficult to measure. Emergency funds are saved in a variety of storage vehicles, including outside of formal bank accounts, and often rely on family, friends, and social network obligations. Finally, short-term savings needs to be considered in the context of overall financial security or health. The goal of liquidity is to help families better manage their household balance sheets, avoiding high-cost credit and maintaining consumption even when income falls short. In the long run, such resilience should help people build longer-term assets to pay for higher education, a home or business, a comfortable retirement, and other goals.

Key Themes

Several key themes emerge from the earlier chapters. To start, a fundamental issue is that while the exact timing of emergency expenditures may be unpredictable, expenses can be predicted to some extent. Next, there are many causes of insufficient emergency savings beyond a lack of income. In addition, a lack of liquidity can come at a high cost, in the form of late fees and other fees associated with high-cost financial products. Another theme is that emergency savings efforts need to be well targeted to particular moments (such as tax-filing season, when families have windfalls in the form of tax refunds). Furthermore, when people tap savings for an emergency, there need to be mechanisms to rebuild savings to prepare for the next unexpected expenditure. The political reality of any new savings policy is fraught with challenges. Overcoming these challenges requires a deeper understanding of both the benefits and drawbacks of using scarce subsidy dollars to support unrestricted savings.

Many emergencies are predictable. Although individuals cannot predict exactly when automobile repairs, unexpected medical or childcare needs, appliance replacement, or home repairs will arise, emergency expenses are quite likely to occur at some point over the course of a year. Unlike other insurable events, the occurrence of these and similar emergencies are quite predictable within the span of a year or two. Overconfidence can result in a failure to adequately appreciate the likelihood of these expenses, and it may be inappropriate to expect low-income savers to completely manage their own risks.

Lack of income is not the only cause of insufficient liquidity. Flat or declining real incomes for working families constrain the amount of money households can withhold from consumption for smoothing in later periods. For low-income families, there is little margin for savings. A "rainy day" fund for unexpected expenses is uncommon among individuals and households with low incomes, but the availability of such funds remains important even among households with fewer resource constraints. Having liquid funds to maintain cash flows requires foresight and planning, and behavioral biases and a lack of useful financial products can create impediments to such savings.

A lack of emergency funds can be costly. Low-income people have experience juggling due dates on bills, managing a variety of formal and informal income sources, curbing or forgoing certain expenses, and strategically maneuvering program eligibility to make ends meet. Payday loans, late fees, overdrafts, pawn loans, and title loans are some of the tools these families use to get through the week or month. Introducing emergency savings may not eliminate these higher-cost products, but it may reduce the extent to which low-income people rely on them. (Consumer protection efforts play an important role by removing deceptive or fraudulent products from the marketplace.) Facilitating contingency savings may also help people increase their own capability to manage expenses and income, giving them more "tools in the toolbox" and increasing their ability to plan and use these tools more effectively.

Choosing a targeted moment is critical. The innovations described in this volume target individuals at different moments in the life course, from younger adults enrolling in community college, to low-income families buying their first home, to individuals filing income tax returns, and even exiting from a homeless shelter. At some of these points, people are on upward economic trajectories, and liquidity may help stabilize bumps in the road, while at other points, individuals are likely to face continuous economic stress. Opportunities to save or tap credit must be designed differently for each targeted moment. In addition, more research is needed on whether consumers draw down liquid savings at optimal moments in the life course.

Savings must be reestablished after an emergency. One of the realities of planning for an unexpected expense is that people will tap liquidity they have accumulated to meet such expenses. At this point, savings balances will decline and debt may increase. The process of building a contingency reserve must begin again. Given that this is an inevitable step in the process, innovations must incorporate ways to reestablish contingency savings. In this context, contingency should be thought of as cyclical. Maintaining continuity for participants as they move into and out of various programs and services is important; technology may facilitate this process.

Using scarce subsidy dollars to support unrestricted savings has both benefits and drawbacks. Although a wide range of programs subsidize matched savings for education and homeownership, there are few examples offering matched savings for unrestricted uses. The role of subsidies in building emergency savings may depend on whether the goal is to encourage individuals to start saving (the extensive margin) or to encourage individuals to supplement existing savings (the intensive margin). Subsidizing the initiation of saving could help individuals overcome behavioral biases and other barriers, while subsidizing ongoing savings might not have the same benefit. On the other hand, subsidies might be used to build a savings "habit" that persists over time. The exact goals and benefits of using subsidies need further elaboration and study.

The chapters also highlight the potential roles for supports other than subsidies, including nonmonetary rewards and incentives, peer support, financial coaching and counseling, savings reminders, goal setting and tracking assistance, norms development, mandated participation or participation incorporated into another program, assistance in maintaining motivation over time, mechanisms to increase participants' sense of control, loss aversion mechanisms, and default saving mechanisms (such as a split tax refund, with one portion sent directly to a savings account). Supports and monitoring programs must be low touch (that is, require limited infrastructure support) and low cost.

Housing-based programs may be one potential path, but they face challenges. Most people allocate some portion of their income to housing. Although housing shocks can be expensive and involve large irregular expenditures, housing expenses are predictable on a monthly basis. There are opportunities to use housing and variation in housing payments as a context for saving, using liquidity, and stabilizing living standards. However, these mechanisms have some important limitations. Low-income housing programs and their participants are already resource constrained. In addition, regulations related to mortgages and mortgage servicing may limit the extent to which saving or borrowing can be built into housing payments or how much low-income homeowners can tap home equity. Community-based organizations and innovative local public housing authorities are sources of a number of savings strategies aimed at families and children. There is much room for entrepreneurial approaches and new strategies to pilot in communities, as well as avenues for replication. The challenge is finding organizations with the capacity and vision to test promising strategies.

To be sustainable, programs must incorporate incentives for both participants and providers. Any new emergency savings initiative must include compelling financial or behavioral benefits for the ultimate users. At a minimum, programs must be simple, easy to use, and inexpensive. Further, new savings initiatives cannot depend solely on nonprofits that must perennially seek grants and donations to maintain programs. Thus, to be scalable, programs must incorporate incentives for financial services firms to participate. While regulatory pressures may encourage some firms to participate, a robust and dynamic marketplace will allow private firms to receive fees or other revenue. For government, the incentive may be lower human services costs. Increasing the financial stability of individuals and households that are one shock away from needing additional government resources may prove an efficient use of government funds. The ability to build on existing infrastructures, including government programs and large firms, also makes scalability more feasible.

We must be realistic about the political reality of any new savings policy. If savings programs are to garner political support, they need to be successful at scale, the goals of these efforts must not be limited to increasing contingency savings by having a certain number of people save or having people save a certain dollar amount. Programs must focus on bigger-picture impacts; in the current policy environment, benefits such as increased social equity or small financial improvements among low-income families are unconvincing. Policymakers are likely to be more convinced by arguments that outline the potentially positive impacts on society of increased emergency savings—namely, reduced use of public services and improved health and well-being outcomes for families. Connecting programs and products to the amelioration of social problems that are expensive for local and state governments (such as homelessness) would be beneficial. In addition, the recent economic crisis is reshaping the financial landscape, and the current transition poses an opportunity to rethink the social contract.

Conclusion

Savings can take a multitude of forms, ranging from small reserve funds used over a few days to regular payroll deductions into formal accounts. The diversity of definitions is reflected in the variation in approaches described in this volume. The broader discussion must address how liquid savings fit into the societal response to the increasing economic volatility families face. With a less robust social safety net, fewer structured supports provided through employers or labor unions, and greater exposure to global equity and labor markets, families today have to develop new ways to deal with volatility in income and expenses. Clearly, these factors cut across many other policy realms, but the result of these shifts is an increase in the types and magnitude of volatility that households face. Savings will remain an important means by which families make ends meet when unexpected circumstances arise.

Liquidity—what people may call "cash in a pinch"—exists in households today. People access liquidity by using credit, borrowing from family and friends, selling assets, and tapping savings. These resources are not all typically considered part of financial asset building, but they all have a place along the continuum of asset- and wealth-building strategies. The key is how prudently households develop and use these approaches.

Some argue that the concepts described in this book, and the idea of encouraging emergency savings, are strategies designed to address a symptom— short-term cash flow problems—rather than the reasons why people have shortfalls in the first place. If the goal of a savings program is to prevent predatory lending, a more straightforward approach might be to regulate such lenders. Nonetheless, centralized, restrictive policies may in fact reduce the liquidity households can access and thereby reduce their economic resilience over time. The ideas captured in this book do not solve the liquidity problems families face, but they do offer structures and policies that take new approaches to a solution. Community-based designs present an opportunity to allow ideas to evolve organically from the field; history suggests these ideas will change over time but may offer a glimpse of policies to come.

It is also important to maintain a commitment to research on emergency savings. This includes incorporating better measures of savings and liquidity in national surveys, as well as supporting investments in well-designed program and product evaluations. An innovative approach may quickly become too popular, before the evidence of need, approach, and impact can be developed. By segmenting households by culture, social networks, and shared experiences, programs can develop greater sensitivity to unique opportunities. The market and ultimately the families who use new programs (or choose not to) can also serve as a crucial test of efficacy.

Finally, the entire discussion around savings for low-income people has an intriguing political dynamic. The ideas that planning for the future and savings are good for families and for society are widely believed. The political support for tax subsidies for small-dollar savings is likely to be divided, but the narrative of helping people to plan ahead and set aside resources for the unexpected is likely to garner support in some form from a wide range of political players. The models and ideas discussed in this book present a set of ideas that can help to further this dialogue and foster the development of approaches that increase the ability of families to maintain a fragile balance using savings and liquid resources.

Contributors

Dan Ariely is the James B. Duke Professor of Psychology & Behavioral Economics at Duke University, holds appointments at Duke's Fuqua School of Business, Center for Cognitive Neuroscience, Department of Economics, and School of Medicine, and is a senior fellow at the Kenan Institute for Ethics at Duke. He is a founding member of the Center for Advanced Hindsight and the author of the *New York Times* bestsellers *Predictably Irrational*, *The Upside of Irrationality*, and *The Honest Truth About Dishonesty.*

Sonya Caesar is a doctoral student at the University of Maryland-Baltimore County (UMBC) in the interdisciplinary Language, Literacy, and Culture program; her research explores antipoverty strategies for economically vulnerable communities. At UMBC, she redesigned the financial literacy component of the mandatory freshman orientation class and is working to expand the college's financial capability initiatives.

J. Michael Collins is faculty director of the Center for Financial Security at the University of Wisconsin-Madison, where he teaches in the public affairs and consumer science departments. Collins studies consumer decision making in the financial marketplace, including the role of public policy in influencing credit, savings, and investment choices.

Krista Comer is a program manager at the Center for Social Development at Washington University in St. Louis, where she plays an instrumental role in developing the Refund to Savings interventions and experimental research.

Jessica Dorrance is a research associate at the UNC Center for Community Capital. She helps lead the center's consumer financial services evaluation work focusing on research and analysis to understand what products and programs promote economic security and mobility for low-wealth households.

Karan Gill is the senior policy analyst and community liaison at the King County Council in Washington State, where he works on various policy issues as well as communications and community outreach efforts for the 5th Legislative District. He also serves as a board member of the Washington Asset Building Coalition and community advisory board member for the Washington State Budget & Policy Center.

Leah Gjertson is a senior research assistant with the Center for Financial Security and a PhD candidate in the School of Social Work at the University of Wisconsin-Madison. Her current areas of research include emergency savings, the financial well-being of youth exiting the foster care system, and the impact financial capability interventions.

Michal Grinstein-Weiss is an associate professor at the Brown School of Social Work at Washington University in St. Louis and the associate director of the Center for Social Development. She is a national expert in policy research related to issues of economic inequality, household financial security, and social development.

Jayson Halladay is the CEO and cofounder of Piggymojo, the company behind MagicMojo. Jayson leads the development of the company's patented method of impulse savings, which combine goal visualization, social dynamics, and mobile technologies.

Karen Heisler has been the director of Asset Development at Rural Dynamics Inc. for the past eight years. She leads the policy, financial education, and asset development strategies for the organization and is passionate about creating programs that systemically move people toward financial security.

Sharon Henderson is senior vice president of Prosperity Works and president of Asset Development Strategies. She has provided technical assistance to municipalities and tribal and community-based organizations in the area of developing assets in lower-income families for over 20 years.

Ingrid Holguin is the director of Savings Programs for Opportunity Fund, a Community Development Financial Institution with headquarters in San Jose, California. At Opportunity Fund and elsewhere, she has worked on micro-lending and micro-savings, housing microfinance, and microfinance institutional investing and fund management.

Clinton Key is a research officer studying savings and financial security at the Pew Charitable Trusts. The research included in this volume was conducted while he was a research manager at the University of North Carolina School of Social Work and the Center for Social Development at Washington University in St. Louis.

Ed Khashadourian is the president and CEO of Opportunity to Assets, a startup social enterprise that offers technology and technical support to community-based organizations launching asset-building programs. Ed has an extensive research background in the areas of savings, wealth building, and economics.

Ezra Levin is associate director of Government Affairs at the Corporation for Enterprise Development, where he focuses on tax policy, wealth-building, and economic opportunity. Previously, he served as deputy policy director for US Representative Lloyd Doggett, and as an AmeriCorps VISTA in the Homeless Services Division of the San Jose Housing Department. He sits on the board of directors of the National Coalition for the Homeless.

Cäzilia Loibl is an associate professor at the Department of Human Sciences at The Ohio State University and Marie Curie Fellow at the Centre for Decision Research at Leeds University Business School, United Kingdom. Her research focuses on consumer financial decision making.

Seth Lutter is the director of Counseling and has been part of the Rural Dynamics, Inc. (RDI) team since 2008. He currently manages the financial counseling department and has previously worked on housing and education programs at RDI.

Kim Manturuk manages research and evaluation initiatives at the Duke University Center for Instructional Technology. She has expertise in all aspects of evaluation planning and execution including survey design, research protocol development, attrition analysis, statistical methods, propensity score analysis, and stakeholder identification.

Margaret McKenna is the owner and principal of the program evaluation consulting firm ConTEXT, which has partnered with The Prosperity Agenda to evaluate asset-building initiatives and financial coaching programs. She is an anthropologist who brings diverse experiences evaluating human service programs and systems to The Prosperity Agenda's work in anti-poverty strategies.

Dana Mills manages human resources, business operations, and strategic planning for The Prosperity Agenda. Her studies have focused on behavioral economics and health policy. She coauthored *TANF Bank Accounts* during her research internship with The Prosperity Agenda in 2013.

Jonathan Mintz is the founding president and CEO of the Cities for Financial Empowerment Fund and founder and cochair of the Cities for Financial Empowerment Coalition, which brings together pioneering municipal governments from across the country to advance innovative financial empowerment initiatives.

Stephanie Moulton is an associate professor at the John Glenn School of Public Affairs, The Ohio State University, and a research affiliate with the University of Wisconsin's Center for Financial Security. Moulton studies the implementation and evaluation of housing and consumer finance policies and programs.

Dana Perantie is a project manager at the Center for Social Development at Washington University in St. Louis. With a background in quantitative and qualitative research methods and extensive experience with data management and analysis, she offers insight into considerations for research design and instrument development.

Blair Russell is a senior research analyst with the Center for Social Development. His research interests center on quantitative policy analysis and program evaluation across a number of substantive areas, including asset building, housing, economic development, and education.

Anya Samek is an assistant professor in the School of Human Ecology at the University of Wisconsin-Madison and an affiliate of the Economics Department, the Center for Financial Security, and the Institute for Research on Poverty. Samek's research fields are experimental economics, public economics, health economics, and visual analytics.

Thomas Shapiro directs the Institute on Assets and Social Policy and is the Pokross Professor of Law and Social Policy at The Heller School for Social Policy and Management, Brandeis University. Shapiro's primary interest is in racial inequality and public policy. He is a leader in the asset development field with a particular focus on closing the racial wealth gap.

Index

Printed and bound in the United States of America